Kotlin Coroutines

Deep Dive

Marcin Moskała

CW01467071

Kotlin Coroutines

Deep Dive

Marcin Moskała

ISBN 978-83-963958-3-2

© 2021 - 2023 Marcin Moskała

For my beloved wife, Maja.

Contents

Introduction   1

Part 1: Understanding Kotlin Coroutines   7
   Why Kotlin Coroutines?   8
   Sequence builder   21
   How does suspension work?   27
   Coroutines under the hood   39
   Coroutines: built-in support vs library   57

Part 2: Kotlin Coroutines library   59
   Coroutine builders   60
   Coroutine context   76
   Jobs and awaiting children   88
   Cancellation   101
   Exception handling   117
   Coroutine scope functions   128
   Dispatchers   148
   Constructing a coroutine scope   168
   The problem with shared state   178
   Testing Kotlin Coroutines   193

Part 3: Channel and Flow   229
   Channel   230
   Select   252
   Hot and cold data sources   258
   Flow introduction   266
   Understanding Flow   278
   Flow building   290
   Flow lifecycle functions   302
   Flow processing   313
   SharedFlow and StateFlow   340
   Testing flow   354

Part 4: Kotlin Coroutines in practice   **371**
    Common use cases   372
    Recipes   397
    Using coroutines from other languages   412
    Launching coroutines vs. suspending functions   425
    Best practices   429

The End   **445**

Introduction

Why do you want to learn about Kotlin Coroutines? I often ask my workshop attendees this question. "Because they're cool" and "Because everyone is talking about them" are common answers. Then, when I dig deeper, I hear responses like "because they are lighter threads", "because they are easier than RxJava", or "because they enable concurrency while maintaining an imperative code style." However, coroutines are much more than that. They are the holy grail of concurrency. As a concept, they have been known in Computer Science since the 1960s, but in mainstream programming, they have only been used in a very limited form (such as async/await). This changed with Golang, which introduced much more general-purpose coroutines. Kotlin built on that, creating what I believe is currently the most powerful and practical implementation of this idea.

The importance of concurrency is growing, but traditional techniques are not enough. Current trends suggest that coroutines are the direction in which our industry is clearly heading, and Kotlin Coroutines represent a significant step forward. Let me introduce them to you, along with examples of how well they handle common use cases. I hope you will have a lot of fun reading this book.

Who is this book for?

As a developer experienced in both backend and Android, I primarily focus on these two perspectives in this book. These are currently the two major industry applications of Kotlin, and it's evident that coroutines were largely designed to suit these use cases well[1]. So, you might say that this book is mainly designed for Android and backend developers, but it should be just as useful for other developers using Kotlin.

This book assumes that readers know Kotlin well. If you do not, I recommend starting with my other book, *Kotlin Essentials*.

---

[1]Google's Android team cooperated in designing and creating some features we will present in this book.

1

The structure of this book

The book is divided into the following parts:

- **Part 1: Understanding Kotlin Coroutines** - dedicated to explaining what Kotlin Coroutines are and how they really work.
- **Part 2: Kotlin Coroutines library** - explaining the most important concepts from the kotlinx.coroutines library and how to use them well.
- **Part 3: Channel and Flow** - focused on Channel and Flow from the kotlinx.coroutines library.
- **Part 4: Kotlin Coroutines in practice** - reviewing common use cases and the most important best practices for using Kotlin Coroutines.

What will be covered?

This book is based on a workshop I conduct. During its iterations I have been able to observe what interested attendees and what did not. These are the elements that are most often mentioned by attendees:

- **How do coroutines really work?** (Part 1)
- **How to use coroutines in practice?** (Part 2, 3 and especially 4)
- **What are the best practices?** (Part 2, 3 and especially 4)
- **Testing Kotlin coroutines** (Testing Kotlin Coroutines in Part 2 and Testing Flow in Part 3)
- **What is Flow and how does it work?** (Part 3)

The Kotlin for Developers series

This book is a part of a series of books called Kotlin for Developers, which includes the following books:

- Kotlin Essentials, which covers all the basic Kotlin features.
- Functional Kotlin, which is dedicated to functional Kotlin features, including function types, lambda expressions, collection processing, DSLs, and scope functions.
- Kotlin Coroutines, which covers all the features of Kotlin Coroutines, including how to use and test them, using flow, best practices, and the most common mistakes.

- Advanced Kotlin, which is dedicated to advanced Kotlin features, including generic variance modifiers, delegation, multiplatform programming, annotation processing, KSP, and compiler plugins.
- Effective Kotlin, which is dedicated to the best practices of Kotlin programming.

Conventions

When I use a concrete element from code, I will use code-font. When naming a concept, I will capitalize the word. To reference an arbitrary element of some type, I will use lowercase. For example:

- `Flow` is a type or an interface, it is printed with code-font (like in "Function needs to return `Flow`");
- Flow represents a concept, so it starts with an uppercase letter (like in "This explains the essential difference between Channel and Flow");
- a flow is an instance, like a list or a set, therefore it is in lowercase (like in "Every flow consists of a few elements").

Another example: `List` means an interface or a type ("The type of `l` is `List`"); List represents a concept (a data structure), while a list is one of many lists ("the `list` variable holds a list").

I have used American English in the book, except for the spelling of "cancellation/cancelled", which I chose due to the spelling of the "Cancelled" coroutine state.

Code conventions

Most of the presented snippets are executable code with no import statements. Some chapters of this book are published as articles on the Kt. Academy website, where most snippets can be executed, and readers can play with the code. The source code of all the snippets is published in the following repository:

https://github.com/MarcinMoskala/coroutines_sources[2]

Snippet results are presented using the `println` function. The result will often be placed at the end of these snippets in comments. If there is a delay between output lines, it will be shown in brackets. Here is an example:

---

[2]https://github.com/MarcinMoskala/coroutines_sources

```
suspend fun main(): Unit = coroutineScope {
  launch {
      delay(1000L)
      println("World!")
  }
  println("Hello,")
}
// Hello,
// (1 sec)
// World!
```

Sometimes, some parts of code or a result are shortened with . . . . In such cases, you can read it as "there should be more here, but it is not relevant to the example".

```
launch(CoroutineName("Name1")) { ... }
launch(CoroutineName("Name2") + Job()) { ... }
```

In some cases, I will show comments next to the line that prints them. I do this when the order is clear:

```
suspend fun main(): Unit = coroutineScope {
  println("Hello,") // Hello,
  delay(1000L) // (1 sec)
  println("World!") // World!
}
```

In a few snippets I have added a number after the line to more easily explain the snippet's behavior. This is what it might look like:

```
suspend fun main(): Unit = coroutineScope {
    println("Hello,") // 1
    delay(1000L) // 2
    println("World!") // 3
}
```

At 1 we print "Hello,", then we wait for a second because line 2 contains delay, and we print "World!" at line 3.

Acknowledgments

This book would not be so good without the reviewers' great suggestions and comments. I would like to thank all of them. Here is the whole list of reviewers, starting from the most active ones.

Nicola Corti - a Google Developer Expert for Kotlin. He has been working with the language since before version 1.0, and he is the maintainer of several open-source libraries and tools for mobile developers (Detekt, Chucker, AppIntro). He's currently working in the React Native core team at Meta, building one of the most popular cross-platform mobile frameworks. Furthermore, he is an active member of the developer community. His involvement goes from speaking at international conferences to being a member of CFP committees and supporting developer communities across Europe. In his free time, he also loves baking, podcasting, and running.

Garima Jain - a Google Developer Expert in Android from India. She is also known around the community as @ragdroid. Garima works as a Principal Android Engineer at GoDaddy. She is also an international speaker and an active technical blogger. She enjoys interacting with other people from the community and sharing her thoughts with them. In her leisure time, she loves watching television shows, playing TT, and basketball. Due to her love for fiction and coding, she loves to mix technology with fiction and then shares her ideas with others through talks and blog posts.

Ilmir Usmanov - a software developer at JetBrains, working on coroutine support in the Kotlin compiler since 2017. Was responsible for stabilization and implementation of the coroutines design. Since then, he has moved to other features, namely inline classes. Currently, his work with coroutines is limited to bug fixing and optimization, since coroutines as a language feature is complete and stable and does not require much attention.

Sean McQuillan - a Developer Advocate at Google. With a decade of experience at Twilio and other San Francisco startups, he is an expert at building apps that scale. Sean is passionate about using great tooling to build high-quality apps quickly. When he is not working on Android, you can find him fiddling on the piano or crocheting hats.

Igor Wojda - a passionate engineer with over a decade of software development experience. He is deeply interested in Android application architecture and the Kotlin language, and he is an active member of the open-source community. Igor is a conference speaker, technical proofreader for the 'Kotlin In Action' book, and author of the 'Android Development with Kotlin' book. Igor enjoys sharing his passion for coding with other developers.

Jana Jarolimova - an Android developer at Avast. She started her career teaching Java classes at Prague City University, before moving on to mobile development, which inevitably led to Kotlin and her love thereof.

Richard Schielek - an experienced developer and an early adopter of Kotlin and coroutines, using both in production before they became stable. Worked in the European space industry for several years.

Vsevolod Tolstopyatov - a team lead of the Kotlin Libraries team. He works at JetBrains and is interested in API design, concurrency, JVM internals, performance tuning and methodologies.

Lukas Lechner, **Ibrahim Yilmaz**, **Dean Djermanović** and **Dan O'Neill**.

I would also like to thank **Michael Timberlake**, our language reviewer, for his excellent corrections to the whole book.

Part 1: Understanding Kotlin Coroutines

Before we begin our adventure with the Kotlin Coroutines library, let's start with some more basic concepts. What are coroutines? How does suspension work? What does it all look like under the hood? We will explore all this while learning some useful tools and practices.

Why Kotlin Coroutines?

Why do we need to learn Kotlin Coroutines? We already have well-established JVM libraries like RxJava or Reactor. Moreover, Java itself has support for multithreading, while many people also choose to just use plain old callbacks instead. Clearly, we already have many options for performing asynchronous operations.

Kotlin Coroutines offer much more than that. They are an implementation of a concept that was first described in 1963[3] but waited years for a proper industry-ready implementation[4]. Kotlin Coroutines connects powerful capabilities presented by half-century-old papers to a library that is designed to perfectly help in real-life use cases. What is more, Kotlin Coroutines are multiplatform, which means they can be used across all Kotlin platforms (like JVM, JS, iOS, and also in the common modules). Finally, they do not change the code structure drastically. We can use most Kotlin coroutines' capabilities nearly effortlessly (which we cannot say about RxJava or callbacks). This makes them beginner-friendly[5].

Let's see it in practice. We will explore how different common use cases are solved by coroutines and other well-known approaches. I will show two typical use cases: Android and backend business logic implementation. Let's start with the first one.

---

[3]Conway, Melvin E. (July 1963). "Design of a Separable Transition-diagram Compiler". Communications of the ACM. ACM. 6 (7): 396–408. doi:10.1145/366663.366704. ISSN 0001-0782. S2CID 10559786

[4]I believe that the first industry-ready and universal coroutines were introduced by Go in 2009. However, it is worth mentioning that coroutines were also implemented in some older languages, like Lisp, but they didn't become popular. I believe this is because their implementation wasn't designed to support real-life cases. Lisp (just like Haskell) was mostly treated as a playground for scientists rather than as a language for professionals.

[5]This does not change the fact that we should understand coroutines to use them well.

Coroutines on Android (and other frontend platforms)

When you implement application logic on the frontend, what you most often need to do is:

1. get some data from one or many sources (API, view element, database, preferences, another application);
2. process this data;
3. do something with this data (display it in the view, store it in a database, send it to an API).

To make our discussion more practical, let's first assume we are developing an Android application. We will start with a situation in which we need to get news from an API, sort it, and display it on the screen. This is a direct representation of what we want our function to do:

```
fun onCreate() {
    val news = getNewsFromApi()
    val sortedNews = news
        .sortedByDescending { it.publishedAt }
    view.showNews(sortedNews)
}
```

Sadly, this cannot be done so easily. On Android, each application has only one thread that can modify the view. This thread is very important and should never be blocked. That is why the above function cannot be implemented in this way. If it were started on the main thread, getNewsFromApi would block it, and our application would crash. If we started it on another thread, our application would crash when we call showNews because it needs to run on the main thread.

Thread switching

We could solve these problems by switching threads. First to a thread that can be blocked, and then to the main thread.

```
fun onCreate() {
  thread {
      val news = getNewsFromApi()
      val sortedNews = news
          .sortedByDescending { it.publishedAt }
      runOnUiThread {
          view.showNews(sortedNews)
      }
  }
}
```

Such thread switching can still be found in some applications, but it is known for being problematic for several reasons:

- There is no mechanism here to cancel these threads, so we often face memory leaks.
- Making so many threads is costly.
- Frequently switching threads is confusing and hard to manage.
- The code will unnecessarily get bigger and more complicated.

To see those problems clearly, imagine the following situation: You open and quickly close a view. While opening, you might have started multiple threads that fetch and process data. Without cancelling them, they will still be doing their job and trying to modify a view that no longer exists. This means unnecessary work for your device, possible exceptions in the background, and who knows what other unexpected results.

Considering all these problems, let's look for a better solution.

Callbacks

Callbacks are another pattern that might be used to solve our problems. The idea is that we make our functions non-blocking, but we pass to them a function that should be executed once the process started by the callback function has finished. This is how our function might look if we use this pattern:

```
fun onCreate() {
  getNewsFromApi { news ->
      val sortedNews = news
          .sortedByDescending { it.publishedAt }
      view.showNews(sortedNews)
  }
}
```

Notice that this implementation does not support cancellation. We might make cancellable callback functions, but it is not easy. Not only does each callback function need to be specially implemented for cancellation, but to cancel them we need to collect all the objects separately.

```
fun onCreate() {
  startedCallbacks += getNewsFromApi { news ->
      val sortedNews = news
          .sortedByDescending { it.publishedAt }
      view.showNews(sortedNews)
  }
}
```

Callback architecture solves this simple problem, but it has many downsides. To explore them, let's discuss a more complex case in which we need to get data from three endpoints:

```
fun showNews() {
  getConfigFromApi { config ->
      getNewsFromApi(config) { news ->
          getUserFromApi { user ->
              view.showNews(user, news)
          }
      }
  }
}
```

This code is far from perfect for several reasons:

- Getting news and user data might be parallelized, but our current callback architecture doesn't support that (it would be hard to achieve this with callbacks).

- As mentioned before, supporting cancellation would require a lot of additional effort.
- The increasing number of indentations make this code hard to read (code with multiple callbacks is often considered highly unreadable). Such a situation is called "callback hell", which can be found especially in some older Node.JS projects:

```
describe('.totalValue', function(){
    it('should calculate the total value of items in a space', function(done){
        var table = new Item('table', 'dining room','07/23/2014', '1','3000');
        var chair = new Item('chair', 'living room','07/23/2014', '3','300');
        var couch = new Item('couch', 'living room','07/23/2014', '2','1100');
        var chair2 = new Item('chair', 'dining room','07/23/2014', '4','500');
        var bed = new Item('bed', 'bed room','07/23/2014', '1','2000');

        table.save(function(){
          chair.save(function(){
            couch.save(function(){
              chair2.save(function(){
                bed.save(function(){
                  Item.totalValue({room: 'dining room'}, function(totalValue){
                    expect(totalValue).to.equal(5000);
                    done();
                    });
                  });
                });
              });
            });
          });
        });
      });
    });
```

- When we use callbacks, it is hard to control what happens after what. The following way of showing a progress indicator will not work:

```
fun onCreate() {
  showProgressBar()
  showNews()
  hideProgressBar() // Wrong
}
```

The progress bar will be hidden just after **starting** the process of showing news, so practically immediately after it has been shown. To make this work, we would need to make showNews a callback function as well.

```
fun onCreate() {
  showProgressBar()
  showNews {
      hideProgressBar()
  }
}
```

That's why the callback architecture is far from perfect for non-trivial cases. Let's take a look at another approach: RxJava and other reactive streams.

RxJava and other reactive streams

An alternative approach that is popular in Java (both in Android and backend) is using reactive streams (or Reactive Extensions): RxJava or its successor Reactor. With this approach, all operations happen inside a stream of data that can be started, processed, and observed. These streams support thread-switching and concurrent processing, so they are often used to parallelize processing in applications.

This is how we might solve our problem using RxJava:

```
fun onCreate() {
  disposables += getNewsFromApi()
      .subscribeOn(Schedulers.io())
      .observeOn(AndroidSchedulers.mainThread())
      .map { news ->
          news.sortedByDescending { it.publishedAt }
      }
      .subscribe { sortedNews ->
          view.showNews(sortedNews)
      }
}
```

The disposables in the above example are needed to cancel this stream if (for example) the user exits the screen.

This is definitely a better solution than callbacks: no memory leaks, cancellation is supported, proper use of threads. The only problem is that it is complicated. If you compare it with the "ideal" code from the beginning (also shown below), you'll see that they have very little in common.

```
fun onCreate() {
  val news = getNewsFromApi()
  val sortedNews = news
      .sortedByDescending { it.publishedAt }
  view.showNews(sortedNews)
}
```

All these functions, like subscribeOn, observeOn, map, or subscribe, need to be learned. Cancelling needs to be explicit. Functions need to return objects wrapped inside Observable or Single classes. In practice, when we introduce RxJava, we need to reorganize our code a lot.

```
fun getNewsFromApi(): Single<List<News>>
```

Think of the second problem, for which we need to call three endpoints before showing the data. This can be solved properly with RxJava, but it is even more complicated.

```
fun showNews() {
  disposables += Observable.zip(
      getConfigFromApi().flatMap { getNewsFromApi(it) },
      getUserFromApi(),
      Function2 { news: List<News>, config: Config ->
          Pair(news, config)
      })
      .subscribeOn(Schedulers.io())
      .observeOn(AndroidSchedulers.mainThread())
      .subscribe { (news, config) ->
          view.showNews(news, config)
      }
}
```

This code is truly concurrent and has no memory leaks, but we need to introduce RxJava functions such as `zip` and `flatMap`, pack a value into `Pair`, and destructure it. This is a correct implementation, but it's quite complicated. So finally, let's see what coroutines offer us.

Using Kotlin Coroutines

The core functionality that Kotlin Coroutines introduce is the ability to suspend a coroutine at some point and resume it in the future. Thanks to that, we might run our code on the Main thread and suspend it when we request data from an API. When a coroutine is suspended, the thread is not blocked and is free to go, therefore it can be used to change the view or process other coroutines. Once the data is ready, the coroutine waits for the Main thread (this is a rare situation, but there might be a queue of coroutines waiting for it); once it gets the thread, it can continue from the point where it stopped.

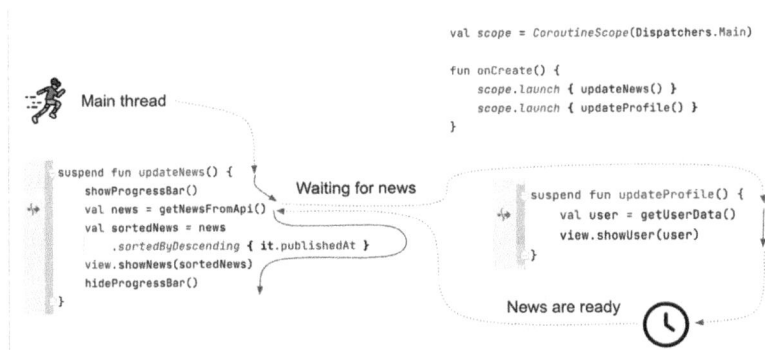

This picture shows updateNews and updateProfile functions running on the Main thread in separate coroutines. They can do this interchangeably because they suspend their coroutines instead of blocking the thread. When the updateNews function is waiting for a network response, the Main thread is used by updateProfile. Here, it's assumed that getUserData did not suspend because the user's data was already cached, therefore it can run until its completion. This wasn't enough time for the network response, so the main thread is not used at that time (it can be used by other functions). Once the data appears, we grab the Main thread and use it to resume the updateNews function, starting from the point straight after getNewsFromApi().

By definition, coroutines are components that can be suspended and resumed. Concepts like async/await and generators, which can be found in languages like JavaScript,

Rust or Python, also use coroutines, but their capabilities are very limited.

So, our first problem might be solved by using Kotlin coroutines in the following way:

```
fun onCreate() {
  viewModelScope.launch {
      val news = getNewsFromApi()
      val sortedNews = news
          .sortedByDescending { it.publishedAt }
      view.showNews(sortedNews)
  }
}
```

In the above code, I used viewModelScope, which is currently quite common on Android. We might instead use a custom scope. We will discuss both options later.

This code is nearly identical to what we've wanted since the beginning! In this solution, the code runs on the Main thread but it never blocks it. Thanks to the suspension mechanism, we are suspending (instead of blocking) the coroutine when we need to wait for data. When the coroutine is suspended, the Main thread can go do other things, like drawing a beautiful progress bar animation. Once the data is ready, our coroutine takes the Main thread again and starts from where it previously stopped.

How about the other problem with three calls? It could be solved similarly:

```
fun showNews() {
  viewModelScope.launch {
      val config = getConfigFromApi()
      val news = getNewsFromApi(config)
      val user = getUserFromApi()
      view.showNews(user, news)
  }
}
```

This solution looks good, but how it works is not optimal. These calls will happen sequentially (one after another), so if each of them takes 1 second, the whole function will take 3 seconds instead of 2 seconds, which we can achieve if the API calls execute in parallel. This is where the Kotlin coroutines library helps us with functions like async, which can be used to immediately start another coroutine with some request and wait for its result to arrive later (with the await function).

```kotlin
fun showNews() {
  viewModelScope.launch {
      val config = async { getConfigFromApi() }
      val news = async { getNewsFromApi(config.await()) }
      val user = async { getUserFromApi() }
      view.showNews(user.await(), news.await())
  }
}
```

This code is still simple and readable. It uses the async/await pattern that is popular in other languages, including JavaScript or C#. It is also efficient and does not cause memory leaks. The code is both simple and well implemented.

With Kotlin coroutines, we can easily implement different use cases and use other Kotlin features. For instance, they do not block us from using for-loops or collection-processing functions. Below, you can see how the next pages might be downloaded in parallel or one after another.

```kotlin
// all pages will be loaded simultaneously
fun showAllNews() {
  viewModelScope.launch {
      val allNews = (0 until getNumberOfPages())
          .map { page -> async { getNewsFromApi(page) } }
          .flatMap { it.await() }
      view.showAllNews(allNews)
  }
}

// next pages are loaded one after another
fun showPagesFromFirst() {
```

```
viewModelScope.launch {
    for (page in 0 until getNumberOfPages()) {
        val news = getNewsFromApi(page)
        view.showNextPage(news)
    }
  }
}
```

Coroutines on the backend

In my opinion, the biggest advantage of using coroutines on the backend is simplicity. Unlike RxJava, using coroutines barely changes
how our code looks. In most cases, migrating from threads to coroutines only involves adding the suspend modifier. When we do this, we
can easily introduce concurrence, test concurrent behavior, cancel
coroutines, and use all the other powerful features we will explore
in this book.

```
suspend fun getArticle(
  articleKey: String,
  lang: Language
): ArticleJson? {
  return articleRepository.getArticle(articleKey, lang)
      ?.let { toArticleJson(it) }
}

suspend fun getAllArticles(
  userUuid: String?,
  lang: Language
): List<ArticleJson> = coroutineScope {
  val user = async { userRepo.findUserByUUID(userUuid) }
  val articles = articleRepo.getArticles(lang)
  articles
      .filter { hasAccess(user.await(), it) }
      .map { toArticleJson(it) }
}
```

Except for all these features, there is one more important reason to
use coroutines: threads are costly. They need to be created, main-

tained, and they need their memory allocated[6]. If your application is used by millions of users and you are blocking whenever you wait for a response from a database or another service, this adds up to a significant cost in memory and processor use (for the creation, maintenance, and synchronization of these threads).

This problem can be visualized with the following snippets that simulate a backend service with 100,000 users asking for data. The first snippet starts 100,000 threads and makes them sleep for a second (to simulate waiting for a response from a database or other service). If you run it on your computer, you will see it takes a while to print all those dots, or it will break with an OutOfMemoryError exception. This is the cost of running so many threads. The second snippet uses coroutines instead of threads and suspends them instead of making them sleep. If you run it, the program will wait for a second and then print all the dots. The cost of starting all these coroutines is so cheap that it is barely noticeable.

```
fun main() {
    repeat(100_000) {
        thread {
            Thread.sleep(1000L)
            print(".")
        }
    }
}
```

```
fun main() = runBlocking {
    repeat(100_000) {
        launch {
            delay(1000L)
            print(".")
        }
    }
}
```

---

[6]Most often, the default size of the thread stack is 1 MB. Due to Java optimizations, this does not necessarily mean 1 MB times the number of threads will be used, but a lot of extra memory is spent just because we create threads.

Conclusion

I hope you feel convinced to learn more about Kotlin coroutines now. They are much more than just a library, and they make concurrent programming as easy as possible with modern tools. If we have that settled, let's start learning. For the rest of this chapter, we will explore how suspension works: first from the usage point of view, then under the hood.

Sequence builder

In some other languages, like Python or JavaScript, you can find structures that use limited forms of coroutines:

- async functions (also called async/await);
- generator functions (functions in which subsequent values are yielded).

We've already seen how async can be used in Kotlin, but this will be explained in detail in the *Coroutine builders* chapter. Instead of generators, Kotlin provides a sequence builder - a function used to create a sequence[7].

A Kotlin sequence is a similar concept to a collection (like List or Set), but it is evaluated lazily, meaning the next element is always calculated on demand, when it is needed. As a result, sequences:

- do the minimal number of required operations;
- can be infinite;
- are more memory-efficient[8].

Due to these characteristics, it makes a lot of sense to define a builder where subsequent elements are calculated and "yielded" on demand. We define it using the function sequence. Inside its lambda expression, we can call the yield function to produce the next elements of this sequence.

```
val seq = sequence {
    yield(1)
    yield(2)
    yield(3)
}
```

---

[7]Even better, it offers flow builders. Flow is a similar but much more powerful concept which we will explain later in the book.

[8]See item *Prefer Sequence for big collections with more than one processing step* in the Effective Kotlin.

```
fun main() {
  for (num in seq) {
      print(num)
  } // 123
}
```

The `sequence` function here is a small DSL. Its argument is a lambda expression with a receiver (suspend `SequenceScope<T>.()` -> `Unit`). Inside it, the receiver `this` refers to an object of type `SequenceScope<T>`. It has functions like `yield`. When we call `yield(1)`, it is equivalent to calling `this.yield(1)` because `this` can be used implicitly. If this is your first contact with lambda expressions with receivers, I recommend starting from learning about them and about DSL creation, as they are used intensively in Kotlin Coroutines.

What is essential here is that each number is generated on demand, not in advance. You can observe this process clearly if we print something in both the builder and in the place where we handle our sequence.

```
val seq = sequence {
    println("Generating first")
    yield(1)
    println("Generating second")
    yield(2)
    println("Generating third")
    yield(3)
    println("Done")
}

fun main() {
    for (num in seq) {
        println("The next number is $num")
    }
}
// Generating first
// The next number is 1
// Generating second
```

```
// The next number is 2
// Generating third
// The next number is 3
// Done
```

Let's analyze how it works. We ask for the first number, so we enter the builder. We print "Generating first", and we yield number 1. Then we get back to the loop with the yielded value, and so "Next number is 1" is printed. Then something crucial happens: execution jumps to the place where we previously stopped to find another number. This would be impossible without a suspension mechanism, as it wouldn't be possible to stop a function in the middle and resume it from the same point in the future. Thanks to suspension, we can do this as execution can jump between main and the sequence generator.

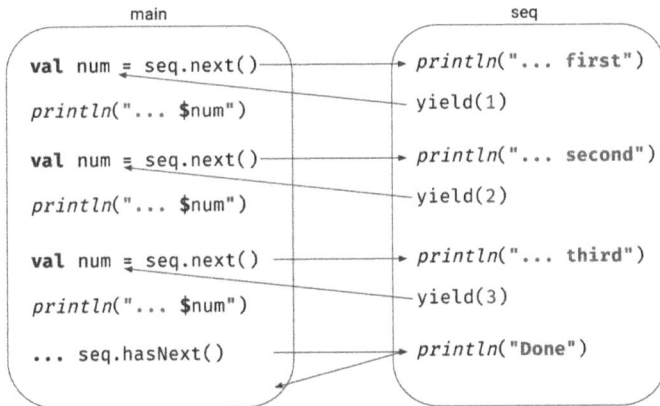

When we ask for the next value in the sequence, we resume in the builder straight after the previous yield.

To see it more clearly, let's manually ask for a few values from the sequence.

```kotlin
val seq = sequence {
    println("Generating first")
    yield(1)
    println("Generating second")
    yield(2)
    println("Generating third")
    yield(3)
    println("Done")
}

fun main() {
    val iterator = seq.iterator()
    println("Starting")
    val first = iterator.next()
    println("First: $first")
    val second = iterator.next()
    println("Second: $second")
    // ...
}

// Prints:
// Starting
// Generating first
// First: 1
// Generating second
// Second: 2
```

Here, we used an iterator to get the next values. At any point, we can call it again to jump into the middle of the builder function and generate the next value. Would this be possible without coroutines? Maybe, if we dedicated a thread for that. Such a thread would need to be maintained, and that would be a huge cost. With coroutines, it is fast and simple. Moreover, we can keep this iterator for as long as we wish as it costs nearly nothing. Soon we will learn how this mechanism works under the hood (in the *Suspension under the hood* chapter).

Real-life usages

There are a few use cases where sequence builders are used. The most typical one is generating a mathematical sequence, like a Fibonacci sequence.

```
val fibonacci: Sequence<BigInteger> = sequence {
    var first = 0.toBigInteger()
    var second = 1.toBigInteger()
    while (true) {
        yield(first)
        val temp = first
        first += second
        second = temp
    }
}

fun main() {
    print(fibonacci.take(10).toList())
}
// [0, 1, 1, 2, 3, 5, 8, 13, 21, 34]
```

This builder can also be used to generate random numbers or texts.

```
fun randomNumbers(
    seed: Long = System.currentTimeMillis()
): Sequence<Int> = sequence {
    val random = Random(seed)
    while (true) {
        yield(random.nextInt())
    }
}

fun randomUniqueStrings(
    length: Int,
    seed: Long = System.currentTimeMillis()
): Sequence<String> = sequence {
    val random = Random(seed)
    val charPool = ('a'..'z') + ('A'..'Z') + ('0'..'9')
```

```
    while (true) {
        val randomString = (1..length)
            .map { i -> random.nextInt(charPool.size) }
            .map(charPool::get)
            .joinToString("");
        yield(randomString)
    }
}.distinct()
```

The sequence builder should not use suspending operations other than yielding operations[9]. If you need, for instance, to fetch data, it's better to use Flow, as will be explained later in the book. The way its builder works is similar to the sequence builder, but Flow has support for other coroutine features.

```
fun allUsersFlow(
  api: UserApi
): Flow<User> = flow {
  var page = 0
  do {
      val users = api.takePage(page++) // suspending
      emitAll(users)
  } while (!users.isNullOrEmpty())
}
```

We've learned about the sequence builder and why it needs suspension to work correctly. Now that we've seen suspension in action, it is time to dive even deeper to understand how suspension works when we use it directly.

---

[9]And it cannot be, since SequenceScope is annotated with RestrictsSuspension, which prevents the suspend function being called unless its receiver is SequenceScope.

How does suspension work?

Suspending functions are the hallmark of Kotlin coroutines. The suspension capability is the single most essential feature upon which all other Kotlin Coroutines concepts are built. That is why our goal in this chapter is to forge a solid understanding of how it works.

Suspending a coroutine means stopping it in the middle. It is similar to stopping a video game: you save at a checkpoint, turn off the game, and both you and your computer can focus on doing different things. Then, when you would like to continue some time later, you turn on the game again, resume from the saved checkpoint, and thus you can play from where you previously left off. This is an analogy to coroutines. When they are suspended, they return a Continuation. It is like a save in a game: we can use it to continue from the point where we stopped.

Notice that this is very different from a thread, which cannot be saved, only blocked. A coroutine is much more powerful. When suspended, it does not consume any resources. A coroutine can be resumed on a different thread, and (at least in theory) a continuation can be serialized, deserialized and then resumed.

Resume

So let's see it in action. For this, we need a coroutine. We start coroutines using coroutine builders (like runBlocking or launch), which we will introduce later. Although there is also a simpler way, we can use a suspending main function.

Suspending functions are functions that can suspend a coroutine. This means that they must be called from a coroutine (or another suspending function). In the end, they need to have something to suspend. Function main is the starting point, so Kotlin will start it in a coroutine when we run it.

```kotlin
suspend fun main() {
    println("Before")

    println("After")
}
// Before
// After
```

This is a simple program that will print "Before" and "After". What will happen if we suspend in between these two prints? For that, we can use the suspendCoroutine function provided by the standard Kotlin library[10].

```
suspend fun main() {
    println("Before")

    suspendCoroutine<Unit> { }

    println("After")
}
// Before
```

If you call the above code, you will not see the "After", and the code will not stop running (as our main function never finished). The coroutine is suspended after "Before". Our game was stopped and never resumed. So, how can we resume? Where is this aforementioned Continuation?

Take a look again at the suspendCoroutine invocation and notice that it ends with a lambda expression ({ }). The function passed as an argument will be invoked **before** the suspension. This function gets a continuation as an argument.

```
suspend fun main() {
    println("Before")

    suspendCoroutine<Unit> { continuation ->
        println("Before too")
    }

    println("After")
}
// Before
// Before too
```

---

[10]It directly calls suspendCoroutineUninterceptedOrReturn, which is a primitive function, that means a function with intrinsic implementation.

Such a function calling another function in place is nothing new. This is similar to let, apply, or useLines. The suspendCoroutine function is designed in the same way, which makes it possible to use the continuation just before the suspension. After the suspendCoroutine call, it would be too late. So, the lambda expression passed as a parameter to the suspendCoroutine function is invoked just before the suspension. This lambda is used to store this continuation somewhere or to plan whether to resume it.

We could use it to resume immediately:

```
suspend fun main() {
    println("Before")

    suspendCoroutine<Unit> { continuation ->
        continuation.resume(Unit)
    }

    println("After")
}
// Before
// After
```

Notice that "After" in the example above is printed because we call resume in suspendCoroutine[11].

> Since Kotlin 1.3, the definition of Continuation has been changed. Instead of resume and resumeWithException, there is one resumeWith function that expects Result. The resume and resumeWithException functions we are using are extension functions from the standard library that use resumeWith.

---

[11]This statement is true, but I need to clarify. You might imagine that here we suspend and immediately resume. This is a good intuition, but the truth is that there is an optimization that prevents a suspension if resuming is immediate.

```
inline fun <T> Continuation<T>.resume(value: T): Unit =
    resumeWith(Result.success(value))

inline fun <T> Continuation<T>.resumeWithException(
    exception: Throwable
): Unit = resumeWith(Result.failure(exception))
```

We could also start a different thread that will sleep for a set duration and resume after that time:

```
suspend fun main() {
    println("Before")

    suspendCoroutine<Unit> { continuation ->
        thread {
            println("Suspended")
            Thread.sleep(1000)
            continuation.resume(Unit)
            println("Resumed")
        }
    }

    println("After")
}
// Before
// Suspended
// (1 second delay)
// After
// Resumed
```

This is an important observation. Notice that we can make a function that will resume our continuation after a defined period. In such a case, the continuation is captured by the lambda expression, as shown in the code snippet below.

```
fun continueAfterSecond(continuation: Continuation<Unit>) {
    thread {
        Thread.sleep(1000)
        continuation.resume(Unit)
    }
}

suspend fun main() {
    println("Before")

    suspendCoroutine<Unit> { continuation ->
        continueAfterSecond(continuation)
    }

    println("After")
}
// Before
// (1 sec)
// After
//sampleEnd
```

Such a mechanism works, but it unnecessarily creates threads only to end them after just a second of inactivity. Threads are not cheap, so why waste them? A better way would be to set up an "alarm clock". In JVM, we can use `ScheduledExecutorService` for that. We can set it to call some `continuation.resume(Unit)` after a defined amount of time.

```
private val executor =
    Executors.newSingleThreadScheduledExecutor {
        Thread(it, "scheduler").apply { isDaemon = true }
    }

suspend fun main() {
    println("Before")

    suspendCoroutine<Unit> { continuation ->
        executor.schedule({
            continuation.resume(Unit)
```

```
        }, 1000, TimeUnit.MILLISECONDS)
    }

    println("After")
}
// Before
// (1 second delay)
// After
```

Suspending for a set amount of time seems like a useful feature. Let's extract it into a function. We will name it delay.

```
private val executor =
    Executors.newSingleThreadScheduledExecutor {
        Thread(it, "scheduler").apply { isDaemon = true }
    }

suspend fun delay(timeMillis: Long): Unit =
    suspendCoroutine { cont ->
        executor.schedule({
            cont.resume(Unit)
        }, timeMillis, TimeUnit.MILLISECONDS)
    }

suspend fun main() {
    println("Before")

    delay(1000)

    println("After")
}
// Before
// (1 second delay)
// After
```

The executor still uses a thread, but it is one thread for all coroutines using the delay function. This is much better than blocking one thread every time we need to wait for some time.

This is exactly how `delay` from the Kotlin Coroutines library used to be implemented. The current implementation is more complicated, mainly so as to support testing, but the essential idea remains the same.

Resuming with a value

One thing that might concern you is why we passed `Unit` to the `resume` function. You might also be wondering why we used `Unit` as a type argument for the `suspendCoroutine`. The fact that these two are the same is no coincidence. `Unit` is also returned from the function and is the generic type of the `Continuation` parameter.

```
val ret: Unit =
    suspendCoroutine<Unit> { cont: Continuation<Unit> ->
        cont.resume(Unit)
    }
```

When we call `suspendCoroutine`, we can specify which type will be returned in its continuation. The same type needs to be used when we call `resume`.

```
suspend fun main() {
    val i: Int = suspendCoroutine<Int> { cont ->
        cont.resume(42)
    }
    println(i) // 42

    val str: String = suspendCoroutine<String> { cont ->
        cont.resume("Some text")
    }
    println(str) // Some text

    val b: Boolean = suspendCoroutine<Boolean> { cont ->
        cont.resume(true)
    }
    println(b) // true
}
```

This does not fit well with the game analogy. I don't know of any game in which you can put something inside the game when resuming a save[12] (unless you cheated and googled how to solve the next challenge). However, it makes perfect sense with coroutines. Often we are suspended because we are waiting for some data, such as a network response from an API. This is a common scenario. Your thread is running business logic until it reaches a point where it needs some data. So, it asks your network library to deliver it. Without coroutines, this thread would then need to sit and wait. This would be a huge waste as threads are expensive, especially if this is an important thread, like the Main Thread on Android. With coroutines, it just suspends and gives the library a continuation with the instruction "Once you've got this data, just send it to the resume function". Then the thread can go do other things. Once the data is there, the thread will be used to resume from the point where the coroutine was suspended.

To see this in action, let's see how we might suspend until we receive some data. In the example below, we use a callback function requestUser that is implemented externally.

```kotlin
suspend fun main() {
    println("Before")
    val user = suspendCoroutine<User> { cont ->
        requestUser { user ->
            cont.resume(user)
        }
    }
    println(user)
    println("After")
}
// Before
// (1 second delay)
// User(name=Test)
// After
```

---

[12]During a workshop discussion it turned out there is such a game: in *Don't Starve Together*, when you resume, you can change players. I haven't played it myself, but this sounds like a nice metaphor for resuming with a value.

Calling suspendCoroutine directly is not convenient. We would prefer to have a suspending function instead. We can extract it ourselves.

```kotlin
suspend fun requestUser(): User {
    return suspendCoroutine<User> { cont ->
        requestUser { user ->
            cont.resume(user)
        }
    }
}

suspend fun main() {
    println("Before")
    val user = requestUser()
    println(user)
    println("After")
}
```

Currently, suspending functions are already supported by many popular libraries, such as Retrofit and Room. This is why we rarely need to use callback functions in suspending functions. However, if you have such a need, I recommend using suspendCancellableCoroutine (instead of suspendCoroutine), which will be explained in the *Cancellation* chapter.

```kotlin
suspend fun requestUser(): User {
    return suspendCancellableCoroutine<User> { cont ->
        requestUser { user ->
            cont.resume(user)
        }
    }
}
```

You might wonder what happens if the API gives us not data but some kind of problem. What if the service is dead or responds with an error? In such a case, we cannot return data; instead, we should throw an exception from the place where the coroutine was suspended. This is where we need to resume with an exception.

Resume with an exception

Every function we call might return some value or throw an exception. The same is true for suspendCoroutine. When resume is called, it returns data passed as an argument. When resumeWithException is called, the exception that is passed as an argument is conceptually thrown from the suspension point.

```kotlin
class MyException : Throwable("Just an exception")

suspend fun main() {
    try {
        suspendCoroutine<Unit> { cont ->
            cont.resumeWithException(MyException())
        }
    } catch (e: MyException) {
        println("Caught!")
    }
}
// Caught!
```

This mechanism is used for different kinds of problems. For instance, to signal network exceptions.

```kotlin
suspend fun requestUser(): User {
    return suspendCancellableCoroutine<User> { cont ->
        requestUser { resp ->
            if (resp.isSuccessful) {
                cont.resume(resp.data)
            } else {
                val e = ApiException(
                    resp.code,
                    resp.message
                )
                cont.resumeWithException(e)
            }
        }
    }
}
```

```
suspend fun requestNews(): News {
    return suspendCancellableCoroutine<News> { cont ->
        requestNews(
            onSuccess = { news -> cont.resume(news) },
            onError = { e -> cont.resumeWithException(e) }
        )
    }
}
```

Suspending a coroutine, not a function

One thing that needs to be emphasized here is that we suspend a coroutine, not a function. Suspending functions are not coroutines, just functions that can suspend a coroutine[13]. Imagine that we store a function in some variable and try to resume it after the function call.

```
// Do not do this
var continuation: Continuation<Unit>? = null

suspend fun suspendAndSetContinuation() {
    suspendCoroutine<Unit> { cont ->
        continuation = cont
    }
}

suspend fun main() {
    println("Before")

    suspendAndSetContinuation()
    continuation?.resume(Unit)

    println("After")
}
// Before
```

---

[13]Suspending main function is a special case. Kotlin compiler starts it in a coroutine.

This makes no sense. It is equivalent to stopping a game and planning to resume it at a later point in the game. resume will never be called. You will only see "Before", and your program will never end unless we resume on another thread or another coroutine. To show this, we can set another coroutine to resume after a second.

```
// Do not do this, potential memory leak
var continuation: Continuation<Unit>? = null

suspend fun suspendAndSetContinuation() {
    suspendCoroutine<Unit> { cont ->
        continuation = cont
    }
}

suspend fun main() = coroutineScope {
    println("Before")

    launch {
        delay(1000)
        continuation?.resume(Unit)
    }

    suspendAndSetContinuation()
    println("After")
}
// Before
// (1 second delay)
// After
```

Summary

I hope now you have a clear picture of how suspension works from the user's point of view. It is important, and we will see it throughout the book. It is also practical, as now you can take callback functions and make them suspending functions. If you are like me and like to know exactly how things work, you are likely still wondering about how it is implemented. If you're curious about this, it will be covered in the next chapter. If you don't feel you need to know, just skip it. It is not very practical, it just reveals the magic of Kotlin coroutines.

Coroutines under the hood

There is a certain kind of person who cannot accept that a car can just be driven. They need to open its hood to understand how it works. I am one of these people, so I just had to find out how coroutines work. If you're like this too, you will enjoy this chapter. If not, you can just skip it.

This chapter won't introduce any new tools that you might use. It is purely explanatory. It tries to explain to a satisfactory level how coroutines work. The key lessons are:

- Suspending functions are like state machines, with a possible state at the beginning of the function and after each suspending function call.
- Both the number identifying the state and the local data are kept in the continuation object.
- Continuation of a function decorates a continuation of its caller function; as a result, all these continuations represent a call stack that is used when we resume or a resumed function completes.

If you are interested in learning some internals (simplified, of course), read on.

Continuation-passing style

There are a few ways in which suspending functions could have been implemented, but the Kotlin team decided on an option called **continuation-passing style**[14]. This means that continuations (explained in the previous chapter) are passed from function to function as arguments. By convention, a continuation takes the last parameter position.

---

[14]https://en.wikipedia.org/wiki/Continuation-passing_style

```
suspend fun getUser(): User?
suspend fun setUser(user: User)
suspend fun checkAvailability(flight: Flight): Boolean

// under the hood is
fun getUser(continuation: Continuation<*>): Any?
fun setUser(user: User, continuation: Continuation<*>): Any
fun checkAvailability(
  flight: Flight,
  continuation: Continuation<*>
): Any
```

You might have also noticed that the result type under the hood is different from the originally declared one. It has changed to Any or Any?. Why so? The reason is that a suspending function might be suspended, and so it might not return a declared type. In such a case, it returns a special COROUTINE_SUSPENDED marker, which we will later see in practice. For now, just notice that since getUser might return User? or COROUTINE_SUSPENDED (which is of type Any), its result type must be the closest supertype of User? and Any, so it is Any?. Perhaps one day Kotlin will introduce union types, in which case we will have User? | COROUTINE_SUSPENDED instead.

A very simple function

To dive deeper, let's start with a very simple function that prints something before and after a delay.

```
suspend fun myFunction() {
  println("Before")
  delay(1000) // suspending
  println("After")
}
```

You can already deduce how the myFunction function signature will look under the hood:

```
fun myFunction(continuation: Continuation<*>): Any
```

The next thing is that this function needs its own continuation in order to remember its state. Let's name it MyFunctionContinuation (the actual continuation is an object expression and has no name, but it will be easier to explain this way). At the beginning of its body, myFunction will wrap the continuation (the parameter) with its own continuation (MyFunctionContinuation).

```
val continuation = MyFunctionContinuation(continuation)
```

This should be done only if the continuation isn't wrapped already. If it is, this is part of the resume process, and we should keep the continuation unchanged[15] (this might be confusing now, but later you will better see why).

```
val continuation =
  if (continuation is MyFunctionContinuation) continuation
  else MyFunctionContinuation(continuation)
```

This condition can be simplified to:

```
val continuation = continuation as? MyFunctionContinuation
  ?: MyFunctionContinuation(continuation)
```

Finally, let's talk about the body of our function.

```
suspend fun myFunction() {
  println("Before")
  delay(1000) // suspending
  println("After")
}
```

The function could be started from two places: either from the beginning (in the case of a first call) or from the point after suspension (in the case of resuming from continuation). To identify the current state, we use a field called label. At the start, it is 0, therefore the function will start from the beginning. However, it is set to the next state before each suspension point so that we start from just after the suspension point after a resume.

---

[15]The actual mechanism here is a little more complicated as the first bit of the label is also changed, and this change is checked by the suspending function. This mechanism is needed for suspending functions in order to support recurrence. This has been skipped for the sake of simplicity.

```kotlin
// A simplified picture of how myFunction looks under the hood
fun myFunction(continuation: Continuation<Unit>): Any {
    val continuation = continuation as? MyFunctionContinuation
        ?: MyFunctionContinuation(continuation)

    if (continuation.label == 0) {
        println("Before")
        continuation.label = 1
        if (delay(1000, continuation) == COROUTINE_SUSPENDED){
            return COROUTINE_SUSPENDED
        }
    }
    if (continuation.label == 1) {
        println("After")
        return Unit
    }
    error("Impossible")
}
```

The last important piece is also presented in the snippet above. When delay is suspended, it returns COROUTINE_SUSPENDED, then myFunction returns COROUTINE_SUSPENDED; the same is done by the function that called it, and the function that called this function, and all other functions until the top of the call stack[16]. This is how a suspension ends all these functions and leaves the thread available for other runnables (including coroutines) to be used.

Before we go any further, let's analyze the code above. What would happen if this delay call didn't return COROUTINE_SUSPENDED? What if it just returned Unit instead (we know it won't, but let's hypothesize)? Notice that if the delay just returned Unit, we would just move to the next state, and the function would behave like any other.

Now, let's talk about the continuation, which is implemented as an anonymous class. Simplified, it looks like this:

---

[16]More concretely, COROUTINE_SUSPENDED is propagated until it reaches either the builder function or the 'resume' function.

```
cont = object : ContinuationImpl(continuation) {
    var result: Any? = null
    var label = 0

    override fun invokeSuspend(`$result`: Any?): Any? {
        this.result = `$result`;
        return myFunction(this);
    }
};
```

To improve the readability of our function, I decided to represent it as a class named MyFunctionContinuation. I also decided to hide the inheritance by inlining the ContinuationImpl body. The resulting class is simplified: I've skipped many optimizations and functionalities so as to keep only what is essential.

> In JVM, type arguments are erased during compilation; so, for instance, both Continuation<Unit> or Continuation<String> become just Continuation. Since everything we present here is Kotlin representation of JVM bytecode, you should not worry about these type arguments at all.

The code below presents a complete simplification of how our function looks under the hood:

```
fun myFunction(continuation: Continuation<Unit>): Any {
    val continuation = continuation as? MyFunctionContinuation
        ?: MyFunctionContinuation(continuation)

    if (continuation.label == 0) {
        println("Before")
        continuation.label = 1
        if (delay(1000, continuation) == COROUTINE_SUSPENDED){
            return COROUTINE_SUSPENDED
        }
    }
    if (continuation.label == 1) {
        println("After")
        return Unit
```

```kotlin
    }
    error("Impossible")
}

class MyFunctionContinuation(
    val completion: Continuation<Unit>
) : Continuation<Unit> {
    override val context: CoroutineContext
        get() = completion.context

    var label = 0
    var result: Result<Any>? = null

    override fun resumeWith(result: Result<Unit>) {
        this.result = result
        val res = try {
            val r = myFunction(this)
            if (r == COROUTINE_SUSPENDED) return
            Result.success(r as Unit)
        } catch (e: Throwable) {
            Result.failure(e)
        }
        completion.resumeWith(res)
    }
}
```

If you want to analyze by yourself what suspending functions are under the hood, open the function in IntelliJ IDEA, use Tools > Kotlin > Show Kotlin bytecode, and click the "Decompile" button. As a result, you will see this code decompiled to Java (so more or less how this code would look if it were written in Java).

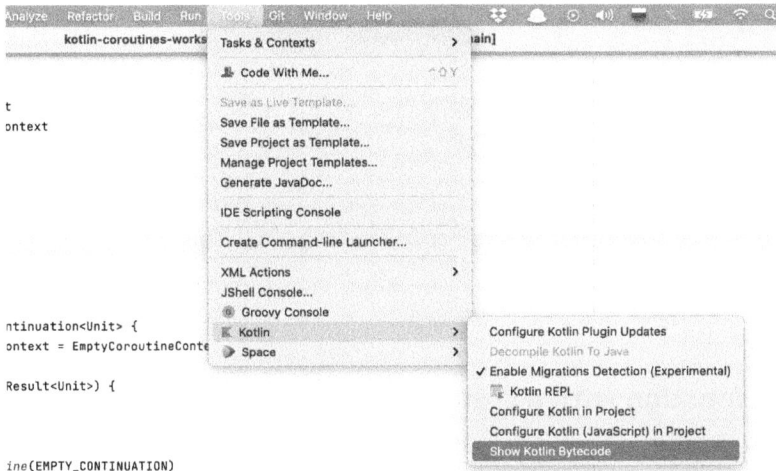

How to show the bytecode generated from the file.

The bytecode generated from the file. Notice the "Decompile" button, which lets us decompile this bytecode to Java.

```
Object $result = ((<undefinedtype>)$continuation).result;
Object var5 = IntrinsicsKt.getCOROUTINE_SUSPENDED();
String var1;
boolean var2;
switch(((<undefinedtype>)$continuation).label) {
case 0:
    ResultKt.throwOnFailure($result);
    var1 = "Before";
    var2 = false;
    System.out.println(var1);
    ((<undefinedtype>)$continuation).label = 1;
    if (DelayKt.delay( timeMillis: 1000L, (Continuation)$continuation) == var5) {
        return var5;
    }
}
```

Bytecode from the Kotlin suspending function decompiled into Java.

A function with a state

If a function has some state (like local variables or parameters) that
needs to be restored after suspension, this state needs to be kept in
this function's continuation. Let's consider the following function:

```
suspend fun myFunction() {
    println("Before")
    var counter = 0
    delay(1000) // suspending
    counter++
    println("Counter: $counter")
    println("After")
}
```

Here `counter` is needed in two states (for a label equal to 0 and 1),
so it needs to be kept in the continuation. It will be stored right before suspension. Restoring these kinds of properties happens at the
beginning of the function. So, this is how the (simplified) function
looks under the hood:

```kotlin
fun myFunction(continuation: Continuation<Unit>): Any {
    val continuation = continuation as? MyFunctionContinuation
        ?: MyFunctionContinuation(continuation)

    var counter = continuation.counter

    if (continuation.label == 0) {
        println("Before")
        counter = 0
        continuation.counter = counter
        continuation.label = 1
        if (delay(1000, continuation) == COROUTINE_SUSPENDED){
            return COROUTINE_SUSPENDED
        }
    }
    if (continuation.label == 1) {
        counter = (counter as Int) + 1
        println("Counter: $counter")
        println("After")
        return Unit
    }
    error("Impossible")
}

class MyFunctionContinuation(
    val completion: Continuation<Unit>
) : Continuation<Unit> {
    override val context: CoroutineContext
        get() = completion.context

    var result: Result<Unit>? = null
    var label = 0
    var counter = 0

    override fun resumeWith(result: Result<Unit>) {
        this.result = result
        val res = try {
            val r = myFunction(this)
            if (r == COROUTINE_SUSPENDED) return
```

```
        Result.success(r as Unit)
    } catch (e: Throwable) {
        Result.failure(e)
    }
    completion.resumeWith(res)
  }
}
```

A function resumed with a value

The situation is slightly different if we actually expect some data from the suspension. Let's analyze the function below:

```
suspend fun printUser(token: String) {
  println("Before")
  val userId = getUserId(token) // suspending
  println("Got userId: $userId")
  val userName = getUserName(userId, token) // suspending
  println(User(userId, userName))
  println("After")
}
```

Here there are two suspending functions: getUserId and getUserName. We also added a parameter token, and our suspending function also returns some values. This all needs to be stored in the continuation:

- token, because it is needed in states 0 and 1,
- userId, because it is needed in states 1 and 2,
- result of type Result, which represents how this function was resumed.

If the function was resumed with a value, the result will be Result.Success(value). In such a case, we can get and use this value. If it was resumed with an exception, the result will be Result.Failure(exception). In such a case, this exception will be thrown.

```kotlin
fun printUser(
    token: String,
    continuation: Continuation<*>
): Any {
    val continuation = continuation as? PrintUserContinuation
        ?: PrintUserContinuation(
            continuation as Continuation<Unit>,
            token
        )

    var result: Result<Any>? = continuation.result
    var userId: String? = continuation.userId
    val userName: String

    if (continuation.label == 0) {
        println("Before")
        continuation.label = 1
        val res = getUserId(token, continuation)
        if (res == COROUTINE_SUSPENDED) {
            return COROUTINE_SUSPENDED
        }
        result = Result.success(res)
    }
    if (continuation.label == 1) {
        userId = result!!.getOrThrow() as String
        println("Got userId: $userId")
        continuation.label = 2
        continuation.userId = userId
        val res = getUserName(userId, continuation)
        if (res == COROUTINE_SUSPENDED) {
            return COROUTINE_SUSPENDED
        }
        result = Result.success(res)
    }
    if (continuation.label == 2) {
        userName = result!!.getOrThrow() as String
        println(User(userId as String, userName))
        println("After")
        return Unit
```

```kotlin
    }
    error("Impossible")
}

class PrintUserContinuation(
    val completion: Continuation<Unit>,
    val token: String
) : Continuation<String> {
    override val context: CoroutineContext
        get() = completion.context

    var label = 0
    var result: Result<Any>? = null
    var userId: String? = null

    override fun resumeWith(result: Result<String>) {
        this.result = result
        val res = try {
            val r = printUser(token, this)
            if (r == COROUTINE_SUSPENDED) return
            Result.success(r as Unit)
        } catch (e: Throwable) {
            Result.failure(e)
        }
        completion.resumeWith(res)
    }
}
```

The call stack

When function a calls function b, the virtual machine needs to store
the state of a somewhere, as well as the address where execution
should return once b is finished. All this is stored in a structure called
call stack[17]. The problem is that when we suspend, we free a thread;
as a result, we clear our call stack. Therefore, the call stack is not
useful when we resume. Instead, the **continuations** serve as a call

_____

[17]The call stack has limited space. When it has all been used,
StackOverflowError occurs. Does this remind you of some popular
website we use to ask or answer technical questions?

stack. Each continuation keeps the state where we suspended (as a label) the function's local variables and parameters (as fields), and the reference to the continuation of the function that called this function. One continuation references another, which references another, etc. As a result, our continuation is like a huge onion: it keeps everything that is generally kept on the call stack. Take a look at the following example:

```
suspend fun a() {
    val user = readUser()
    b()
    b()
    b()
    println(user)
}

suspend fun b() {
    for (i in 1..10) {
        c(i)
    }
}

suspend fun c(i: Int) {
    delay(i * 100L)
    println("Tick")
}
```

A sample continuation could be represented as follows:

```
CContinuation(
  i = 4,
  label = 1,
  completion = BContinuation(
      i = 4,
      label = 1,
      completion = AContinuation(
          label = 2,
          user = User@1234,
          completion = ...
```

```
    )
  )
)
```

Looking at the above representation, how many times was "Tick" already printed (assume readUser is not a suspending function)[18]?

When a continuation is resumed, each continuation first calls its function; once this is done, that continuation resumes the continuation of the function that called the function. This continuation calls its function, and the process repeats until the top of the stack is reached.

```
override fun resumeWith(result: Result<String>) {
    this.result = result
    val res = try {
        val r = printUser(token, this)
        if (r == COROUTINE_SUSPENDED) return
        Result.success(r as Unit)
    } catch (e: Throwable) {
        Result.failure(e)
    }
    completion.resumeWith(res)
}
```

For example, think of a situation where function a calls function b, which calls function c, which is suspended. During resuming, the c continuation first resumes the c function. Once this function is done, the c continuation resumes the b continuation that calls the b function. Once it is done, the b continuation resumes the a continuation, which calls the a function.

The whole process can be visualized with the following sketch:

---

[18]The answer is 13. Since the label on AContinuation is 2, one b function call has already finished (this means 10 ticks). Since i equals 4, three ticks have already been printed in this b function.

Normal call stack   Resume on c

It's similar with exceptions: an uncaught exception is caught in resumeWith and then wrapped with Result.failure(e), and then the function that called our function is resumed with this result.

I hope this all gives you some picture of what is going on when we suspend. The state needs to be stored in a continuation, and the suspension mechanism needs to be supported. When we resume, we need to restore the state from the continuation and either use the result or throw an exception.

```
println( Got userId: $userId )           Setting next label
continuation.label = 2                    Setting next label
continuation.userId = userId              Storing state on continuation
val res = getUserName(userId, continuation)   Calling suspending function
if (res == COROUTINE_SUSPENDED) {
    return COROUTINE_SUSPENDED            Suspension
}
result = Result.success(res)              Setting result if not suspended
}
if (continuation.label == 2) {
    result!!.throwOnFailure()             Throwing is resumed with exception
    userName = result.getOrNull() as String   Reading result value
    println(User(userId as String, userName))
```

The actual code

The actual code that continuations and suspending functions are compiled to is more complicated as it includes optimizations and some additional mechanisms, like:

- constructing a better exceptions stack trace;
- adding coroutine suspension interception (we will talk about this feature later);
- optimizations on different levels (like removing unused variables or tail-call optimization).

Here is a part of the `BaseContinuationImpl` from Kotlin version "1.5.30"; it shows the actual `resumeWith` implementation (other methods and some comments skipped):

```kotlin
internal abstract class BaseContinuationImpl(
    val completion: Continuation<Any?>?
) : Continuation<Any?>, CoroutineStackFrame, Serializable {
    // This implementation is final. This fact is used to
    // unroll resumeWith recursion.
    final override fun resumeWith(result: Result<Any?>) {
        // This loop unrolls recursion in
        // current.resumeWith(param) to make saner and
        // shorter stack traces on resume
        var current = this
        var param = result
        while (true) {
            // Invoke "resume" debug probe on every resumed
            // continuation, so that a debugging library
            // infrastructure can precisely track what part
            // of suspended call stack was already resumed
            probeCoroutineResumed(current)
            with(current) {
                val completion = completion!! // fail fast
                // when trying to resume continuation
                // without completion
                val outcome: Result<Any?> =
                    try {
```

```
                val outcome = invokeSuspend(param)
                if (outcome === COROUTINE_SUSPENDED)
                    return
                Result.success(outcome)
            } catch (exception: Throwable) {
                Result.failure(exception)
            }
        releaseIntercepted()
        // this state machine instance is terminating
        if (completion is BaseContinuationImpl) {
            // unrolling recursion via loop
            current = completion
            param = outcome
        } else {
            // top-level completion reached --
            // invoke and return
            completion.resumeWith(outcome)
            return
        }
        }
        }
    }

    // ...
}
```

As you can see, it uses a loop instead of recursion. This change allows the actual code to make some optimizations and simplifications.

The performance of suspending functions

What is the cost of using suspending functions instead of regular ones? When looking under the hood, many people might have an impression that the cost is significant, but this is not true. Dividing a function into states is cheap as number comparison and execution jumping costs nearly nothing. Saving a state in a continuation is also cheap. We do not copy local variables: we make new variables point to the same points in memory. The only operation that costs something is creating a continuation class, but this is still not a big deal. If you are not worried about the performance of RxJava or callbacks, you should definitely not worry about the performance of suspending functions.

Summary

What is actually under the hood is more complicated than what I've described, but I hope that you've got some idea of the internals of coroutines. The key lessons are:

- Suspending functions are like state machines, with a possible state at the beginning of the function and after each suspending function call.
- Both the label identifying the state and the local data are kept in the continuation object.
- Continuation of one function decorates a continuation of its caller function; as a result, all these continuations represent a call stack that is used when we resume or a resumed function completes.

Coroutines: built-in support vs library

When talking about coroutines, it's common to refer to them as a single concept. In fact, they consist of two components: built-in support provided by the Kotlin language (compiler support and elements in the Kotlin standard library), and the Kotlin Coroutines library (named kotlinx.coroutines). Sometimes they are treated as the same entity, but they are very different from each other.

Built-in language support is designed to be minimalistic and give as much freedom as possible. It can be used to reproduce practically any concurrency style known from other programming languages, but it is not convenient to use it directly. Most of its elements, such as suspendCoroutine or Continuation, are supposed to be used by library creators rather than by application developers.

On the other hand, we have the kotlinx.coroutines library. This is a separate dependency that needs to be added to the project. It's built on top of the built-in language support. It is way easier to use and gives developers a concrete concurrence style.

Built-in support	kotlinx.coroutines library
Compiler support and elements in the Kotlin standard library.	Separate dependency needs to be added to the project.
Elements are in the `kotlin.coroutines` package.	Elements are in the `kotlinx.coroutines` package.
Minimalistic, provides a few basic elements (like `Continuation` or `suspendCoroutine`) and the `suspend` keyword.	Provides many elements (like `launch`, `async`, `Deferred`).
Hard to use directly.	Designed for direct use.
Allows nearly any concurrence style.	Designed for one concrete concurrence style.

Currently, built-in support and the kotlinx.coroutines library are nearly always used together, but that's not a requirement. Many computer science papers[19] show the universality of the suspension concept. It was also shown by the team working on the Kotlin Coroutines library. When looking for the best concurrency style, they used built-in Kotlin support to reproduce the concurrency styles from many other languages (like Go's Goroutines). The current concurrency style offered by kotlinx.coroutines is elegant, convenient, and aligned with other patterns in the programming ecosystem. However, patterns and programming styles change over time. Maybe one day our community will come up with a better concurrency style. If so, someone will most likely be able to implement it by using built-in Kotlin support and ship it as a separate library. This promising new library might even replace the kotlinx.coroutines library. Who knows what the future will bring?

So far in this book we have mostly only focussed on the built-in support. From now on, we will be concentrating on the kotlinx.coroutines library.

---

[19]For example, Revisiting coroutines (2009) by Ana Lúcia De Moura and Roberto Ierusalimschy, and Continuations and coroutines (1984), by Christopher T. Haynes, Daniel P. Friedman, and Mitchell Wand.

Part 2: Kotlin Coroutines library

Now that we understand how built-in support works, it is time to concentrate on the kotlinx.coroutines library. In this part, we will learn everything that is needed to use it properly. We will explore coroutine builders, different coroutine contexts, and how cancellation works. We will finish with practical knowledge on how to set up coroutines, how to test them, and how to safely access a shared state.

Coroutine builders

Suspending functions need to pass continuations to one another. They do not have any trouble calling normal functions, but normal functions cannot call suspending functions.

```kotlin
suspend fun suspendingFun() {
    // ...
    normalFun()
}
```

```kotlin
fun normalFun() {
    // ...
    suspendingFun()
}
```

> Suspend function 'suspendingFun' should be called only from a coroutine or another suspend function
>
> Make normalFun suspend ⌥⇧↵   More actions... ⌥↵
>
> *Main.kt*
> public suspend fun **suspendingFun**(): Unit
> · kotlin-coroutines-workshop.main

Every suspending function needs to be called by another suspending function, which is called by another suspending function, and so on. This all needs to start somewhere. It starts with a **coroutine builder**, a bridge from the normal to the suspending world[20].

We are going to explore the three essential coroutine builders provided by the kotlinx.coroutines library:

- launch
- runBlocking
- async

Each has its own use cases. Let's explore them.

---

[20]It can also start from a suspending main, but even though we use it in a lot in examples, it is not helpful when we write Android or backend applications. It is also good to know that a suspending main is also just started by a builder, but we don't see it because Kotlin does that for us.

`launch` builder

The way `launch` works is conceptually similar to starting a new thread (`thread` function). We just start a coroutine, and it will run independently, like a firework that is launched into the air. This is how we use `launch` - to start a process.

```kotlin
fun main() {
    GlobalScope.launch {
        delay(1000L)
        println("World!")
    }
    GlobalScope.launch {
        delay(1000L)
        println("World!")
    }
    GlobalScope.launch {
        delay(1000L)
        println("World!")
    }
    println("Hello,")
    Thread.sleep(2000L)
}
// Hello,
// (1 sec)
// World!
// World!
// World!
```

The `launch` function is an extension function on the `CoroutineScope` interface. This is part of an important mechanism called *structured concurrency*, whose purpose is to build a relationship between the parent coroutine and a child coroutine. Later in this chapter, we will learn about structured concurrency, but for now we will avoid this topic by calling `launch` (and later `async`) on the `GlobalScope` object. This is not a standard practice though as we should rarely use `GlobalScope` in real-life projects.

Another thing you might have noticed is that at the end of the `main` function we need to call `Thread.sleep`. Without doing this, this function would end immediately after launching the coroutines, so they wouldn't have a chance to do their job. This is because `delay` does not block the thread: it suspends a coroutine. You might remember from the *How does suspension work?*[21] chapter that `delay` just sets a timer to resume after a set amount of time, and suspends a coroutine until then. If the thread is not blocked, nothing is busy, so nothing stops the program from finishing (later we will see that if we use structured concurrency, `Thread.sleep` is not needed).

To some degree, how `launch` works is similar to a daemon thread[22] but much cheaper. This metaphor is useful initially but it becomes problematic later. Maintaining a blocked thread is always costly, while maintaining a suspended coroutine is almost free (as explained in the *Coroutines under the hood* chapter). They both start some independent processes and need something that will prevent the program ending before they are done (in the example below, this is `Thread.sleep(2000L)`).

```kotlin
fun main() {
    thread(isDaemon = true) {
        Thread.sleep(1000L)
        println("World!")
    }
    thread(isDaemon = true) {
        Thread.sleep(1000L)
        println("World!")
    }
    thread(isDaemon = true) {
        Thread.sleep(1000L)
        println("World!")
    }
    println("Hello,")
    Thread.sleep(2000L)
}
```

runBlocking builder

The general rule is that coroutines should never block threads, only suspend them. On the other hand, there are cases in which blocking

---

[21]https://kt.academy/article/cc-suspension

[22]A daemon thread is a low-priority thread that runs in the background. Here I compare `launch` to a daemon thread because both do not stop the program from ending.

is necessary. Like in the main function, we need to block the thread, otherwise our program will end too early. For such cases, we might use runBlocking.

runBlocking is a very atypical builder. It blocks the thread it has been started on whenever its coroutine is suspended[23] (similar to suspending main). This means that delay(1000L) inside runBlocking will behave like Thread.sleep(1000L)[24].

```kotlin
fun main() {
    runBlocking {
        delay(1000L)
        println("World!")
    }
    runBlocking {
        delay(1000L)
        println("World!")
    }
    runBlocking {
        delay(1000L)
        println("World!")
    }
    println("Hello,")
}
// (1 sec)
// World!
// (1 sec)
// World!
// (1 sec)
// World!
// Hello,
```

---

[23]To be more precise, it runs a new coroutine and blocks the current thread interruptibly until its completion.

[24]Using a dispatcher, we can make runBlocking run on a different thread. But still, the thread on which this builder has been started will be blocked until the coroutine is done.

```kotlin
fun main() {
    Thread.sleep(1000L)
    println("World!")
    Thread.sleep(1000L)
    println("World!")
    Thread.sleep(1000L)
    println("World!")
    println("Hello,")
}
// (1 sec)
// World!
// (1 sec)
// World!
// (1 sec)
// World!
// Hello,
```

There are actually a couple of specific use cases in which `runBlocking` is used. The first one is the main function, where we need to block the thread, because otherwise the program will end. Another common use case is unit tests, where we need to block the thread for the same reason.

```kotlin
fun main() = runBlocking {
    // ...
}

class MyTests {

    @Test
    fun `a test`() = runBlocking {

    }
}
```

We might use `runBlocking` in our example to replace `Thread.sleep(2000)` with `delay(2000)`. Later we will see that it is even more useful once we introduce structured concurrency.

```
fun main() = runBlocking {
    GlobalScope.launch {
        delay(1000L)
        println("World!")
    }
    GlobalScope.launch {
        delay(1000L)
        println("World!")
    }
    GlobalScope.launch {
        delay(1000L)
        println("World!")
    }
    println("Hello,")
    delay(2000L) // still needed
}
// Hello,
// (1 sec)
// World!
// World!
// World!
```

runBlocking used to be an important builder, but in modern programming it is used rather rarely. In unit tests, we often use its successor runTest instead, which makes coroutines operate in virtual time (a very useful feature for testing which we will describe in the *Testing coroutines* chapter). For the main function, we often make it suspending.

```
suspend fun main() {
    GlobalScope.launch {
        delay(1000L)
        println("World!")
    }
    GlobalScope.launch {
        delay(1000L)
        println("World!")
    }
    GlobalScope.launch {
```

```
        delay(1000L)
        println("World!")
    }
    println("Hello,")
    delay(2000L)
}
// Hello,
// (1 sec)
// World!
// World!
// World!
```

Suspending main is convenient, but for now we will keep using runBlocking[25].

async **builder**

The async coroutine builder is similar to launch, but it is designed to produce a value. This value needs to be returned by the lambda expression[26]. The async function returns an object of type Deferred<T>, where T is the type of the produced value. Deferred has a suspending method await, which returns this value once it is ready. In the example below, the produced value is 42, and its type is Int, so Deferred<Int> is returned, and await returns 42 of type Int.

```
fun main() = runBlocking {
    val resultDeferred: Deferred<Int> = GlobalScope.async {
        delay(1000L)
        42
    }
    // do other stuff...
    val result: Int = resultDeferred.await() // (1 sec)
    println(result) // 42
    // or just
```

[25]The reason is that runBlocking creates a scope, while suspending main does not unless we use the coroutineScope function, which we will introduce later.

[26]To be strict with wording: by the argument of a functional type placed in the last position.

```
    println(resultDeferred.await()) // 42
}
```

Just like the `launch` builder, `async` starts a coroutine immediately when it is called. So, it is a way to start a few processes at once and then await all their results. The returned `Deferred` stores a value inside itself once it is produced, so once it is ready it will be immediately returned from `await`. However, if we call `await` before the value is produced, we are suspended until the value is ready.

```
fun main() = runBlocking {
    val res1 = GlobalScope.async {
        delay(1000L)
        "Text 1"
    }
    val res2 = GlobalScope.async {
        delay(3000L)
        "Text 2"
    }
    val res3 = GlobalScope.async {
        delay(2000L)
        "Text 3"
    }
    println(res1.await())
    println(res2.await())
    println(res3.await())
}
// (1 sec)
// Text 1
// (2 sec)
// Text 2
// Text 3
```

How the `async` builder works is very similar to `launch`, but it has additional support for returning a value. If all `launch` functions were replaced with `async`, the code would still work fine. But don't do that! `async` is about producing a value, so if we don't need a value, we should use `launch`.

```
fun main() = runBlocking {
    // Don't do that!
    // this is misleading to use async as launch
    GlobalScope.async {
        delay(1000L)
        println("World!")
    }
    println("Hello,")
    delay(2000L)
}
// Hello,
// (1 sec)
// World!
```

The async builder is often used to parallelize two processes, such as obtaining data from two different places, to combine them together.

```
scope.launch {
    val news = async {
        newsRepo.getNews()
            .sortedByDescending { it.date }
    }
    val newsSummary = newsRepo.getNewsSummary()
    // we could wrap it with async as well,
    // but it would be redundant
    view.showNews(
        newsSummary,
        news.await()
    )
}
```

Structured Concurrency

If a coroutine is started on GlobalScope, the program will not wait for it. As previously mentioned, coroutines do not block any threads, and nothing prevents the program from ending. This is why, in the below example, an additional delay at the end of runBlocking needs to be called if we want to see "World!" printed.

```
fun main() = runBlocking {
    GlobalScope.launch {
        delay(1000L)
        println("World!")
    }
    GlobalScope.launch {
        delay(2000L)
        println("World!")
    }
    println("Hello,")
    //    delay(3000L)
}
// Hello,
```

Why do we need this GlobalScope in the first place? It is because launch and async are extension functions on CoroutineScope. However, if you take a look at the definitions of these and of runBlocking, you will see that the block parameter is a function type whose receiver type is also CoroutineScope.

```
fun <T> runBlocking(
    context: CoroutineContext = EmptyCoroutineContext,
    block: suspend CoroutineScope.() -> T
): T

fun CoroutineScope.launch(
    context: CoroutineContext = EmptyCoroutineContext,
    start: CoroutineStart = CoroutineStart.DEFAULT,
    block: suspend CoroutineScope.() -> Unit
): Job

fun <T> CoroutineScope.async(
    context: CoroutineContext = EmptyCoroutineContext,
    start: CoroutineStart = CoroutineStart.DEFAULT,
    block: suspend CoroutineScope.() -> T
): Deferred<T>
```

This means that we can get rid of the GlobalScope; instead, launch can be called on the receiver provided by runBlocking, so with this.launch or simply launch. As a result, launch becomes a child of runBlocking. As parents might recognize, a parental responsibility is to wait for all their children, so runBlocking will suspend until all its children are finished.

```kotlin
fun main() = runBlocking {
    this.launch { // same as just launch
        delay(1000L)
        println("World!")
    }
    launch { // same as this.launch
        delay(2000L)
        println("World!")
    }
    println("Hello,")
}
// Hello,
// (1 sec)
// World!
// (1 sec)
// World!
```

A parent provides a scope for its children, and they are called in this scope. This builds a relationship that is called a *structured concurrency*. Here are the most important effects of the parent-child relationship:

- children inherit context from their parent (but they can also overwrite it, as will be explained in the *Coroutine context* chapter);
- a parent suspends until all the children are finished (this will be explained in the *Job and children awaiting* chapter);
- when the parent is cancelled, its child coroutines are cancelled too (this will be explained in the *Cancellation* chapter);
- when a child raises an error, it destroys the parent as well (this will be explained in the *Exception handling* chapter).

Notice that, unlike other coroutine builders, runBlocking is not an extension function on CoroutineScope. This means that it cannot be a child: it can only be used as a root coroutine (the parent of all the children in a hierarchy). This means that runBlocking will be used in different cases than other coroutines. As we mentioned before, this is very different from other builders.

The bigger picture

Suspending functions need to be called from other suspending functions. This all needs to start with a coroutine builder. Except for runBlocking, builders need to be started on CoroutineScope. In our simple examples, the scope is provided by runBlocking, but in bigger applications it is either constructed by us (we will explain how to do this in the *Constructing coroutine scope* chapter) or it is provided by the framework we use (for instance, Ktor on a backend or Android KTX on Android). Once the first builder is started on a scope, other builders can be started on the scope of the first builder, and so on. This is in essence how our applications are structured.

Here are a few examples of how coroutines are used in real-life projects. The first two are typical for both backend and Android. MainPresenter represents a case typical for Android. UserController represents a case typical for backend applications.

```
class NetworkUserRepository(
    private val api: UserApi,
) : UserRepository {
    suspend fun getUser(): User = api.getUser().toDomainUser()
}

class NetworkNewsRepository(
    private val api: NewsApi,
    private val settings: SettingsRepository,
) : NewsRepository {

    suspend fun getNews(): List<News> = api.getNews()
        .map { it.toDomainNews() }

    suspend fun getNewsSummary(): List<News> {
        val type = settings.getNewsSummaryType()
        return api.getNewsSummary(type)
    }
}
```

```kotlin
class MainPresenter(
    private val view: MainView,
    private val userRepo: UserRepository,
    private val newsRepo: NewsRepository
) : BasePresenter {

    fun onCreate() {
        scope.launch {
            val user = userRepo.getUser()
            view.showUserData(user)
        }
        scope.launch {
            val news = async {
                newsRepo.getNews()
                    .sortedByDescending { it.date }
            }
            val newsSummary = async {
                newsRepo.getNewsSummary()
            }
            view.showNews(newsSummary.await(), news.await())
        }
    }
}

@Controller
class UserController(
    private val tokenService: TokenService,
    private val userService: UserService,
) {
    @GetMapping("/me")
    suspend fun findUser(
        @PathVariable userId: String,
        @RequestHeader("Authorization") authorization: String
    ): UserJson {
        val userId = tokenService.readUserId(authorization)
        val user = userService.findUserById(userId)
        return user.toJson()
    }
```

```
}
```

There is one problem though: what about suspending functions? We can suspend there, but we do not have any scope. Passing scope as an argument is not a good solution (as we will see in the *Scoping functions* chapter). Instead, we should use the `coroutineScope` function, which is a suspending function that creates a scope for builders.

Using `coroutineScope`

Imagine that in some repository function you need to asynchronously load two resources, for example user data and a list of articles. In this case, you want to return only those articles that should be seen by the user. To call `async`, we need a scope, but we don't want to pass it to a function[27]. To create a scope out of a suspending function, we use the `coroutineScope` function.

```
suspend fun getArticlesForUser(
    userToken: String?,
): List<ArticleJson> = coroutineScope {
    val articles = async { articleRepository.getArticles() }
    val user = userService.getUser(userToken)
    articles.await()
        .filter { canSeeOnList(user, it) }
        .map { toArticleJson(it) }
}
```

`coroutineScope` is just a suspending function that creates a scope for its lambda expression. The function returns whatever is returned by the lambda expression (like `let`, `run`, `use`, or `runBlocking`). So, in the above example, it returns `List<ArticleJson>` because this is what is returned from the lambda expression.

`coroutineScope` is a standard function we use when we need a scope inside a suspending function. It is really important. The way it is designed is perfect for this use case, but to analyze it we first need to learn a bit about context, cancelling, and exception handling. This is why the function will be explained in detail later in a dedicated chapter (*Coroutine scope functions*).

---

[27]In the *Coroutine scope functions* chapter, we will explain in detail why.

We can also start using the suspending main function together with
coroutineScope, which is a modern alternative to using the main
function with runBlocking.

```kotlin
suspend fun main(): Unit = coroutineScope {
  launch {
      delay(1000L)
      println("World!")
  }
  println("Hello,")
}
// Hello,
// (1 sec)
// World!
```

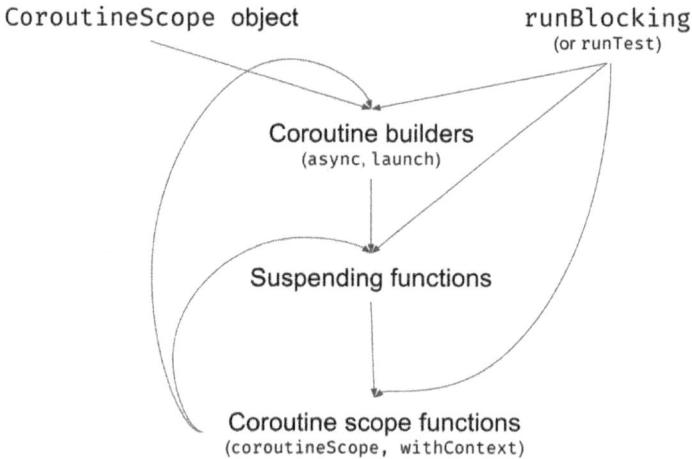

A diagram showing how different kinds of elements of the kotlinx.coroutines library are
used. We generally start with a scope or runBlocking. In these, we can call other builders
or suspending functions. We cannot run builders on suspending functions, so we use
coroutine scope functions (like coroutineScope).

Summary

This knowledge is enough for most Kotlin coroutine usages. In most
cases, we just have suspending functions calling other suspending or

normal functions. If we need to introduce concurrent processing, we wrap a function with `coroutineScope` and use builders in its scope. Everything needs to start with some builders called in some scope. We will learn in later parts how to construct such a scope, but for most projects it needs to be defined once and is touched only rarely.

Even though we have learned the essentials, there is still a lot to learn about. In the next chapters, we will dive deeper into coroutines. We will learn to use different contexts, how to tame cancellations, exception handling, how to test coroutines, etc. There are still a lot of great features to discover.

Coroutine context

If you take a look at the coroutine builders' definitions, you will see that their first parameter is of type CoroutineContext.

```
public fun CoroutineScope.launch(
    context: CoroutineContext = EmptyCoroutineContext,
    start: CoroutineStart = CoroutineStart.DEFAULT,
    block: suspend CoroutineScope.() -> Unit
): Job {
    ...
}
```

The receiver and the last argument's receiver are of type CoroutineScope[28]. This CoroutineScope seems to be an important concept, so let's check out its definition:

```
public interface CoroutineScope {
    public val coroutineContext: CoroutineContext
}
```

It seems to be just a wrapper around CoroutineContext. So, you might want to recall how Continuation is defined.

```
public interface Continuation<in T> {
    public val context: CoroutineContext
    public fun resumeWith(result: Result<T>)
}
```

Continuation contains CoroutineContext as well. This type is used by the most important Kotlin coroutine elements. This must be a really important concept, so what is it?

---

[28]Let's clear up the nomenclature. launch is an extension function on CoroutineScope, so CoroutineScope is its receiver type. The extension function's receiver is the object we reference with this.

`CoroutineContext` interface

`CoroutineContext` is an interface that represents an element or a collection of elements. It is conceptually similar to a map or a set collection: it is an indexed set of `Element` instances like `Job`, `CoroutineName`, `CouroutineDispatcher`, etc. The unusual thing is that each `Element` is also a `CoroutineContext`. So, every element in a collection is a collection in itself.

This concept is quite intuitive. Imagine a mug. It is a single element, but it is also a collection that contains a single element. When you add another mug, you have a collection with two elements.

In order to allow convenient context specification and modification, each `CoroutineContext` element is a `CoroutineContext` itself, as in the example below (adding contexts and setting a coroutine builder context will be explained later). Just specifying or adding contexts is much easier than creating an explicit set.

```
launch(CoroutineName("Name1")) { ... }
launch(CoroutineName("Name2") + Job()) { ... }
```

Every element in this set has a unique `Key` that is used to identify it. These keys are compared by reference.

For example `CoroutineName` or `Job` implement `CoroutineContext.Element`, which implements the `CoroutineContext` interface.

```
fun main() {
    val name: CoroutineName = CoroutineName("A name")
    val element: CoroutineContext.Element = name
    val context: CoroutineContext = element

    val job: Job = Job()
    val jobElement: CoroutineContext.Element = job
    val jobContext: CoroutineContext = jobElement
}
```

It's the same with `SupervisorJob`, `CoroutineExceptionHandler` and dispatchers from the `Dispatchers` object. These are the most important coroutine contexts. They will be explained in the next chapters.

Finding elements in CoroutineContext

Since CoroutineContext is like a collection, we can find an element
with a concrete key using get. Another option is to use square brackets, because in Kotlin the get method is an operator and can be
invoked using square brackets instead of an explicit function call.
Just like in Map: when an element is in the context, it will be returned.
If it is not, null will be returned instead.

```
fun main() {
    val ctx: CoroutineContext = CoroutineName("A name")

    val coroutineName: CoroutineName? = ctx[CoroutineName]
    // or ctx.get(CoroutineName)
    println(coroutineName?.name) // A name
    val job: Job? = ctx[Job] // or ctx.get(Job)
    println(job) // null
```

> CoroutineContext is part of the built-in support
> for Kotlin coroutines, so it is imported from
> kotlin.coroutines, while contexts like Job or
> CoroutineName are part of the kotlinx.coroutines library,
> so they need to be imported from kotlinx.coroutines.

To find a CoroutineName, we use just CoroutineName. This is not a type
or a class: it is a companion object. It is a feature of Kotlin that a name
of a class used by itself acts as a reference to its companion object, so
ctx[CoroutineName] is just a shortcut to ctx[CoroutineName.Key].

```
data class CoroutineName(
    val name: String
) : AbstractCoroutineContextElement(CoroutineName) {

    override fun toString(): String = "CoroutineName($name)"

    companion object Key : CoroutineContext.Key<CoroutineName>
}
```

It is common practice in the kotlinx.coroutines library to use
companion objects as keys to elements with the same name. This

makes it easier to remember[29]. A key might point to a class (like
CoroutineName) or to an interface (like Job) that is implemented by
many classes with the same key (like Job and SupervisorJob).

```
interface Job : CoroutineContext.Element {
    companion object Key : CoroutineContext.Key<Job>

    // ...
}
```

Adding contexts

What makes CoroutineContext truly useful is the ability to merge
two of them together.

When two elements with different keys are added, the resulting
context responds to both keys.

```
fun main() {
    val ctx1: CoroutineContext = CoroutineName("Name1")
    println(ctx1[CoroutineName]?.name) // Name1
    println(ctx1[Job]?.isActive) // null

    val ctx2: CoroutineContext = Job()
    println(ctx2[CoroutineName]?.name) // null
    println(ctx2[Job]?.isActive) // true, because "Active"
    // is the default state of a job created this way

    val ctx3 = ctx1 + ctx2
    println(ctx3[CoroutineName]?.name) // Name1
    println(ctx3[Job]?.isActive) // true
```

When another element with the same key is added, just like in a map,
the new element replaces the previous one.

---

[29]The companion object below is named Key. We can name companion objects, but this changes little in terms of how they are used.
The default companion object name is Companion, so this name is
used when we need to reference this object using reflection or when
we define an extension function on it. Here we use Key instead.

```
fun main() {
    val ctx1: CoroutineContext = CoroutineName("Name1")
    println(ctx1[CoroutineName]?.name) // Name1

    val ctx2: CoroutineContext = CoroutineName("Name2")
    println(ctx2[CoroutineName]?.name) // Name2

    val ctx3 = ctx1 + ctx2
    println(ctx3[CoroutineName]?.name) // Name2
}
```

Empty coroutine context

Since CoroutineContext is like a collection, we also have an empty context. Such a context by itself returns no elements; if we add it to another context, it behaves exactly like this other context.

```
fun main() {
    val empty: CoroutineContext = EmptyCoroutineContext
    println(empty[CoroutineName]) // null
    println(empty[Job]) // null

    val ctxName = empty + CoroutineName("Name1") + empty
    println(ctxName[CoroutineName]) // CoroutineName(Name1)
}
```

Subtracting elements

Elements can also be removed from a context by their key using the minusKey function.

> The minus operator is not overloaded for CoroutineContext. I believe this is because its meaning would not be clear enough, as explained in Effective Kotlin Item 12: *An operator's meaning should be consistent with its function name.*

```
fun main() {
    val ctx = CoroutineName("Name1") + Job()
    println(ctx[CoroutineName]?.name) // Name1
    println(ctx[Job]?.isActive) // true

    val ctx2 = ctx.minusKey(CoroutineName)
    println(ctx2[CoroutineName]?.name) // null
    println(ctx2[Job]?.isActive) // true

    val ctx3 = (ctx + CoroutineName("Name2"))
        .minusKey(CoroutineName)
    println(ctx3[CoroutineName]?.name) // null
    println(ctx3[Job]?.isActive) // true
}
```

Folding context

If we need to do something for each element in a context, we can use the `fold` method, which is similar to `fold` for other collections. It takes:

- an initial accumulator value;
- an operation to produce the next state of the accumulator, based on the current state, and the element it is currently invoked in.

```
fun main() {
    val ctx = CoroutineName("Name1") + Job()

    ctx.fold("") { acc, element -> "$acc$element " }
        .also(::println)
    // CoroutineName(Name1) JobImpl{Active}@dbab622e

    val empty = emptyList<CoroutineContext>()
    ctx.fold(empty) { acc, element -> acc + element }
        .joinToString()
        .also(::println)
    // CoroutineName(Name1), JobImpl{Active}@dbab622e
}
```

Coroutine context and builders

So CoroutineContext is just a way to hold and pass data. By default, the parent passes its context to the child, which is one of the parent-child relationship effects. We say that the child inherits context from its parent.

```
fun CoroutineScope.log(msg: String) {
    val name = coroutineContext[CoroutineName]?.name
    println("[$name] $msg")
}


fun main() = runBlocking(CoroutineName("main")) {
    log("Started") // [main] Started
    val v1 = async {
        delay(500)
        log("Running async") // [main] Running async
        42
    }
    launch {
        delay(1000)
        log("Running launch") // [main] Running launch
    }
    log("The answer is ${v1.await()}")
    // [main] The answer is 42
}
```

Each child might have a specific context defined in the argument. This context overrides the one from the parent.

```
fun main() = runBlocking(CoroutineName("main")) {
    log("Started") // [main] Started
    val v1 = async(CoroutineName("c1")) {
        delay(500)
        log("Running async") // [c1] Running async
        42
    }
    launch(CoroutineName("c2")) {
        delay(1000)
```

```
        log("Running launch") // [c2] Running launch
    }
    log("The answer is ${v1.await()}")
    // [main] The answer is 42
}
```

A simplified formula to calculate a coroutine context is:

```
defaultContext + parentContext + childContext
```

Since new elements always replace old ones with the same key, the child context always overrides elements with the same key from the parent context. The defaults are used only for keys that are not specified anywhere else. Currently, the defaults only set Dispatchers.Default when no ContinuationInterceptor is set, and they only set CoroutineId when the application is in debug mode.

There is a special context called Job, which is mutable and is used to communicate between a coroutine's child and its parent. The next chapters will be dedicated to the effects of this communication.

Accessing context in a suspending function

CoroutineScope has a coroutineContext property that can be used to access the context. But what if we are in a regular suspending function? As you might remember from the *Coroutines under the hood* chapter, context is referenced by continuations, which are passed to each suspending function. So, it is possible to access a parent's context in a suspending function. To do this, we use the coroutineContext property, which is available in every suspending scope.

```
suspend fun printName() {
    println(coroutineContext[CoroutineName]?.name)
}

suspend fun main() = withContext(CoroutineName("Outer")) {
    printName() // Outer
    launch(CoroutineName("Inner")) {
        printName() // Inner
```

```
    }
    delay(10)
    printName() // Outer
}
```

Creating our own context

It is not a common need, but we can create our own coroutine context pretty easily. To do this, the easiest way is to create a class that implements the CoroutineContext.Element interface. Such a class needs a property key of type CoroutineContext.Key<*>. This key will be used as the key that identifies this context. The common practice is to use this class's companion object as a key. This is how a very simple coroutine context can be implemented:

```
class MyCustomContext : CoroutineContext.Element {

    override val key: CoroutineContext.Key<*> = Key

    companion object Key :
        CoroutineContext.Key<MyCustomContext>
}
```

Such a context will behave a lot like CoroutineName: it will propagate from parent to child, but any children will be able to override it with a different context with the same key. To see this in practice, below you can see an example context that is designed to print consecutive numbers.

```
class CounterContext(
    private val name: String
) : CoroutineContext.Element {
    override val key: CoroutineContext.Key<*> = Key
    private var nextNumber = 0

    fun printNext() {
        println("$name: $nextNumber")
        nextNumber++
    }
```

```
    companion object Key :CoroutineContext.Key<CounterContext>
}

suspend fun printNext() {
    coroutineContext[CounterContext]?.printNext()
}

suspend fun main(): Unit =
    withContext(CounterContext("Outer")) {
        printNext() // Outer: 0
        launch {
            printNext() // Outer: 1
            launch {
                printNext() // Outer: 2
            }
            launch(CounterContext("Inner")) {
                printNext() // Inner: 0
                printNext() // Inner: 1
                launch {
                    printNext() // Inner: 2
                }
            }
        }
        printNext() // Outer: 3
    }
```

I have seen custom contexts in use as a kind of dependency injection -
to easily inject different values in production than in tests. However,
I don't think this will become standard practice.

```
data class User(val id: String, val name: String)

abstract class UuidProviderContext :
    CoroutineContext.Element {

    abstract fun nextUuid(): String

    override val key: CoroutineContext.Key<*> = Key
```

```
    companion object Key :
        CoroutineContext.Key<UuidProviderContext>
}


class RealUuidProviderContext : UuidProviderContext() {
    override fun nextUuid(): String =
        UUID.randomUUID().toString()
}


class FakeUuidProviderContext(
    private val fakeUuid: String
) : UuidProviderContext() {
    override fun nextUuid(): String = fakeUuid
}


suspend fun nextUuid(): String =
    checkNotNull(coroutineContext[UuidProviderContext]) {
        "UuidProviderContext not present"
    }
        .nextUuid()


// function under test
suspend fun makeUser(name: String) = User(
    id = nextUuid(),
    name = name
)


suspend fun main(): Unit {
    // production case
    withContext(RealUuidProviderContext()) {
        println(makeUser("Michał"))
        // e.g. User(id=d260482a-..., name=Michał)
    }

    // test case
    withContext(FakeUuidProviderContext("FAKE_UUID")) {
        val user = makeUser("Michał")
        println(user) // User(id=FAKE_UUID, name=Michał)
```

```
            assertEquals(User("FAKE_UUID", "Michał"), user)
    }
}
```

Summary

CoroutineContext is conceptually similar to a map or a set collection. It is an indexed set of Element instances, where each Element is also a CoroutineContext. Every element in it has a unique Key that is used to identify it. This way, CoroutineContext is just a universal way to group and pass objects to coroutines. These objects are kept by the coroutines and can determine how these coroutines should be running (what their state is, in which thread, etc). In the next chapters, we will discuss the most essential coroutine contexts in the Kotlin coroutines library.

Jobs and awaiting children

In the *Structured Concurrency* chapter, we mentioned the following consequences of the parent-child relationship:

- children inherit context from their parent;
- a parent suspends until all the children are finished;
- when the parent is cancelled, its child coroutines are also cancelled;
- when a child is destroyed, it also destroys the parent.

The fact that a child inherits its context from its parent is a basic part of a coroutine builder's behavior.

```kotlin
fun main(): Unit = runBlocking(CoroutineName("main")) {
    val name = coroutineContext[CoroutineName]?.name
    println(name) // main
    launch {
        delay(1000)
        val name = coroutineContext[CoroutineName]?.name
        println(name) // main
    }
}
```

The other three important consequences of structured concurrency depend fully on the Job context. Furthermore, Job can be used to cancel coroutines, track their state, and much more. It is really important and useful, so this and the next two chapters are dedicated to the Job context and the essential Kotlin Coroutine mechanisms that are connected to it.

What is Job?

Conceptually, a job represents a cancellable thing with a lifecycle. Formally, Job is an interface, but it has a concrete contract and state, so it might be treated similarly to an abstract class.

A job lifecycle is represented by its state. Here is a graph of states and the transitions between them:

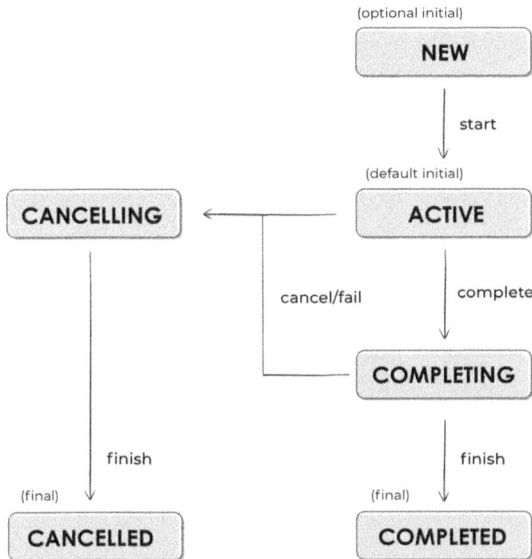

(optional initial)

NEW

start

(default initial)

CANCELLING ← **ACTIVE**

cancel/fail   complete

COMPLETING

finish   finish

(final)   (final)

CANCELLED   **COMPLETED**

A diagram of job (so also coroutine) states.

In the "Active" state, a job is running and doing its job. If the job is created with a coroutine builder, this is the state where the body of this coroutine will be executed. In this state, we can start child coroutines. Most coroutines will start in the "Active" state. Only those that are started lazily will start with the "New" state. These need to be started in order for them to move to the "Active" state. When a coroutine is executing its body, it is surely in the "Active" state. When it is done, its state changes to "Completing", where it waits for its children. Once all its children are done, the job changes its state to "Completed", which is a terminal one. Alternatively, if a job cancels or fails when running (in the "Active" or "Completing" state), its state will change to "Cancelling". In this state, we have the last chance to do some clean-up, like closing connections or freeing resources (we will see how to do this in the next chapter). Once this is done, the job will
move to the "Cancelled" state.

The state is displayed in a job's toString[30]. In the example below, we see different jobs as their states change. The last one is started lazily, which means it does not start automatically. All the others will immediately become active once created.

The code below presents Job in different states. I use join to await coroutine completion. This will be explained later.

```kotlin
suspend fun main() = coroutineScope {
    // Job created with a builder is active
    val job = Job()
    println(job) // JobImpl{Active}@ADD
    // until we complete it with a method
    job.complete()
    println(job) // JobImpl{Completed}@ADD

    // launch is initially active by default
    val activeJob = launch {
        delay(1000)
    }
    println(activeJob) // StandaloneCoroutine{Active}@ADD
    // here we wait until this job is done
    activeJob.join() // (1 sec)
    println(activeJob) // StandaloneCoroutine{Completed}@ADD

    // launch started lazily is in New state
    val lazyJob = launch(start = CoroutineStart.LAZY) {
        delay(1000)
    }
    println(lazyJob) // LazyStandaloneCoroutine{New}@ADD
    // we need to start it, to make it active
    lazyJob.start()
    println(lazyJob) // LazyStandaloneCoroutine{Active}@ADD
    lazyJob.join() // (1 sec)
    println(lazyJob) //LazyStandaloneCoroutine{Completed}@ADD
}
```

---

[30]I hope I do not need to remind the reader that toString should be used for debugging and logging purposes; it should not be parsed in code as this would break this function's contract, as I described in *Effective Kotlin*.

To check the state in code, we use the properties isActive, isCompleted, and isCancelled.

State	isActive	isCompleted	isCancelled
New (optional initial state)	false	false	false
Active (default initial state)	true	false	false
Completing (transient state)	true	false	false
Cancelling (transient state)	false	false	true
Cancelled (final state)	false	true	true
Completed (final state)	false	true	false

As mentioned above, each coroutine has its own job. Let's see how we can access and use it.

Coroutine builders create their jobs based on their parent job

Every coroutine builder from the Kotlin Coroutines library creates its own job. Most coroutine builders return their jobs, so it can be used elsewhere. This is clearly visible for launch, where Job is an explicit result type.

```
fun main(): Unit = runBlocking {
    val job: Job = launch {
        delay(1000)
        println("Test")
    }
}
```

The type returned by the async function is Deferred<T>, and Deferred<T> also implements the Job interface, so it can also be used in the same way.

```
fun main(): Unit = runBlocking {
    val deferred: Deferred<String> = async {
        delay(1000)
        "Test"
    }
    val job: Job = deferred
}
```

Since `Job` is a coroutine context, we can access it using
`coroutineContext[Job]`. However, there is also an extension
property `job`, which lets us access the job more easily.

```
// extension
val CoroutineContext.job: Job
    get() = get(Job) ?: error("Current context doesn't...")

// usage
fun main(): Unit = runBlocking {
    print(coroutineContext.job.isActive) // true
}
```

There is a very important rule: `Job` is the only coroutine context that
is not inherited by a coroutine from a coroutine. Every coroutine creates its own `Job`, and the job from an argument or parent coroutine
is used as a parent of this new job.

```
fun main(): Unit = runBlocking {
    val name = CoroutineName("Some name")
    val job = Job()

    launch(name + job) {
        val childName = coroutineContext[CoroutineName]
        println(childName == name) // true
        val childJob = coroutineContext[Job]
        println(childJob == job) // false
        println(childJob == job.children.first()) // true
    }
}
```

The parent can reference all its children, and the children can refer to the parent. This parent-child relationship (Job reference storing) enables the implementation of cancellation and exception handling inside a coroutine's scope.

```kotlin
fun main(): Unit = runBlocking {
    val job: Job = launch {
        delay(1000)
    }

    val parentJob: Job = coroutineContext.job
    // or coroutineContext[Job]!!
    println(job == parentJob) // false
    val parentChildren: Sequence<Job> = parentJob.children
    println(parentChildren.first() == job) // true
}
```

Structured concurrency mechanisms will not work if a new `Job` context replaces the one from the parent. To see this, we might use the `Job()` function, which creates a `Job` context (this will be explained later).

```kotlin
fun main(): Unit = runBlocking {
  launch(Job()) { // the new job replaces one from parent
    delay(1000)
    println("Will not be printed")
  }
}
// (prints nothing, finishes immediately)
```

In the above example, the parent does not wait for its children because it has no relation with them. This is because the child uses the job from the argument as a parent, so it has no relation to the `runBlocking`.

When a coroutine has its own (independent) job, it has nearly no relation to its parent. It only inherits other contexts, but other results of the parent-child relationship will not apply. This causes us to lose structured concurrency, which is a problematic situation that should be avoided.

Waiting for children

The first important advantage of a job is that it can be used to wait until the coroutine is completed. For that, we use the join method. This is a suspending function that suspends until a concrete job reaches a final state (either Completed or Cancelled).

```
fun main(): Unit = runBlocking {
    val job1 = launch {
        delay(1000)
        println("Test1")
    }
    val job2 = launch {
        delay(2000)
        println("Test2")
    }

    job1.join()
    job2.join()
    println("All tests are done")
}
// (1 sec)
// Test1
// (1 sec)
// Test2
// All tests are done
```

The Job interface also exposes a children property that lets us reference all its children. We might as well use it to wait until all children are in a final state.

```
fun main(): Unit = runBlocking {
    launch {
        delay(1000)
        println("Test1")
    }
    launch {
        delay(2000)
        println("Test2")
```

```
    }

    val children = coroutineContext[Job]
        ?.children

    val childrenNum = children?.count()
    println("Number of children: $childrenNum")
    children?.forEach { it.join() }
    println("All tests are done")
}
// Number of children: 2
// (1 sec)
// Test1
// (1 sec)
// Test2
// All tests are done
```

Job factory function

A Job can be created without a coroutine using the Job() factory function. It creates a job that isn't associated with any coroutine and can be used as a context. This also means that we can use such a job as a parent of many coroutines.

A common mistake is to create a job using the Job() factory function, use it as a parent for some coroutines, and then use join on the job. Such a program will never end because Job is still in an active state, even when all its children are finished. This is because this context is still ready to be used by other coroutines.

```
suspend fun main(): Unit = coroutineScope {
    val job = Job()
    launch(job) { // the new job replaces one from parent
        delay(1000)
        println("Text 1")
    }
    launch(job) { // the new job replaces one from parent
        delay(2000)
        println("Text 2")
    }
```

```
    job.join() // Here we will await forever
    println("Will not be printed")
}
// (1 sec)
// Text 1
// (1 sec)
// Text 2
// (runs forever)
```

A better approach would be to join all the current children of the job.

```
suspend fun main(): Unit = coroutineScope {
    val job = Job()
    launch(job) { // the new job replaces one from parent
        delay(1000)
        println("Text 1")
    }
    launch(job) { // the new job replaces one from parent
        delay(2000)
        println("Text 2")
    }
    job.children.forEach { it.join() }
}
// (1 sec)
// Text 1
// (1 sec)
// Text 2
```

Job() is a great example of a factory function. At first, you might think that you're calling a constructor of Job, but you might then realize that Job is an interface, and interfaces cannot have constructors. The reality is that it is a fake constructor[31] - a simple function that looks like a constructor. Moreover, the actual type returned by this function is not a Job but its subinterface CompletableJob.

---

[31]A pattern that is well described in Effective Kotlin Item 33: Consider factory functions instead of constructors.

```
public fun Job(parent: Job? = null): CompletableJob
```

The CompletableJob interface extends the functionality of the Job interface by providing two additional methods:

- complete(): Boolean - used to complete a job. Once it is used, all the child coroutines will keep running until they are all done, but new coroutines cannot be started in this job. The result is true if this job was completed as a result of this invocation; otherwise, it is false (if it was already completed).

```
fun main() = runBlocking {
    val job = Job()

    launch(job) {
        repeat(5) { num ->
            delay(200)
            println("Rep$num")
        }
    }

    launch {
        delay(500)
        job.complete()
    }

    job.join()

    launch(job) {
        println("Will not be printed")
    }

    println("Done")
}
// Rep0
// Rep1
// Rep2
// Rep3
```

```
// Rep4
// Done
```

  • completeExceptionally(exception: Throwable):   Boolean
    - Completes this job with a given exception. This means
    that all children will be cancelled immediately (with
    CancellationException wrapping the exception provided
    as an argument). The result, just like in the above function,
    responds to the question: "Was this job finished because of the
    invocation?".

```
fun main() = runBlocking {
    val job = Job()

    launch(job) {
        repeat(5) { num ->
            delay(200)
            println("Rep$num")
        }
    }

    launch {
        delay(500)
        job.completeExceptionally(Error("Some error"))
    }

    job.join()

    launch(job) {
        println("Will not be printed")
    }

    println("Done")
}
// Rep0
// Rep1
// Done
```

The complete function is often used after we start the last coroutine

on a job. Thanks to this, we can just wait for the job completion using
the join function.

```
suspend fun main(): Unit = coroutineScope {
    val job = Job()
    launch(job) { // the new job replaces one from parent
        delay(1000)
        println("Text 1")
    }
    launch(job) { // the new job replaces one from parent
        delay(2000)
        println("Text 2")
    }
    job.complete()
    job.join()
}
// (1 sec)
// Text 1
// (1 sec)
// Text 2
```

You can pass a reference to the parent as an argument of the Job
function. Thanks to this, such a job will be cancelled when the parent
is.

```
suspend fun main(): Unit = coroutineScope {
  val parentJob = Job()
  val job = Job(parentJob)
  launch(job) {
      delay(1000)
      println("Text 1")
  }
  launch(job) {
      delay(2000)
      println("Text 2")
  }
  delay(1100)
  parentJob.cancel()
  job.children.forEach { it.join() }
```

```
}
// Text 1
```

The next two chapters describe cancellation and exception handling in Kotlin Coroutines. These two important mechanisms fully depend on the child-parent relationship created using `Job`.

Cancellation

A very important functionality of Kotlin Coroutines is *cancellation*. It is so important that some classes and libraries use suspending functions primarily to support cancellation[32]. There is a good reason for this: a good cancellation mechanism is worth its weight in gold[33]. Just killing a thread is a terrible solution as there should be an opportunity to close connections and free resources. Forcing developers to frequently check if some state is still active isn't convenient either. The problem of cancellation waited for a good solution for a very long time, but what Kotlin Coroutines offer is surprisingly simple: they are convenient and safe. This is the best cancellation mechanism I've seen in my career. Let's explore it.

Basic cancellation

The `Job` interface has a `cancel` method, which allows its cancellation. Calling it triggers the following effects:

- Such a coroutine ends the job at the first suspension point (`delay` in the example below).
- If a job has some children, they are also cancelled (but its parent is not affected).
- Once a job is cancelled, it cannot be used as a parent for any new coroutines. It is first in the "Cancelling" and then in the "Cancelled" state.

---

[32]A good example is `CoroutineWorker` on Android, where according to the presentation *Understand Kotlin Coroutines on Android* on Google I/O'19 by Sean McQuillan and Yigit Boyar (both working on Android at Google), support for coroutines was added primarily to use the cancellation mechanism.

[33]Actually, it's worth much more since the code is currently not very heavy (it used to be, when it was stored on punched cards).

```
suspend fun main(): Unit = coroutineScope {
    val job = launch {
        repeat(1_000) { i ->
            delay(200)
            println("Printing $i")
        }
    }

    delay(1100)
    job.cancel()
    job.join()
    println("Cancelled successfully")
}
// Printing 0
// Printing 1
// Printing 2
// Printing 3
// Printing 4
// Cancelled successfully
```

We might cancel with a different exception (by passing an exception as an argument to the cancel function) to specify the cause. This cause needs to be a subtype of CancellationException, because only an exception of this type can be used to cancel a coroutine.

After cancel, we often also add join to wait for the cancellation to finish before we can proceed. Without this, we would have some race conditions. The snippet below shows an example in which without join we will see "Printing 4" after "Cancelled successfully".

```
suspend fun main() = coroutineScope {
    val job = launch {
        repeat(1_000) { i ->
            delay(100)
            Thread.sleep(100) // We simulate long operation
            println("Printing $i")
        }
    }

    delay(1000)
```

```
    job.cancel()
    println("Cancelled successfully")
}
// Printing 0
// Printing 1
// Printing 2
// Printing 3
// Cancelled successfully
// Printing 4
```

Adding job.join() would change this because it suspends until a coroutine has finished cancellation.

```
suspend fun main() = coroutineScope {
    val job = launch {
        repeat(1_000) { i ->
            delay(100)
            Thread.sleep(100) // We simulate long operation
            println("Printing $i")
        }
    }

    delay(1000)
    job.cancel()
    job.join()
    println("Cancelled successfully")
}
// Printing 0
// Printing 1
// Printing 2
// Printing 3
// Printing 4
// Cancelled successfully
```

To make it easier to call cancel and join together, the kotlinx.coroutines library offers a convenient extension function with a self-descriptive name, cancelAndJoin.

```
// The most explicit function name I've ever seen
public suspend fun Job.cancelAndJoin() {
  cancel()
  return join()
}
```

A job created using the `Job()` factory function can be cancelled in
the same way. This is often used to make it easy to cancel many
coroutines at once.

```
suspend fun main(): Unit = coroutineScope {
    val job = Job()
    launch(job) {
        repeat(1_000) { i ->
            delay(200)
            println("Printing $i")
        }
    }
    delay(1100)
    job.cancelAndJoin()
    println("Cancelled successfully")
}
// Printing 0
// Printing 1
// Printing 2
// Printing 3
// Printing 4
// Cancelled successfully
```

This is a crucial capability. On many platforms, we often need to
cancel a group of concurrent tasks. For instance, in Android, we
cancel all the coroutines started in a view when a user leaves this
view.

```kotlin
class ProfileViewModel : ViewModel() {
    private val scope =
        CoroutineScope(Dispatchers.Main + SupervisorJob())

    fun onCreate() {
        scope.launch { loadUserData() }
    }

    override fun onCleared() {
        scope.coroutineContext.cancelChildren()
    }

    // ...
}
```

How does cancellation work?

When a job is cancelled, it changes its state to "Cancelling". Then, at the first suspension point, a CancellationException is thrown. This exception can be caught using a try-catch, but it is recommended to rethrow it.

```kotlin
suspend fun main(): Unit = coroutineScope {
    val job = Job()
    launch(job) {
        try {
            repeat(1_000) { i ->
                delay(200)
                println("Printing $i")
            }
        } catch (e: CancellationException) {
            println(e)
            throw e
        }
    }
    delay(1100)
    job.cancelAndJoin()
    println("Cancelled successfully")
    delay(1000)
```

```
}
// Printing 0
// Printing 1
// Printing 2
// Printing 3
// Printing 4
// JobCancellationException...
// Cancelled successfully
```

Keep in mind that a cancelled coroutine is not just stopped: it is cancelled internally using an exception. Therefore, we can freely clean up everything inside the `finally` block. For instance, we can use a `finally` block to close a file or a database connection. Since most resource-closing mechanisms rely on the `finally` block (for instance, if we read a file using `useLines`), we simply do not need to worry about them.

```
suspend fun main(): Unit = coroutineScope {
    val job = Job()
    launch(job) {
        try {
            delay(Random.nextLong(2000))
            println("Done")
        } finally {
            print("Will always be printed")
        }
    }
    delay(1000)
    job.cancelAndJoin()
}
// Will always be printed
// (or)
// Done
// Will always be printed
```

Just one more call

Since we can catch `CancellationException` and invoke more oper-ations before the coroutine truly ends, you might be wondering where the limit is. The coroutine can run as long as it needs to clean up all the resources. However, suspension is no longer allowed. The Job is already in a "Cancelling" state, in which suspension or starting another coroutine is not possible at all. If we try to start another coroutine, it will just be ignored. If we try to suspend, it will throw CancellationException.

```kotlin
suspend fun main(): Unit = coroutineScope {
    val job = Job()
    launch(job) {
        try {
            delay(2000)
            println("Job is done")
        } finally {
            println("Finally")
            launch { // will be ignored
                println("Will not be printed")
            }
            delay(1000) // here exception is thrown
            println("Will not be printed")
        }
    }
    delay(1000)
    job.cancelAndJoin()
    println("Cancel done")
}
// (1 sec)
// Finally
// Cancel done
```

Sometimes, we truly need to use a suspending call when a coroutine is already cancelled. For instance, we might need to roll back changes in a database. In this case, the preferred way is to wrap this call with the withContext(NonCancellable) function. We will later explain in detail how withContext works. For now, all we need to know is that it changes the context of a block of code. Inside withContext, we used the NonCancellable object, which is a Job that cannot be cancelled. So, inside the block the job is in the active state, and we can call whatever suspending functions we want.

```
suspend fun main(): Unit = coroutineScope {
    val job = Job()
    launch(job) {
        try {
            delay(200)
            println("Coroutine finished")
        } finally {
            println("Finally")
            withContext(NonCancellable) {
                delay(1000L)
                println("Cleanup done")
            }
        }
    }
    delay(100)
    job.cancelAndJoin()
    println("Done")
}
// Finally
// Cleanup done
// Done
```

invokeOnCompletion

Another mechanism that is often used to free resources is the
invokeOnCompletion function from Job. It is used to set a handler
to be called when the job reaches a terminal state, namely either
"Completed" or "Cancelled".

```
suspend fun main(): Unit = coroutineScope {
    val job = launch {
        delay(1000)
    }
    job.invokeOnCompletion { exception: Throwable? ->
        println("Finished")
    }
    delay(400)
    job.cancelAndJoin()
```

```
}
// Finished
```

One of this handler's parameters is an exception:

- null if the job finished with no exception;
- CancellationException if the coroutine was cancelled;
- the exception that finished a coroutine (more about this in the next chapter).

If a job was completed before invokeOnCompletion was called, the handler will be invoked immediately. The onCancelling[34] and invokeImmediately[35] parameters allow further customization.

```
suspend fun main(): Unit = coroutineScope {
    val job = launch {
        delay(Random.nextLong(2400))
        println("Finished")
    }
    delay(800)
    job.invokeOnCompletion { exception: Throwable? ->
        println("Will always be printed")
        println("The exception was: $exception")
    }
    delay(800)
    job.cancelAndJoin()
}
// Will always be printed
// The exception was:
// kotlinx.coroutines.JobCancellationException
// (or)
// Finished
// Will always be printed
// The exception was null
```

---

[34]If true, the function is called in the "Cancelling" state (i.e., before "Cancelled"). false by default.

[35]This parameter determines whether the handler should be called immediately if the handler is set when a coroutine is already in the desired state. true by default.

`invokeOnCompletion` is called synchronously during cancellation, and we do not control the thread in which it will be running.

Stopping the unstoppable

Because cancellation happens at the suspension points, it will not happen if there is no suspension point. To simulate such a situation, we could use `Thread.sleep` instead of `delay`. This is a terrible practice, so please don't do this in any real-life projects. We are just trying to simulate a case in which we are using our coroutines extensively but not suspending them. In practice, such a situation might happen if we have some complex calculations, like neural network learning (yes, we also use coroutines for such cases in order to simplify processing parallelization), or when we need to do some blocking calls (for instance, reading files).

The example below presents a situation in which a coroutine cannot be cancelled because there is no suspension point inside it (we use `Thread.sleep` instead of `delay`). The execution needs over 3 minutes, even though it should be cancelled after 1 second.

```
suspend fun main(): Unit = coroutineScope {
    val job = Job()
    launch(job) {
        repeat(1_000) { i ->
            Thread.sleep(200) // We might have some
            // complex operations or reading files here
            println("Printing $i")
        }
    }
    delay(1000)
    job.cancelAndJoin()
    println("Cancelled successfully")
    delay(1000)
}
// Printing 0
// Printing 1
// Printing 2
// ... (up to 1000)
```

There are a few ways to deal with such situations. The first one is to use the `yield()` function from time to time. This function suspends and immediately resumes a coroutine. This gives an opportunity to do whatever is needed during suspension (or resuming), including cancellation (or changing a thread using a dispatcher).

```kotlin
suspend fun main(): Unit = coroutineScope {
    val job = Job()
    launch(job) {
        repeat(1_000) { i ->
            Thread.sleep(200)
            yield()
            println("Printing $i")
        }
    }
    delay(1100)
    job.cancelAndJoin()
    println("Cancelled successfully")
    delay(1000)
}
// Printing 0
// Printing 1
// Printing 2
// Printing 3
// Printing 4
// Cancelled successfully
```

It is a good practice to use yield in suspend functions, between blocks of non-suspended CPU-intensive or time-intensive operations.

```kotlin
suspend fun cpuIntensiveOperations() =
    withContext(Dispatchers.Default) {
        cpuIntensiveOperation1()
        yield()
        cpuIntensiveOperation2()
        yield()
        cpuIntensiveOperation3()
    }
```

Another option is to track the state of the job. Inside a coroutine builder, this (the receiver) references the scope of this builder.

CoroutineScope has a context we can reference using the
coroutineContext property. Thus, we can access the coroutine job
(coroutineContext[Job] or coroutineContext.job) and check what
its current state is. Since a job is often used to check if a coroutine is
active, the Kotlin Coroutines library provides a function to simplify
that:

```
public val CoroutineScope.isActive: Boolean
  get() = coroutineContext[Job]?.isActive ?: true
```

We can use the isActive property to check if a job is still active and
stop calculations when it is inactive.

```
suspend fun main(): Unit = coroutineScope {
    val job = Job()
    launch(job) {
        do {
            Thread.sleep(200)
            println("Printing")
        } while (isActive)
    }
    delay(1100)
    job.cancelAndJoin()
    println("Cancelled successfully")
}
// Printing
// Printing
// Printing
// Printing
// Printing
// Printing
// Cancelled successfully
```

Alternatively, we might use the ensureActive() function, which
throws CancellationException if Job is not active.

```
suspend fun main(): Unit = coroutineScope {
    val job = Job()
    launch(job) {
        repeat(1000) { num ->
            Thread.sleep(200)
            ensureActive()
            println("Printing $num")
        }
    }
    delay(1100)
    job.cancelAndJoin()
    println("Cancelled successfully")
}
// Printing 0
// Printing 1
// Printing 2
// Printing 3
// Printing 4
// Cancelled successfully
```

The result of ensureActive() and yield() seem similar, but they are very different. The function ensureActive() needs to be called on a CoroutineScope (or CoroutineContext, or Job). All it does is throw an exception if the job is no longer active. It is lighter, so generally it should be preferred. The function yield is a regular top-level suspension function. It does not need any scope, so it can be used in regular suspending functions. Since it does suspension and resuming, other effects might arise, such as thread changing if we use a dispatcher with a pool of threads (more about this in the *Dispatchers*[36] chapter). yield is more often used just in suspending functions that are CPU intensive or are blocking threads.

suspendCancellableCoroutine

Here, you might remind yourself of the suspendCancellableCoroutine function introduced in the *How does suspension work?*[37] chapter. It behaves like suspendCoroutine, but its continuation is wrapped into CancellableContinuation<T>, which provides some additional

---

[36]https://kt.academy/article/cc-dispatchers
[37]https://kt.academy/article/cc-suspension

methods. The most important one is `invokeOnCancellation`, which we use to define what should happen when a coroutine is cancelled. Most often we use it to cancel processes in a library or to free some resources.

```kotlin
suspend fun someTask() = suspendCancellableCoroutine { cont ->
    cont.invokeOnCancellation {
        // do cleanup
    }
    // rest of the implementation
}
```

Here is a full example in which we wrap a Retrofit[38] `Call` with a suspending function.

```kotlin
suspend fun getOrganizationRepos(
    organization: String
): List<Repo> =
    suspendCancellableCoroutine { continuation ->
        val orgReposCall = apiService
            .getOrganizationRepos(organization)
        orgReposCall.enqueue(object : Callback<List<Repo>> {
            override fun onResponse(
                call: Call<List<Repo>>,
                response: Response<List<Repo>>
            ) {
                if (response.isSuccessful) {
                    val body = response.body()
                    if (body != null) {
                        continuation.resume(body)
                    } else {
                        continuation.resumeWithException(
                            ResponseWithEmptyBody
                        )
                    }
                } else {
                    continuation.resumeWithException(
```

---

[38]https://square.github.io/retrofit/

```
                        ApiException(
                            response.code(),
                            response.message()
                        )
                    )
                }
            }

            override fun onFailure(
                call: Call<List<Repo>>,
                t: Throwable
            ) {
                continuation.resumeWithException(t)
            }
        })
        continuation.invokeOnCancellation {
            orgReposCall.cancel()
        }
    }
```

It's so good that Retrofit now supports suspending functions!

```
class GithubApi {
  @GET("orgs/{organization}/repos?per_page=100")
  suspend fun getOrganizationRepos(
      @Path("organization") organization: String
  ): List<Repo>
}
```

The `CancellableContinuation<T>` also lets us check the job state (using the `isActive`, `isCompleted` and `isCancelled` properties) and cancel this continuation with an optional cancellation cause.

Summary

Cancellation is a powerful feature. It is generally easy to use, but it can sometimes be tricky. So, it is important to understand how it works.

A properly used cancellation means fewer wasted resources and fewer memory leaks. It is important for our application's performance, and I hope you will use these advantages from now on.

Exception handling

A very important part of how coroutines behave is their exception handling. Just as a program breaks when an uncaught exception slips by, a coroutine breaks in the case of an uncaught exception. This behavior is nothing new: for instance, threads also end in such cases. The difference is that coroutine builders also cancel their parents, and each cancelled parent cancels all its children. Let's look at the example below. Once a coroutine receives an exception, it cancels itself and propagates the exception to its parent (launch). The parent cancels itself and all its children, then it propagates the exception to its parent (runBlocking). runBlocking is a root coroutine (it has no parent), so it just ends the program (runBlocking rethrows the exception).

```
fun main(): Unit = runBlocking {
    launch {
        launch {
            delay(1000)
            throw Error("Some error")
        }

        launch {
            delay(2000)
            println("Will not be printed")
        }

        launch {
            delay(500) // faster than the exception
            println("Will be printed")
        }
    }

    launch {
        delay(2000)
        println("Will not be printed")
    }
}
// Will be printed
// Exception in thread "main" java.lang.Error: Some error...
```

Adding additional `launch` coroutines wouldn't change anything. Exception propagation is bi-directional: the exception is propagated from child to parent, and when those parents are cancelled, they cancel their children. Thus, if exception propagation is not stopped, all coroutines in the hierarchy will be cancelled.

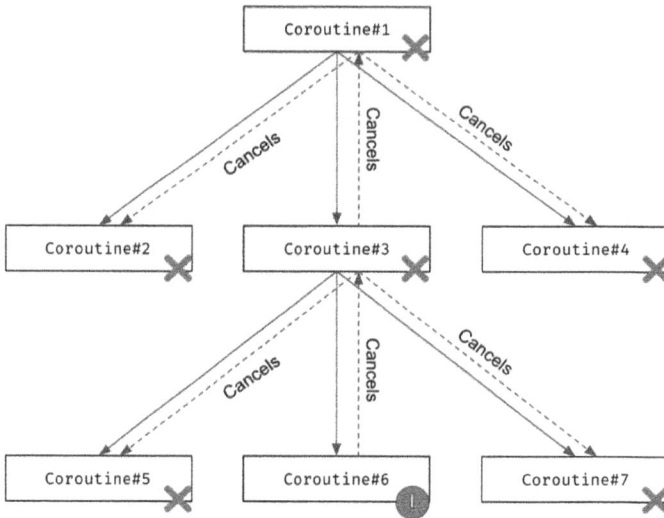

Stop breaking my coroutines

Catching an exception before it breaks a coroutine is helpful, but any later is too late. Communication happens via a job, so wrapping a coroutine builder with a try-catch is not helpful at all.

```kotlin
fun main(): Unit = runBlocking {
    // Don't wrap in a try-catch here. It will be ignored.
    try {
        launch {
            delay(1000)
            throw Error("Some error")
        }
    } catch (e: Throwable) { // nope, does not help here
        println("Will not be printed")
    }
```

```
    launch {
        delay(2000)
        println("Will not be printed")
    }
}
// Exception in thread "main" java.lang.Error: Some error...
```

SupervisorJob

The most important way to stop coroutines breaking is by using a
SupervisorJob. This is a special kind of job that ignores all exceptions
in its children.

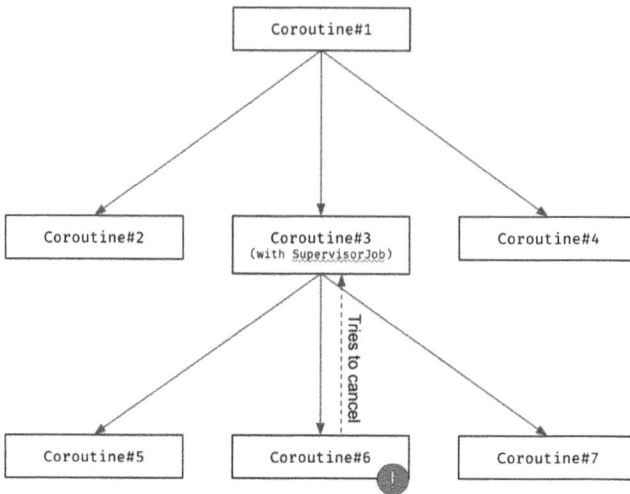

SupervisorJob is generally used as part of a scope in which we start multiple coroutines (more about this in the *Constructing coroutine scope* chapter).

```kotlin
fun main(): Unit = runBlocking {
    val scope = CoroutineScope(SupervisorJob())
    scope.launch {
        delay(1000)
        throw Error("Some error")
    }

    scope.launch {
        delay(2000)
        println("Will be printed")
    }

    delay(3000)
}
// Exception...
// Will be printed
```

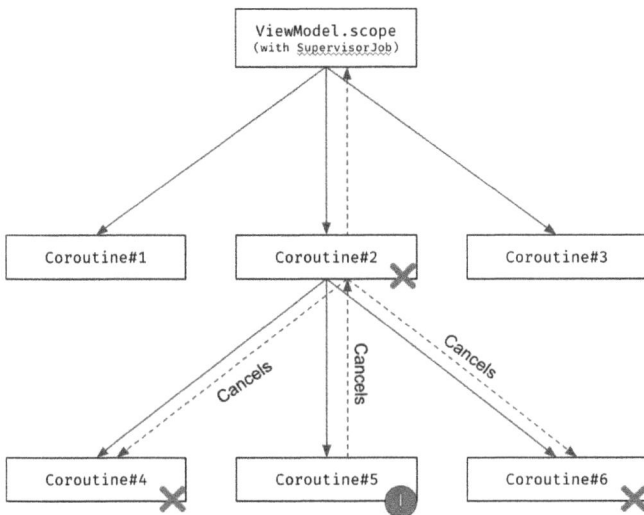

A common mistake is to use a SupervisorJob as an argument to a parent coroutine, like in the code below. It won't help us handle exceptions, because in such a case SupervisorJob has only one direct child, namely the launch defined at 1 that received this SupervisorJob as an argument. So, in such a case there is no advantage of using SupervisorJob over Job (in both cases, the exception will not propagate to runBlocking because we are not using its job).

```
fun main(): Unit = runBlocking {
    // Don't do that, SupervisorJob with one children
    // and no parent works similar to just Job
    launch(SupervisorJob()) { // 1
        launch {
            delay(1000)
            throw Error("Some error")
        }

        launch {
            delay(2000)
            println("Will not be printed")
```

```
        }
    }

    delay(3000)
}
// Exception...
```

It would make more sense if we used the same job as a context for multiple coroutine builders because each of them can be cancelled, but they won't cancel each other.

```
fun main(): Unit = runBlocking {
    val job = SupervisorJob()
    launch(job) {
        delay(1000)
        throw Error("Some error")
    }
    launch(job) {
        delay(2000)
        println("Will be printed")
    }
    job.join()
}
// (1 sec)
// Exception...
// (1 sec)
// Will be printed
```

supervisorScope

Another way to stop exception propagation is to wrap coroutine builders with supervisorScope. This is very convenient as we still keep a connection to the parent, yet any exceptions from the coroutine will be silenced.

```
fun main(): Unit = runBlocking {
    supervisorScope {
        launch {
            delay(1000)
            throw Error("Some error")
        }

        launch {
            delay(2000)
            println("Will be printed")
        }
    }
    delay(1000)
    println("Done")
}
// Exception...
// Will be printed
// (1 sec)
// Done
```

supervisorScope is just a suspending function and can be used to wrap suspending function bodies. This and other functionalities of supervisorScope will be described better in the next chapter. The common way to use it is to start multiple independent tasks.

```
suspend fun notifyAnalytics(actions: List<UserAction>) =
    supervisorScope {
        actions.forEach { action ->
            launch {
                notifyAnalytics(action)
            }
        }
    }
```

Another way to stop exception propagation is to use coroutineScope. Instead of influencing a parent, this function throws an exception that can be caught using try-catch (in contrast to coroutine builders). Both will be described in the next chapter.

Beware, that supervisorScope cannot be replaced with withContext(SupervisorJob())! Take a look at the below snippet.

```
// DON'T DO THAT!
suspend fun sendNotifications(
    notifications: List<Notification>
) = withContext(SupervisorJob()) {
    for (notification in notifications) {
        launch {
            client.send(notification)
        }
    }
}
```

The problem here is that Job is the only context that is not inherited.
Each coroutine needs its own job, and passing a job to a coroutine
makes it a parent. So here SupervisorJob is a parent of withContext
coroutine. When a child has an exception, it propagates to coroutine
coroutine, cancels its Job, cancels children, and throws an exception.
The fact that SupervisorJob is a parent changes nothing.

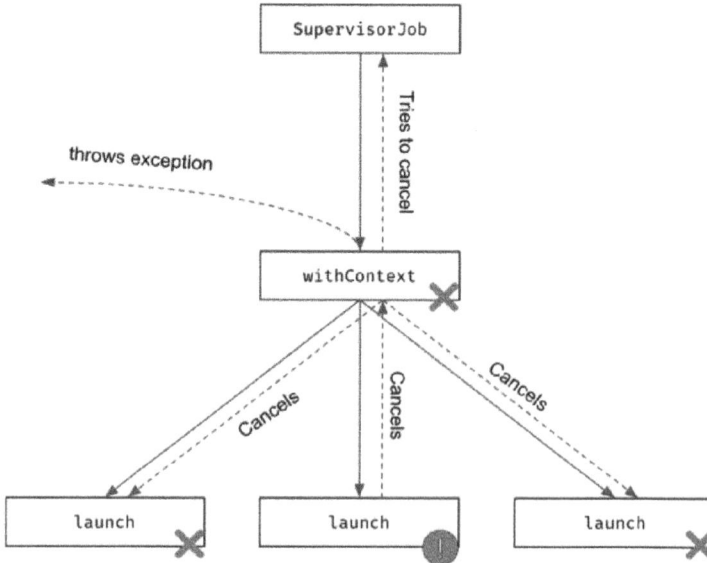

Await

So, we know how to stop exception propagation, but sometimes this is not enough. In the case of an exception, the async coroutine builder breaks its parent, just like launch and other coroutine builders that have a relation with their parents. However, what if this process is silenced (for instance, using SupervisorJob or supervisorScope) and await is called? Let's look at the following example:

```kotlin
class MyException : Throwable()

suspend fun main() = supervisorScope {
    val str1 = async<String> {
        delay(1000)
        throw MyException()
    }

    val str2 = async {
        delay(2000)
        "Text2"
    }

    try {
        println(str1.await())
    } catch (e: MyException) {
        println(e)
    }

    println(str2.await())
}
// MyException
// Text2
```

We have no value to return since the coroutine ended with an exception, so instead the MyException exception is thrown by await. This is why MyException is printed. The other async finishes uninterrupted because we're using the supervisorScope.

CancellationException does not propagate to its parent

If an exception is a subclass of CancellationException, it will not be propagated to its parent. It will only cause cancellation of the current coroutine. CancellationException is an open class, so it can be extended by our own classes or objects.

```
object MyNonPropagatingException : CancellationException()

suspend fun main(): Unit = coroutineScope {
  launch { // 1
      launch { // 2
          delay(2000)
          println("Will not be printed")
      }
      throw MyNonPropagatingException // 3
  }
  launch { // 4
      delay(2000)
      println("Will be printed")
  }
}
// (2 sec)
// Will be printed
```

In the above snippet, we start two coroutines with builders at 1 and 4. At 3, we throw a MyNonPropagatingException exception, which is a subtype of CancellationException. This exception is caught by launch (started at 1). This builder cancels itself, then it also cancels its children, namely the builder defined at 2. The launch started at 4 is not affected, so it prints "Will be printed" after 2 seconds.

Coroutine exception handler

When dealing with exceptions, sometimes it is useful to define default behavior for all of them. This is where the CoroutineExceptionHandler context comes in handy. It does not stop the exception propagating, but it can be used to define what should happen in the case of an exception (by default, it prints the exception stack trace).

```
fun main(): Unit = runBlocking {
  val handler =
      CoroutineExceptionHandler { ctx, exception ->
          println("Caught $exception")
      }
  val scope = CoroutineScope(SupervisorJob() + handler)
  scope.launch {
      delay(1000)
      throw Error("Some error")
  }

  scope.launch {
      delay(2000)
      println("Will be printed")
  }

  delay(3000)
}
// Caught java.lang.Error: Some error
// Will be printed
```

This context is useful on many platforms to add a default way of dealing with exceptions. For Android, it often informs the user about a problem by showing a dialog or an error message.

Summary

Exception handling is an important part of the kotlinx.coroutines library. Over time, we will inevitably come back to these topics. For now, I hope that you understand how exceptions propagate from child to parent in basic builders, and how they can be stopped. Now it's time for a long-awaited, strongly connected topic. Time to talk about coroutine scope functions.

Coroutine scope functions

Imagine that in a suspending function you need to concurrently get data from two (or more) endpoints. Before we explore how to do this correctly, let's see some **suboptimal** approaches.

Approaches that were used before coroutine scope functions were introduced

The first approach is calling suspending functions from a suspending function. The problem with this solution is that it is not concurrent (so, if getting data from one endpoint takes 1 second, a function will take 2 seconds instead of 1).

```
// Data loaded sequentially, not simultaneously
suspend fun getUserProfile(): UserProfileData {
    val user = getUserData() // (1 sec)
    val notifications = getNotifications() // (1 sec)

    return UserProfileData(
        user = user,
        notifications = notifications,
    )
}
```

To make two suspending calls concurrently, the easiest way is by wrapping them with async. However, async requires a scope, and using GlobalScope is not a good idea.

```
// DON'T DO THAT
suspend fun getUserProfile(): UserProfileData {
    val user = GlobalScope.async { getUserData() }
    val notifications = GlobalScope.async {
        getNotifications()
    }

    return UserProfileData(
        user = user.await(), // (1 sec)
```

```
        notifications = notifications.await(),
    )
}
```

`GlobalScope` is just a scope with `EmptyCoroutineContext`.

```
public object GlobalScope : CoroutineScope {
    override val coroutineContext: CoroutineContext
        get() = EmptyCoroutineContext
}
```

If we call `async` on a `GlobalScope`, we will have no relationship to the parent coroutine. This means that the `async` coroutine:

- cannot be cancelled (if the parent is cancelled, functions inside async still run, thus wasting resources until they are done);
- does not inherit a scope from any parent (it will always run on the default dispatcher and will not respect any context from the parent).

The most important consequences are:

- potential memory leaks and redundant CPU usage;
- the tools for unit testing coroutines will not work here, so testing this function is very hard.

This is not a good solution. Let's take a look at another one, in which we pass a scope as an argument:

```
// DON'T DO THAT
suspend fun getUserProfile(
    scope: CoroutineScope
): UserProfileData {
    val user = scope.async { getUserData() }
    val notifications = scope.async { getNotifications() }

    return UserProfileData(
        user = user.await(), // (1 sec)
        notifications = notifications.await(),
```

```
    )
}

// or

// DON'T DO THAT
suspend fun CoroutineScope.getUserProfile(): UserProfileData {
    val user = async { getUserData() }
    val notifications = async { getNotifications() }

    return UserProfileData(
        user = user.await(), // (1 sec)
        notifications = notifications.await(),
    )
}
```

This one is a bit better as cancellation and proper unit testing are now possible. The problem is that this solution requires this scope to be passed from function to function. Also, such functions can cause unwanted side effects in the scope; for instance, if there is an exception in one async, the whole scope will be shut down (assuming it is using Job, not SupervisorJob). What is more, a function that has access to the scope could easily abuse this access and, for instance, cancel this scope with the cancel method. This is why this approach can be tricky and potentially dangerous.

```
data class Details(val name: String, val followers: Int)
data class Tweet(val text: String)

fun getFollowersNumber(): Int =
    throw Error("Service exception")

suspend fun getUserName(): String {
    delay(500)
    return "marcinmoskala"
}

suspend fun getTweets(): List<Tweet> {
    return listOf(Tweet("Hello, world"))
}
```

```
suspend fun CoroutineScope.getUserDetails(): Details {
    val userName = async { getUserName() }
    val followersNumber = async { getFollowersNumber() }
    return Details(userName.await(), followersNumber.await())
}

fun main() = runBlocking {
    val details = try {
        getUserDetails()
    } catch (e: Error) {
        null
    }
    val tweets = async { getTweets() }
    println("User: $details")
    println("Tweets: ${tweets.await()}")
}
// Only Exception...
```

In the above code, we would like to at least see Tweets, even if we have a problem fetching user details. Unfortunately, an exception on getFollowersNumber breaks async, which breaks the whole scope and ends the program. Instead, we would prefer a function that just throws an exception if it occurs. Time to introduce our hero: coroutineScope.

coroutineScope

coroutineScope is a suspending function that starts a scope. It returns the value produced by the argument function.

```
suspend fun <R> coroutineScope(
    block: suspend CoroutineScope.() -> R
): R
```

Unlike async or launch, the body of coroutineScope is called in-place. It formally creates a new coroutine, but it suspends the previous one until the new one is finished, so it does not start any concurrent process. Take a look at the below example, in which both delay calls suspend runBlocking.

```
fun main() = runBlocking {
    val a = coroutineScope {
        delay(1000)
        10
    }
    println("a is calculated")
    val b = coroutineScope {
        delay(1000)
        20
    }
    println(a) // 10
    println(b) // 20
}
// (1 sec)
// a is calculated
// (1 sec)
// 10
// 20
```

The provided scope inherits its `coroutineContext` from the outer
scope, but it overrides the context's `Job`. Thus, the produced scope
respects its parental responsibilities:

- inherits a context from its parent;
- waits for all its children before it can finish itself;
- cancels all its children when the parent is cancelled.

In the example below, you can observe that "After" will be printed at
the end because `coroutineScope` will not finish until all its children
are finished. Also, `CoroutineName` is properly passed from parent to
child.

```
suspend fun longTask() = coroutineScope {
    launch {
        delay(1000)
        val name = coroutineContext[CoroutineName]?.name
        println("[$name] Finished task 1")
    }
    launch {
        delay(2000)
        val name = coroutineContext[CoroutineName]?.name
        println("[$name] Finished task 2")
    }
}

fun main() = runBlocking(CoroutineName("Parent")) {
    println("Before")
    longTask()
    println("After")
}
// Before
// (1 sec)
// [Parent] Finished task 1
// (1 sec)
// [Parent] Finished task 2
// After
```

In the next snippet, you can observe how cancellation works. A cancelled parent leads to the cancellation of unfinished children.

```
suspend fun longTask() = coroutineScope {
    launch {
        delay(1000)
        val name = coroutineContext[CoroutineName]?.name
        println("[$name] Finished task 1")
    }
    launch {
        delay(2000)
        val name = coroutineContext[CoroutineName]?.name
        println("[$name] Finished task 2")
    }
```

```
}

fun main(): Unit = runBlocking {
    val job = launch(CoroutineName("Parent")) {
        longTask()
    }
    delay(1500)
    job.cancel()
}
// [Parent] Finished task 1
```

Unlike coroutine builders, if there is an exception in coroutineScope or any of its children, it cancels all other children and rethrows it. This is why using coroutineScope would fix our previous "Twitter example". To show that the same exception is rethrown, I changed a generic Error into a concrete ApiException.

```
data class Details(val name: String, val followers: Int)
data class Tweet(val text: String)
class ApiException(
    val code: Int,
    message: String
) : Throwable(message)

fun getFollowersNumber(): Int =
    throw ApiException(500, "Service unavailable")

suspend fun getUserName(): String {
    delay(500)
    return "marcinmoskala"
}

suspend fun getTweets(): List<Tweet> {
    return listOf(Tweet("Hello, world"))
}

suspend fun getUserDetails(): Details = coroutineScope {
    val userName = async { getUserName() }
    val followersNumber = async { getFollowersNumber() }
```

```
    Details(userName.await(), followersNumber.await())
}

fun main() = runBlocking<Unit> {
    val details = try {
        getUserDetails()
    } catch (e: ApiException) {
        null
    }
    val tweets = async { getTweets() }
    println("User: $details")
    println("Tweets: ${tweets.await()}")
}
// User: null
// Tweets: [Tweet(text=Hello, world)]
```

This all makes coroutineScope a perfect candidate for most cases when we just need to start a few concurrent calls in a suspending function.

```
suspend fun getUserProfile(): UserProfileData =
    coroutineScope {
        val user = async { getUserData() }
        val notifications = async { getNotifications() }

        UserProfileData(
            user = user.await(), // (1 sec)
            notifications = notifications.await(),
        )
    }
```

As we've already mentioned, coroutineScope is nowadays often used to wrap a suspending main body. You can think of it as the modern replacement for the runBlocking function:

```
suspend fun main(): Unit = coroutineScope {
    launch {
        delay(1000)
        println("World")
    }
    println("Hello, ")
}
// Hello
// (1 sec)
// World
```

The function coroutineScope creates a scope out of a suspending context. It inherits a scope from its parent and supports structured concurrency.

To make it clear, there is practically no difference between the below functions, except that the first one calls getProfile and getFriends sequentially, where the second one calls them simultaneously.

```
suspend fun produceCurrentUserSeq(): User {
    val profile = repo.getProfile()
    val friends = repo.getFriends()
    return User(profile, friends)
}
```

```
suspend fun produceCurrentUserSym(): User = coroutineScope {
    val profile = async { repo.getProfile() }
    val friends = async { repo.getFriends() }
    User(profile.await(), friends.await())
}
```

coroutineScope is a useful function, but it's not the only one of its kind.

Coroutine scope functions

There are more functions that create a scope and behave similarly to coroutineScope. supervisorScope is like coroutineScope but it uses SupervisorJob instead of Job. withContext is a coroutineScope that can modify coroutine context. withTimeout is a coroutineScope

with a timeout. Each of those functions will be better explained in the following parts of this chapter. For now, I just want you to know there are such functions because if there is a group of similar functions, it makes sense that it should have a name. So how should we name this group? Some people call them "scoping functions", but I find this confusing as I am not sure what is meant by "scoping". I guess that whoever started using this term just wanted to make it different from "scope functions" (functions like let, with or apply). It is not really helpful as those two terms are still often confused. This is why I decided to use the term "coroutine scope functions". It is longer but should cause
fewer misunderstandings, and I find it more correct. Just think about that: coroutine scope functions are those that are used to create a coroutine scope in suspending functions.

On the other hand, coroutine scope functions are often confused with coroutine builders, but this is incorrect because they are very different, both conceptually and practically. To clarify this, the table below presents the comparison between them.

Coroutine builders (except for runBlocking)	Coroutine scope functions
launch, async, produce	coroutineScope, supervisorScope, withContext, withTimeout
Are extension functions on CoroutineScope.	Are suspending functions.
Take coroutine context from CoroutineScope receiver.	Take coroutine context from suspending function continuation.
Exceptions are propagated to the parent through Job.	Exceptions are thrown in the same way as they are from/by regular functions.
Starts an asynchronous coroutine.	Starts a coroutine that is called in-place.

Now think about runBlocking. You might notice that it looks like it has more in common with coroutine scope functions than with builders. runBlocking also calls its body in-place and returns its result. The biggest difference is that runBlocking is a blocking function, while coroutine scope functions are suspending functions. This is why runBlocking must be at the top of the hierarchy of coroutines, while coroutine scope functions must be in the middle.

withContext

The withContext function is similar to coroutineScope, but it additionally allows some changes to be made to the scope. The context provided as an argument to this function overrides the context from the parent scope (the same way as in coroutine builders). This means that withContext(EmptyCoroutineContext) and coroutineScope() behave in exactly the same way.

```
fun CoroutineScope.log(text: String) {
    val name = this.coroutineContext[CoroutineName]?.name
    println("[$name] $text")
}

fun main() = runBlocking(CoroutineName("Parent")) {
    log("Before")

    withContext(CoroutineName("Child 1")) {
        delay(1000)
        log("Hello 1")
    }

    withContext(CoroutineName("Child 2")) {
        delay(1000)
        log("Hello 2")
    }

    log("After")
}
// [Parent] Before
// (1 sec)
// [Child 1] Hello 1
// (1 sec)
// [Child 2] Hello 2
// [Parent] After
```

The function withContext is often used to set a different coroutine scope for part of our code. Usually, you should use it together with dispatchers, as will be described in the next chapter.

```
launch(Dispatchers.Main) {
    view.showProgressBar()
    withContext(Dispatchers.IO) {
        fileRepository.saveData(data)
    }
    view.hideProgressBar()
}
```

> You might notice that the way coroutineScope { /*...*/
> } works very similar to async with immediate await:
> async { /*...*/ }.await(). Also withContext(context)
> { /*...*/ } is in a way similar to async(context) {
> /*...*/ }.await(). The biggest difference is that async
> requires a scope, where coroutineScope and withContext
> take the scope from suspension. In both cases, it's better
> to use coroutineScope and withContext, and avoid async
> with immediate await.

supervisorScope

The supervisorScope function also behaves a lot like coroutineScope:
it creates a CoroutineScope that inherits from the outer scope and
calls the specified suspend block in it. The difference is that it overrides the context's Job with SupervisorJob, so it is not cancelled
when a child raises an exception.

```
fun main() = runBlocking {
    println("Before")

    supervisorScope {
        launch {
            delay(1000)
            throw Error()
        }

        launch {
            delay(2000)
            println("Done")
        }
    }
```

```
    println("After")
}
// Before
// (1 sec)
// Exception...
// (1 sec)
// Done
// After
```

supervisorScope is mainly used in functions that start multiple independent tasks.

```
suspend fun notifyAnalytics(actions: List<UserAction>) =
    supervisorScope {
        actions.forEach { action ->
            launch {
                notifyAnalytics(action)
            }
        }
    }
```

If you use async, silencing its exception propagation to the parent is not enough. When we call await and the async coroutine finishes with an exception, then await will rethrow it. This is why if we want to truly ignore exceptions, we should also wrap await calls with a try-catch block.

```
class ArticlesRepositoryComposite(
    private val articleRepositories: List<ArticleRepository>,
) : ArticleRepository {
    override suspend fun fetchArticles(): List<Article> =
        supervisorScope {
            articleRepositories
                .map { async { it.fetchArticles() } }
                .mapNotNull {
                    try {
                        it.await()
                    } catch (e: Throwable) {
```

```
                    e.printStackTrace()
                    null
                }
            }
            .flatten()
            .sortedByDescending { it.publishedAt }
        }
}
```

In my workshops, I am often asked if we can use `withContext(SupervisorJob())` instead of `supervisorScope`. No, we can't. When we use `withContext(SupervisorJob())`, then `withContext` is still using a regular `Job`, and the `SupervisorJob()` becomes its parent. As a result, when one child raises an exception, the other children will be cancelled as well. `withContext` will also throw an exception, so its `SupervisorJob()` is practically useless. This is why I find `withContext(SupervisorJob())` pointless and misleading, and I consider it a bad practice.

```
fun main() = runBlocking {
    println("Before")

    withContext(SupervisorJob()) {
        launch {
            delay(1000)
            throw Error()
        }

        launch {
            delay(2000)
            println("Done")
        }
    }

    println("After")
}
// Before
// (1 sec)
// Exception...
```

withTimeout

Another function that behaves a lot like `coroutineScope` is `withTimeout`. It also creates a scope and returns a value. Actually, `withTimeout` with a very big timeout behaves just like `coroutineScope`. The difference is that `withTimeout` additionally sets a time limit for its body execution. If it takes too long, it cancels this body and throws `TimeoutCancellationException` (a subtype of `CancellationException`).

```
suspend fun test(): Int = withTimeout(1500) {
    delay(1000)
    println("Still thinking")
    delay(1000)
    println("Done!")
    42
}

suspend fun main(): Unit = coroutineScope {
    try {
        test()
    } catch (e: TimeoutCancellationException) {
        println("Cancelled")
    }
    delay(1000) // Extra timeout does not help,
    // `test` body was cancelled
}
// (1 sec)
// Still thinking
// (0.5 sec)
// Cancelled
```

The function `withTimeout` is especially useful for testing. It can be used to test if some function takes more or less than some time. If it is used inside `runTest`, it will operate in virtual time. We also use it inside `runBlocking` to just limit the execution time of some function (this is then like setting `timeout` on `@Test`).

```
class Test {
    @Test
    fun testTime2() = runTest {
        withTimeout(1000) {
            // something that should take less than 1000
            delay(900) // virtual time
        }
    }

    @Test(expected = TimeoutCancellationException::class)
    fun testTime1() = runTest {
        withTimeout(1000) {
            // something that should take more than 1000
            delay(1100) // virtual time
        }
    }

    @Test
    fun testTime3() = runBlocking {
        withTimeout(1000) {
            // normal test, that should not take too long
            delay(900) // really waiting 900 ms
        }
    }
}
```

Beware that `withTimeout` throws `TimeoutCancellationException`, which is a subtype of `CancellationException` (the same exception that is thrown when a coroutine is cancelled). So, when this exception is thrown in a coroutine builder, it only cancels it and does not affect its parent (as explained in the previous chapter).

```kotlin
suspend fun main(): Unit = coroutineScope {
    launch { // 1
        launch { // 2, cancelled by its parent
            delay(2000)
            println("Will not be printed")
        }
        withTimeout(1000) { // we cancel launch
            delay(1500)
        }
    }
    launch { // 3
        delay(2000)
        println("Done")
    }
}
// (2 sec)
// Done
```

In the above example, `delay(1500)` takes longer than `withTimeout(1000)` expects, so it throws `TimeoutCancellationException`. The exception is caught by `launch` from 1, and it cancels itself and its children, so `launch` from 2. `launch` started at 3 is also not affected.

A less aggressive variant of `withTimeout` is `withTimeoutOrNull`, which does not throw an exception. If the timeout is exceeded, it just cancels its body and returns `null`. I find `withTimeoutOrNull` useful for wrapping functions in which waiting times that are too long signal that something went wrong. For instance, network operations: if we wait over 5 seconds for a response, it is unlikely we will ever receive it (some libraries might wait forever).

```kotlin
suspend fun fetchUser(): User {
    // Runs forever
    while (true) {
        yield()
    }
}

suspend fun getUserOrNull(): User? =
    withTimeoutOrNull(5000) {
```

```
        fetchUser()
    }

suspend fun main(): Unit = coroutineScope {
    val user = getUserOrNull()
    println("User: $user")
}
// (5 sec)
// User: null
```

Connecting coroutine scope functions

If you need to use functionalities from two coroutine scope functions, you need to use one inside another. For instance, to set both a timeout and a dispatcher, you can use withTimeoutOrNull inside withContext.

```
suspend fun calculateAnswerOrNull(): User? =
    withContext(Dispatchers.Default) {
        withTimeoutOrNull(1000) {
            calculateAnswer()
        }
    }
```

Additional operations

Imagine a case in which in the middle of some processing you need to execute an additional operation. For example, after showing a user profile you want to send a request for analytics purposes. People often do this with just a regular launch in the same scope:

```
class ShowUserDataUseCase(
    private val repo: UserDataRepository,
    private val view: UserDataView,
) {

    suspend fun showUserData() = coroutineScope {
        val name = async { repo.getName() }
        val friends = async { repo.getFriends() }
```

```
        val profile = async { repo.getProfile() }
        val user = User(
            name = name.await(),
            friends = friends.await(),
            profile = profile.await()
        )
        view.show(user)
        launch { repo.notifyProfileShown() }
    }
}
```

However, there are some problems with this approach. Firstly, this launch does nothing here because coroutineScope needs to await its completion anyway. So if you are showing a progress bar when updating the view, the user needs to wait until this notifyProfileShown is finished as well. This does not make much sense.

```
fun onCreate() {
    viewModelScope.launch {
        _progressBar.value = true
        showUserData()
        _progressBar.value = false
    }
}
```

The second problem is cancellation. Coroutines are designed (by default) to cancel other operations when there is an exception. This is great for essential operations. If getProfile has an exception, we should cancel getName and getFriends because their response would be useless anyway. However, canceling a process just because an analytics call has failed does not make much sense.

So what should we do? When you have an additional (non-essential) operation that should not influence the main process, it is better to start it on a separate scope. Creating your own scope is easy. In this example, we create an analyticsScope.

```
val analyticsScope = CoroutineScope(SupervisorJob())
```

For unit testing and controlling this scope, it is better to inject it via a constructor:

```
class ShowUserDataUseCase(
    private val repo: UserDataRepository,
    private val view: UserDataView,
    private val analyticsScope: CoroutineScope,
) {

    suspend fun showUserData() = coroutineScope {
        val name = async { repo.getName() }
        val friends = async { repo.getFriends() }
        val profile = async { repo.getProfile() }
        val user = User(
            name = name.await(),
            friends = friends.await(),
            profile = profile.await()
        )
        view.show(user)
        analyticsScope.launch { repo.notifyProfileShown() }
    }
}
```

Starting operations on an injected scope object is common. Passing a scope clearly signals that such a class can start independent calls. This means suspending functions might not wait for all the operations they start. If no scope is passed, we can expect that suspending functions will not finish until all their operations are done.

Summary

Coroutine scope functions are really useful, especially since they can be used in any suspending function. Most often they are used to wrap the whole function body. Although they are often used to just wrap a bunch of calls with a scope (especially withContext), I hope you can appreciate their usefulness. They are a very important part of the Kotlin Coroutines ecosystem. You will see how we will use them through the rest of the book.

Dispatchers

An important functionality offered by the Kotlin Coroutines library is letting us decide on which thread (or pool of threads) a coroutine should be running (starting and resuming). This is done using dispatchers.

In the English dictionary, a dispatcher is defined as "a person who is responsible for sending people or vehicles to where they are needed, especially emergency vehicles". In Kotlin coroutines, CoroutineContext determines on which thread a certain coroutine will run.

> Dispatchers in Kotlin Coroutines are a similar concept to RxJava Schedulers.

Default dispatcher

If you don't set any dispatcher, the one chosen by default is Dispatchers.Default, which is designed to run CPU-intensive operations. It has a pool of threads with a size equal to the number of cores in the machine your code is running on (but not less than two). At least theoretically, this is the optimal number of threads, assuming you are using these threads efficiently, i.e., performing CPU-intensive calculations and not blocking them.

To see this dispatcher in action, run the following code:

```
suspend fun main() = coroutineScope {
    repeat(1000) {
        launch { // or launch(Dispatchers.Default) {
            // To make it busy
            List(1000) { Random.nextLong() }.maxOrNull()

            val threadName = Thread.currentThread().name
            println("Running on thread: $threadName")
        }
    }
}
```

Example result on my machine (I have 12 cores, so there are 12 threads in the pool):

```
Running on thread: DefaultDispatcher-worker-1
Running on thread: DefaultDispatcher-worker-5
Running on thread: DefaultDispatcher-worker-7
Running on thread: DefaultDispatcher-worker-6
Running on thread: DefaultDispatcher-worker-11
Running on thread: DefaultDispatcher-worker-2
Running on thread: DefaultDispatcher-worker-10
Running on thread: DefaultDispatcher-worker-4
...
```

> Warning: runBlocking sets its own dispatcher if no other one is set; so, inside it, the Dispatcher.Default is not the one that is chosen automatically. So, if we used runBlocking instead of coroutineScope in the above example, all coroutines would be running on "main".

Limiting the default dispatcher

Let's say that you have an expensive process, and you suspect that it might use all Dispatchers.Default threads and starve other coroutines using the same dispatcher. In such cases, we can use limitedParallelism on Dispatchers.Default to make a dispatcher that runs on the same threads but is limited to using not more than a certain number of them at the same time.

```
private val dispatcher = Dispatchers.Default
    .limitedParallelism(5)
```

This mechanism is used not to limit Dispatchers.Default but it is worth remembering it, because soon we will present limitedParallelism for Dispatchers.IO, which is much more important and common.

> limitedParallelism was introduced in kotlinx-coroutines version 1.6.

Main dispatcher

Android and many other application frameworks have a concept of a main or UI thread, which is generally the most important thread.

On Android, it is the only one that can be used to interact with the UI. Therefore, it needs to be used very often but also with great care. When the Main thread is blocked, the whole application is frozen. To run a coroutine on the Main thread, we use `Dispatchers.Main`.

`Dispatchers.Main` is available on Android if we use the `kotlinx-coroutines-android` artifact. Similarly, it's available on JavaFX if we use `kotlinx-coroutines-javafx`, and on Swing if we use `kotlinx-coroutines-swing`. If you do not have a dependency that defines the main dispatcher, it is not available and cannot be used.

Notice that frontend libraries are typically not used in unit tests, so `Dispatchers.Main` is not defined there. To be able to use it, you need to set a dispatcher using `Dispatchers.setMain(dispatcher)` from `kotlinx-coroutines-test`.

```kotlin
class SomeTest {

    private val dispatcher = Executors
        .newSingleThreadExecutor()
        .asCoroutineDispatcher()

    @Before
    fun setup() {
        Dispatchers.setMain(dispatcher)
    }

    @After
    fun tearDown() {
        // reset main dispatcher to
        // the original Main dispatcher
        Dispatchers.resetMain()
        dispatcher.close()
    }

    @Test
    fun testSomeUI() = runBlocking {
        launch(Dispatchers.Main) {
            // ...
        }
```

```
        }
}
```

On Android, we typically use the Main dispatcher as the default one.
If you use libraries that are suspending instead of blocking, and you
don't do any complex calculations, in practice you can often use only
Dispatchers.Main. If you do some CPU-intensive operations, you
should run them on Dispatchers.Default. These two are enough
for many applications, but what if you need to block the thread?
For instance, if you need to perform long I/O operations (e.g., read
big files) or if you need to use a library with blocking functions.
You cannot block the Main thread, because your application would
freeze. If you block your default dispatcher, you risk blocking all
the threads in the thread pool, in which case you wouldn't be able
to do any calculations. This is why we need a dispatcher for such a
situation, and it is Dispatchers.IO.

IO dispatcher

Dispatchers.IO is designed to be used when we block threads with
I/O operations, for instance, when we read/write files, use Android
shared preferences, or call blocking functions. The code below takes
around 1 second because Dispatchers.IO allows more than 50 active
threads at the same time.

```
suspend fun main() {
    val time = measureTimeMillis {
        coroutineScope {
            repeat(50) {
                launch(Dispatchers.IO) {
                    Thread.sleep(1000)
                }
            }
        }
    }
    println(time) // ~1000
}
```

How does it work? Imagine an unlimited pool of threads. Initially,
it is empty, but as we need more threads, they are created and kept

active until they are not used for some time. Such a pool exists, but it wouldn't be safe to use it directly. With too many active threads, the performance degrades in a slow but unlimited manner, eventually causing out-of-memory errors. This is why we create dispatchers that have a limited number of threads they can use at the same time. `Dispatchers.Default` is limited by the number of cores in your processor. The limit of `Dispatchers.IO` is 64 (or the number of cores if there are more).

```
suspend fun main() = coroutineScope {
    repeat(1000) {
        launch(Dispatchers.IO) {
            Thread.sleep(200)

            val threadName = Thread.currentThread().name
            println("Running on thread: $threadName")
        }
    }
}
// Running on thread: DefaultDispatcher-worker-1
//...
// Running on thread: DefaultDispatcher-worker-53
// Running on thread: DefaultDispatcher-worker-14
```

As we mentioned, both `Dispatchers.Default` and `Dispatchers.IO` share the same pool of threads. This is an important optimization. Threads are reused, and often redispatching is not needed. For instance, let's say you are running on `Dispatchers.Default` and then execution reaches `withContext(Dispatchers.IO) { ... }`. Most often, you will stay on the same thread[39], but what changes is that this thread counts not towards the `Dispatchers.Default` limit but towards the `Dispatchers.IO` limit. Their limits are independent, so they will never starve each other.

---

[39]This mechanism is not deterministic.

```
suspend fun main(): Unit = coroutineScope {
    launch(Dispatchers.Default) {
        println(Thread.currentThread().name)
        withContext(Dispatchers.IO) {
            println(Thread.currentThread().name)
        }
    }
}
// DefaultDispatcher-worker-2
// DefaultDispatcher-worker-2
```

To see this more clearly, imagine that you use both Dispatchers.Default and Dispatchers.IO to the maximum. As a result, your number of active threads will be the sum of their limits. If you allow 64 threads in Dispatchers.IO and you have 8 cores, you will have 72 active threads in the shared pool. This means we have efficient thread reuse and both dispatchers have strong independence.

The most typical case where we use Dispatchers.IO is when we need to call blocking functions from libraries. The best practice is to wrap them with withContext(Dispatchers.IO) to make them suspending functions. Such functions can be used without any special care: they can be treated like all other properly implemented suspending functions.

```
class DiscUserRepository(
    private val discReader: DiscReader
) : UserRepository {
    override suspend fun getUser(): UserData =
        withContext(Dispatchers.IO) {
            UserData(discReader.read("userName"))
        }
}
```

The only problem is when such functions block too many threads. Dispatchers.IO is limited to 64. One service that is massively blocking threads might make all others wait for their turn. To help us deal with this, we again use limitedParallelism.

IO dispatcher with a custom pool of threads

Dispatchers.IO has a special behavior defined for the limitedParallelism function. It creates a new dispatcher with an independent pool of threads. What is more, this pool is not limited to 64 as we can decide to limit it to as many threads as we want.

For example, imagine you start 100 coroutines, each of which blocks a thread for a second. If you run these coroutines on Dispatchers.IO, it will take 2 seconds. If you run them on Dispatchers.IO with limitedParallelism set to 100 threads, it will take 1 second. Execution time for both dispatchers can be measured at the same time because the limits of these two dispatchers are independent anyway.

```
suspend fun main(): Unit = coroutineScope {
    launch {
        printCoroutinesTime(Dispatchers.IO)
        // Dispatchers.IO took: 2074
    }

    launch {
        val dispatcher = Dispatchers.IO
            .limitedParallelism(100)
        printCoroutinesTime(dispatcher)
        // LimitedDispatcher@XXX took: 1082
    }
}

suspend fun printCoroutinesTime(
    dispatcher: CoroutineDispatcher
) {
    val test = measureTimeMillis {
        coroutineScope {
            repeat(100) {
                launch(dispatcher) {
                    Thread.sleep(1000)
                }
            }
        }
```

```
    }
    println("$dispatcher took: $test")
}
```

Conceptually, you might imagine it in the following way:

```
// Dispatcher with an unlimited pool of threads
private val pool = ...
```

```
Dispatchers.IO = pool.limitedParallelism(64)
Dispatchers.IO.limitedParallelism(x) =
  pool.limitedParallelism(x)
```

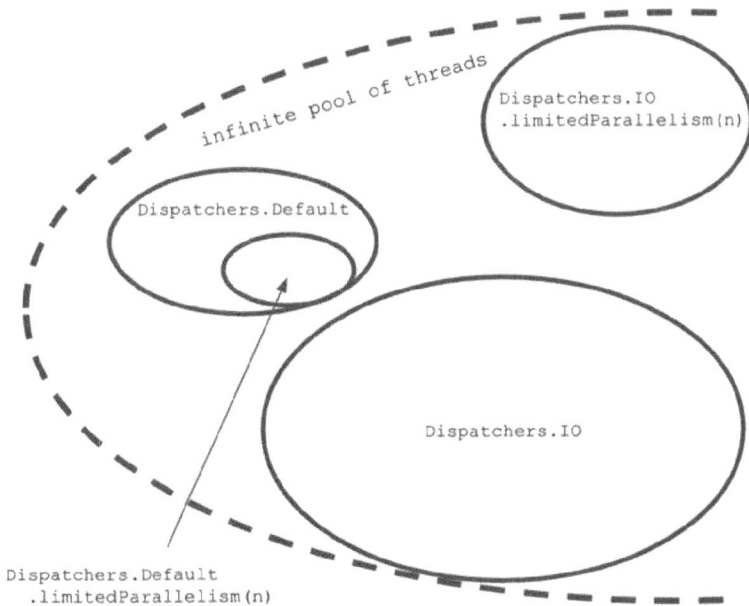

limitedParallelism used on Dispatchers.Default makes a dispatcher with an additional limit. Using limitedParallelism on Dispatcher.IO makes a dispatcher independent of Dispatcher.IO. However, they all share the same infinite pool of threads.

The best practice for classes that might intensively block threads is to define their own dispatchers that have their own independent limits. How big should this limit be? You need to decide for yourself. Too many threads are an inefficient use of our resources. On the other hand, waiting for an available thread is not good for performance. What is most essential is that this limit is independent of Dispatcher.IO and other dispatchers' limits. Thanks to that, one service will not block another.

```kotlin
class DiscUserRepository(
    private val discReader: DiscReader
) : UserRepository {
    private val dispatcher = Dispatchers.IO
        .limitParallelism(5)

    override suspend fun getUser(): UserData =
        withContext(dispatcher) {
            UserData(discReader.read("userName"))
        }
}
```

Dispatcher with a fixed pool of threads

Some developers like to have more control over the pools of threads they use, and Java offers a powerful API for that. For example, we can create a fixed or cached pool of threads with the Executors class. These pools implement the ExecutorService or Executor interfaces, which we can transform into a dispatcher using the asCoroutineDispatcher function.

```kotlin
val NUMBER_OF_THREADS = 20
val dispatcher = Executors
    .newFixedThreadPool(NUMBER_OF_THREADS)
    .asCoroutineDispatcher()
```

> limitedParallelism was introduced in kotlinx-coroutines version 1.6; in previous versions, we often created dispatchers with independent pools of threads using the Executors class.

The biggest problem with this approach is that a dispatcher created with ExecutorService.asCoroutineDispatcher() needs to be closed with the close function. Developers often forget about this, which leads to leaking threads. Another problem is that when you create a fixed pool of threads, you are not using them efficiently. You will keep unused threads alive without sharing them with other services.

Dispatcher limited to a single thread

For all dispatchers using multiple threads, we need to consider the shared state problem. Notice that in the example below 10,000 coroutines are increasing i by 1. So, its value should be 10,000, but it is a smaller number. This is a result of a shared state (i property) modification on multiple threads at the same time.

```
var i = 0

suspend fun main(): Unit = coroutineScope {
    repeat(10_000) {
        launch(Dispatchers.IO) { // or Default
            i++
        }
    }
    delay(1000)
    println(i) // ~9930
}
```

There are many ways to solve this problem (most will be described in the *The problem with state* chapter), but one option is to use a dispatcher with just a single thread. If we use just a single thread at a time, we do not need any other synchronization. The classic way to do this was to create such a dispatcher using Executors.

```
val dispatcher = Executors.newSingleThreadExecutor()
    .asCoroutineDispatcher()

// previously:
// val dispatcher = newSingleThreadContext("My name")
```

The problem is that this dispatcher keeps an extra thread active, and it needs to be closed when it is not used anymore. A modern solution is to use Dispatchers.Default or Dispatchers.IO (if we block threads) with parallelism limited to 1.

```kotlin
var i = 0

suspend fun main(): Unit = coroutineScope {
    val dispatcher = Dispatchers.Default
        .limitedParallelism(1)

    repeat(10000) {
        launch(dispatcher) {
            i++
        }
    }
    delay(1000)
    println(i) // 10000
}
```

The biggest disadvantage is that because we have only one thread, our calls will be handled sequentially if we block it.

```kotlin
suspend fun main(): Unit = coroutineScope {
    val dispatcher = Dispatchers.Default
        .limitedParallelism(1)

    val job = Job()
    repeat(5) {
        launch(dispatcher + job) {
            Thread.sleep(1000)
        }
    }
    job.complete()
    val time = measureTimeMillis { job.join() }
    println("Took $time") // Took 5006
}
```

Using virtual threads from Project Loom

JVM platform introduced a new technology known as Project Loom. Its biggest innovation is the introduction of *virtual threads*, which are much lighter than regular threads. It costs much less to have blocked virtual threads than to have a regular thread blocked.

> Warning! Project Loom is still young, and I do not recommend using it on enterprise applications until it gets stable.

Project Loom does not have much to offer us developers who know Kotlin Coroutines. Kotlin Coroutines have many more amazing features, like effortless cancellation or virtual time for testing[40]. What Project Loom can be truly useful for is that we can use its virtual threads instead of `Dispatcher.IO`, where we cannot avoid blocking threads[41].

To use Project Loom, we need to use JVM in version over 19, and currently, we need to enable preview features using the `--enable-preview` flag. Then we should be able to create an executor using `newVirtualThreadPerTaskExecutor` from `Executors` and transform it into a coroutine dispatcher.

```
val LoomDispatcher = Executors
    .newVirtualThreadPerTaskExecutor()
    .asCoroutineDispatcher()
```

Alternatively, one could make an object that implements `ExecutorCoroutineDispatcher`.

```
object LoomDispatcher : ExecutorCoroutineDispatcher() {

    override val executor: Executor = Executor { command ->
        Thread.startVirtualThread(command)
    }

    override fun dispatch(
        context: CoroutineContext,
        block: Runnable
    ) {
        executor.execute(block)
    }
```

---

[40]We will discuss it in the chapter *Testing Kotlin Coroutines*.

[41]The solution was inspired by the article *Running Kotlin coroutines on Project Loom's virtual threads* by Jan Vladimir Mostert.

```
override fun close() {
    error("Cannot be invoked on Dispatchers.LOOM")
}
}
```

To use this dispatcher similarly to other dispatchers, we can define an extension property on the Dispatchers object. This should also help this dispatcher's discoverability.

```
val Dispatchers.Loom: CoroutineDispatcher
    get() = LoomDispatcher
```

Now we only need to test if our new dispatcher really is an improvement. We expect that when we are blocking threads, it should take less memory and processor attention than other dispatchers. We could set up the environment for precise measurements, or we could construct an example so extreme that anyone can observe the difference. For this book, I decided to use the latter approach. I started 100.000 coroutines, each blocked for 1 second. You can make them do something else, like printing something or incrementing some value, it should not change the result much. Finishing all those coroutines execution on Dispatchers.Loom took a bit more than two seconds.

```
suspend fun main() = measureTimeMillis {
    coroutineScope {
        repeat(100_000) {
            launch(Dispatchers.Loom) {
                Thread.sleep(1000)
            }
        }
    }
}.let(::println) // 2 273
```

Let's compare it to an alternative. Using pure Dispatchers.IO would not be fair, as it is limited to 64 threads, and such function execution will take over 26 minutes. We should increment the threads limit to the number of coroutines. When I did that, such code execution took over 23 seconds, so ten times more.

```
suspend fun main() = measureTimeMillis {
    val dispatcher = Dispatchers.IO
        .limitedParallelism(100_000)
    coroutineScope {
        repeat(100_000) {
            launch(dispatcher) {
                Thread.sleep(1000)
            }
        }
    }
}.let(::println) // 23 803
```

At the moment, Project Loom is still young, and it is hard actually to use it, but I must say it is an exciting substitution for Dispatchers.IO. However, you will likely not need it in the future, as the Kotlin Coroutines team expresses their willingness to use virtual threads by default once Project Loom gets stable. I hope it will happen soon.

Unconfined dispatcher

The last dispatcher we need to discuss is Dispatchers.Unconfined. This dispatcher is different from the previous one as it does not change any threads. When it is started, it runs on the thread on which it was started. If it is resumed, it runs on the thread that resumed it.

```
suspend fun main(): Unit =
    withContext(newSingleThreadContext("Thread1")) {
        var continuation: Continuation<Unit>? = null

        launch(newSingleThreadContext("Thread2")) {
            delay(1000)
            continuation?.resume(Unit)
        }

        launch(Dispatchers.Unconfined) {
            println(Thread.currentThread().name) // Thread1

            suspendCancellableCoroutine<Unit> {
```

```
            continuation = it
        }

        println(Thread.currentThread().name) // Thread2

        delay(1000)

        println(Thread.currentThread().name)
        // kotlinx.coroutines.DefaultExecutor
        // (used by delay)
    }
}
```

This is sometimes useful for unit testing. Imagine that you need
to test a function that calls launch. Synchronizing the time might
not be easy. One solution is to use Dispatchers.Unconfined instead
of all other dispatchers. If it is used in all scopes, everything runs
on the same thread, and we can more easily control the order
of operations. This trick is not needed if we use runTest from
kotlinx-coroutines-test. We will discuss this later in the book.

From the performance point of view, this dispatcher is the cheapest
as it never requires thread switching. So, we might choose it if we
do not care at all on which thread our code is running. However, in
practice, it is not considered good to use it so recklessly. What if, by
accident, we miss a blocking call and we are running on the Main
thread? This could lead to blocking the entire application.

Immediate main dispatching

There is a cost associated with dispatching a coroutine. When
withContext is called, the coroutine needs to be suspended, possibly
wait in a queue, and then resumed. This is a small but unnecessary
cost if we are already on this thread. Look at the function below:

```
suspend fun showUser(user: User) =
    withContext(Dispatchers.Main) {
        userNameElement.text = user.name
        // ...
    }
```

If this function had already been called on the main dispatcher, we would have an unnecessary cost of re-dispatching. What is more, if there were a long queue for the Main thread because of withContext, the user data might be shown with some delay (this coroutine would need to wait for other coroutines to do their job first). To prevent this, there is Dispatchers.Main.immediate, which dispatches only if it is needed. So, if the function below is called on the Main thread, it won't be re-dispatched, it will be called immediately.

```
suspend fun showUser(user: User) =
    withContext(Dispatchers.Main.immediate) {
        userNameElement.text = user.name
        // ...
    }
```

We prefer Dispatchers.Main.immediate as the withContext argument whenever this function might have already been called from the main dispatcher. Currently, the other dispatchers do not support immediate dispatching.

Continuation interceptor

Dispatching works based on the mechanism of continuation interception, which is built into the Kotlin language. There is a coroutine context named ContinuationInterceptor, whose interceptContinuation method is used to modify a continuation when a coroutine is suspended[42]. It also has a releaseInterceptedContinuation method that is called when a continuation is ended.

---

[42]Wrapping needs to happen only once per continuation thanks to the caching mechanism.

```kotlin
public interface ContinuationInterceptor :
    CoroutineContext.Element {

    companion object Key :
        CoroutineContext.Key<ContinuationInterceptor>

    fun <T> interceptContinuation(
        continuation: Continuation<T>
    ): Continuation<T>

    fun releaseInterceptedContinuation(
        continuation: Continuation<*>
    ) {
    }

    //...
}
```

The capability to wrap a continuation gives a lot of control. Dispatchers use `interceptContinuation` to wrap a continuation with `DispatchedContinuation`, which runs on a specific pool of threads. This is how dispatchers work.

The problem is that the same context is also used by many testing libraries, for instance by `runTest` from `kotlinx-coroutines-test`. Each element in a context has to have a unique key. This is why we sometimes inject dispatchers to replace them in unit tests with test dispatchers. We will get back to this topic in the chapter dedicated to coroutine testing.

```kotlin
class DiscUserRepository(
    private val discReader: DiscReader,
    private val dispatcher: CoroutineContext = Dispatchers.IO,
) : UserRepository {
    override suspend fun getUser(): UserData =
        withContext(dispatcher) {
            UserData(discReader.read("userName"))
        }
}
```

```
class UserReaderTests {

    @Test
    fun `some test`() = runTest {
        // given
        val discReader = FakeDiscReader()
        val repo = DiscUserRepository(
            discReader,
            // one of coroutines testing practices
            this.coroutineContext[ContinuationInterceptor]!!
        )
        //...
    }
}
```

Performance of dispatchers against different tasks

To show how different dispatchers perform against different tasks, I made some benchmarks. In all these cases, the task is to run 100 independent coroutines with the same task. Different columns represent different tasks: suspending for a second, blocking for a second, CPU-intensive operation, and memory-intensive operation (where the majority of the time is spent on accessing, allocating, and freeing memory). Different rows represent the different dispatchers used for running these coroutines. The table below shows the average execution time in milliseconds.

	Suspending	Blocking	CPU	Memory
Single thread	1 002	100 003	39 103	94 358
Default (8 threads)	1 002	13 003	8 473	21 461
IO (64 threads)	1 002	2 003	9 893	20 776
100 threads	1 002	1 003	16 379	21 004

There are a few important observations you can make:

1. When we are just suspending, it doesn't really matter how many threads we are using.

2. When we are blocking, the more threads we are using, the faster all these coroutines will be finished.
3. With CPU-intensive operations, Dispatchers.Default is the best option[43].
4. If we are dealing with a memory-intensive problem, more threads might provide some (but not a significant) improvement.

Here is how the tested functions look[44]:

```kotlin
fun cpu(order: Order): Coffee {
    var i = Int.MAX_VALUE
    while (i > 0) {
        i -= if (i % 2 == 0) 1 else 2
    }
    return Coffee(order.copy(customer = order.customer + i))
}


fun memory(order: Order): Coffee {
    val list = List(1_000) { it }
    val list2 = List(1_000) { list }
    val list3 = List(1_000) { list2 }
    return Coffee(
        order.copy(
            customer = order.customer + list3.hashCode()
        )
    )
}


fun blocking(order: Order): Coffee {
    Thread.sleep(1000)
    return Coffee(order)
}
```

---

[43]The main reason is that the more threads we use, the more time the processor needs to spend on switching between them, and so it has less time to do meaningful operations. Also Dispatchers.IO should not be used for CPU-intensive operations because it is used to block operations, and some other process might block all its threads.

[44]The whole code can be found on https://bit.ly/3vqMpYf

```
suspend fun suspending(order: Order): Coffee {
    delay(1000)
    return Coffee(order)
}
```

Summary

Dispatchers determine on which thread or thread pool a coroutine will be running (starting and resuming). The most important options are:

- `Dispatchers.Default`, which we use for CPU-intensive operations;
- `Dispatchers.Main`, which we use to access the Main thread on Android, Swing, or JavaFX;
- `Dispatchers.Main.immediate`, which runs on the same thread as `Dispatchers.Main` but is not re-dispatched if it is not necessary;
- `Dispatchers.IO`, which we use when we need to do some blocking operations;
- `Dispatchers.IO` with limited parallelism or a custom dispatcher with a pool of threads, which we use when we might have a big number of blocking calls;
- `Dispatchers.Default` or `Dispatchers.IO` with parallelism limited to 1, or a custom dispatcher with a single thread, which is used when we need to secure shared state modifications;
- `Dispatchers.Unconfined`, which we use when we do not care where the coroutine will be executed.

Constructing a coroutine scope

In previous chapters, we've learned about the tools needed to construct a proper scope. Now it is time to summarize this knowledge and see how it is typically used. We will see two common examples: one for Android, and one for backend development.

CoroutineScope factory function

`CoroutineScope` is an interface with a single property `coroutineContext`.

```
interface CoroutineScope {
    val coroutineContext: CoroutineContext
}
```

Therefore, we can make a class implement this interface and just directly call coroutine builders in it.

```
class SomeClass : CoroutineScope {
    override val coroutineContext: CoroutineContext = Job()

    fun onStart() {
        launch {
            // ...
        }
    }
}
```

However, this approach is not very popular. On one hand, it is convenient; on the other, it is problematic that in such a class we can directly call other `CoroutineScope` methods like `cancel` or `ensureActive`. Even accidentally, someone might cancel the whole scope, and coroutines will not start anymore. Instead, we generally prefer to hold a coroutine scope as an object in a property and use it to call coroutine builders.

```
class SomeClass {
    val scope: CoroutineScope = ...

    fun onStart() {
        scope.launch {
            // ...
        }
    }
}
```

The easiest way to create a coroutine scope object is by using the CoroutineScope factory function[45]. It creates a scope with provided context (and an additional Job for structured concurrency if no job is already part of the context).

```
public fun CoroutineScope(
    context: CoroutineContext
): CoroutineScope =
    ContextScope(
        if (context[Job] != null) context
        else context + Job()
    )

internal class ContextScope(
    context: CoroutineContext
) : CoroutineScope {
    override val coroutineContext: CoroutineContext = context
    override fun toString(): String =
        "CoroutineScope(coroutineContext=$coroutineContext)"
}
```

Constructing a scope on Android

In most Android applications, we use an architecture that is a descendant of MVC: currently mainly MVVM or MVP. In these architectures, we extract presentation logic into objects called ViewModels

---

[45]A function that looks like a constructor is known as a *fake constructor*. This pattern is explained in Effective Kotlin Item 33: *Consider factory functions instead of constructors.*

or Presenters. This is where coroutines are generally started. In other layers, like in Use Cases or Repositories, we generally just use suspending functions. Coroutines might also be started in Fragments or Activities. Regardless of where coroutines are started on Android, how they are constructed will most likely be the same. Let's take a `MainViewModel` as an example: let's say it needs to fetch some data in `onCreate` (which is called when a user enters the screen). This data fetching needs to happen in a coroutine which needs to be called on some scope object. We will construct a scope in the `BaseViewModel` so it is defined just once for all view models. So, in the `MainViewModel`, we can just use the `scope` property from `BaseViewModel`.

```kotlin
abstract class BaseViewModel : ViewModel() {
    protected val scope = CoroutineScope(TODO())
}

class MainViewModel(
    private val userRepo: UserRepository,
    private val newsRepo: NewsRepository,
) : BaseViewModel {

    fun onCreate() {
        scope.launch {
            val user = userRepo.getUser()
            view.showUserData(user)
        }
        scope.launch {
            val news = newsRepo.getNews()
                .sortedByDescending { it.date }
            view.showNews(news)
        }
    }
}
```

Time to define a context for this scope. Given that many functions in Android need to be called on the Main thread, `Dispatchers.Main` is considered the best option as the default dispatcher. We will use it as a part of our default context on Android.

```
abstract class BaseViewModel : ViewModel() {
    protected val scope = CoroutineScope(Dispatchers.Main)
}
```

Second, we need to make our scope cancellable. It is a common feature to cancel all unfinished processes once a user exits a screen and onDestroy (or onCleared in case of ViewModels) is called. To make our scope cancellable, we need it to have some Job (we do not really need to add it, because if we don't it will be added by the CoroutineScope function anyway, but it is more explicit this way). Then, we can cancel it in onCleared.

```
abstract class BaseViewModel : ViewModel() {
    protected val scope =
        CoroutineScope(Dispatchers.Main + Job())

    override fun onCleared() {
        scope.cancel()
    }
}
```

Even better, it is a common practice to not cancel the whole scope but only its children. Thanks to that, as long as this view model is active, new coroutines can start on its scope property.

```
abstract class BaseViewModel : ViewModel() {
    protected val scope =
        CoroutineScope(Dispatchers.Main + Job())

    override fun onCleared() {
        scope.coroutineContext.cancelChildren()
    }
}
```

We also want different coroutines started on this scope to be independent. When we use Job, if any of the children is cancelled due to an error, the parent and all its other children are cancelled as well. Even if there was an exception when loading user data, it should not stop us from seeing the news. To have such independence, we should use SupervisorJob instead of Job.

```
abstract class BaseViewModel : ViewModel() {
    protected val scope =
        CoroutineScope(Dispatchers.Main + SupervisorJob())

    override fun onCleared() {
        scope.coroutineContext.cancelChildren()
    }
}
```

The last important functionality is the default way of handling uncaught exceptions. On Android, we often define what should happen
in the case of different kinds of exceptions. If we receive a 401
Unauthorized from an HTTP call, we might open the login screen.
For a 503 Service Unavailable API error, we might show a server
problem message. In other cases, we might show dialogs, snackbars,
or toasts. We often define these exception handlers once, for instance in some BaseActivity, and then pass them to view models (often via constructor). Then, we can use CoroutineExceptionHandler
to call this function if there is an unhandled exception.

```
abstract class BaseViewModel(
    private val onError: (Throwable) -> Unit
) : ViewModel() {
    private val exceptionHandler =
        CoroutineExceptionHandler { _, throwable ->
            onError(throwable)
        }

    private val context =
        Dispatchers.Main + SupervisorJob() + exceptionHandler

    protected val scope = CoroutineScope(context)

    override fun onCleared() {
        context.cancelChildren()
    }
}
```

An alternative would be to hold exceptions as a live data property,
which is observed in the BaseActivity or another view element.

```
abstract class BaseViewModel : ViewModel() {
    private val _failure: MutableLiveData<Throwable> =
        MutableLiveData()
    val failure: LiveData<Throwable> = _failure

    private val exceptionHandler =
        CoroutineExceptionHandler { _, throwable ->
            _failure.value = throwable
        }

    private val context =
        Dispatchers.Main + SupervisorJob() + exceptionHandler

    protected val scope = CoroutineScope(context)

    override fun onCleared() {
        context.cancelChildren()
    }
}
```

viewModelScope and lifecycleScope

In modern Android applications, instead of defining your own scope, you can also use viewModelScope (needs androidx.lifecycle:lifecycle-viewmodel-ktx version 2.2.0 or higher) or lifecycleScope (needs androidx.lifecycle:lifecycle-runtime-ktx version 2.2.0 or higher). How they work is nearly identical to what we've just constructed: they use Dispatchers.Main and SupervisorJob, and they cancel the job when the view model or lifecycle owner gets destroyed.

```
// Implementation from lifecycle-viewmodel-ktx version 2.4.0
public val ViewModel.viewModelScope: CoroutineScope
    get() {
        val scope: CoroutineScope? = this.getTag(JOB_KEY)
        if (scope != null) {
            return scope
        }
        return setTagIfAbsent(
            JOB_KEY,
            CloseableCoroutineScope(
                SupervisorJob() +
                    Dispatchers.Main.immediate
            )
        )
    }


internal class CloseableCoroutineScope(
    context: CoroutineContext
) : Closeable, CoroutineScope {
    override val coroutineContext: CoroutineContext = context

    override fun close() {
        coroutineContext.cancel()
    }
}
```

Using viewModelScope and lifecycleScope is convenient and recommended if we do not need any special context as a part of our
scope (like CoroutineExceptionHandler). This is why this approach
is chosen by many (maybe most) Android applications.

```
class ArticlesListViewModel(
    private val produceArticles: ProduceArticlesUseCase,
) : ViewModel() {

    private val _progressBarVisible =
        MutableStateFlow(false)
    val progressBarVisible: StateFlow<Boolean> =
        _progressBarVisible
```

```kotlin
private val _articlesListState =
    MutableStateFlow<ArticlesListState>(Initial)
val articlesListState: StateFlow<ArticlesListState> =
    _articlesListState

fun onCreate() {
    viewModelScope.launch {
        _progressBarVisible.value = true
        val articles = produceArticles.produce()
        _articlesListState.value =
            ArticlesLoaded(articles)
        _progressBarVisible.value = false
    }
}
}
```

Constructing a coroutine on the backend

Many backend frameworks have built-in support for suspending functions. Spring Boot allows controller functions to be suspended. In Ktor, all handlers are suspending functions by default. Thanks to that, we rarely need to create a scope ourselves. However, assuming that we do (maybe because we need to start a task or work with an older version of Spring), what we most likely need is:

- a custom dispatcher with a pool of threads (or `Dispatchers.Default`);
- `SupervisorJob` to make different coroutines independent;
- probably some `CoroutineExceptionHandler` to respond with proper error codes, send dead letters[46], or log problems.

---

[46]This is a popular microservices pattern that is used when we use a software bus, like in Apache Kafka.

```
@Configuration
public class CoroutineScopeConfiguration {

    @Bean
    fun coroutineDispatcher(): CoroutineDispatcher =
        Dispatchers.IO.limitedParallelism(5)

    @Bean
    fun coroutineExceptionHandler() =
        CoroutineExceptionHandler { _, throwable ->
            FirebaseCrashlytics.getInstance()
                .recordException(throwable)
        }

    @Bean
    fun coroutineScope(
        coroutineDispatcher: CoroutineDispatcher,
        coroutineExceptionHandler: CoroutineExceptionHandler,
    ) = CoroutineScope(
        SupervisorJob() +
            coroutineDispatcher +
            coroutineExceptionHandler
    )
}
```

Such a scope is most often injected into classes via the constructor. Thanks to that, the scope can be defined once to be used by many classes, and it can be easily replaced with a different scope for testing purposes.

Constructing a scope for additional calls

As explained in the *Additional operations* section of the *Coroutine scope functions* chapter, we often make scopes for starting additional operations. These scopes are then typically injected via arguments to functions or the constructor. If we only plan to use these scopes to suspend calls, it is enough if they just have a SupervisorScope.

```
val analyticsScope = CoroutineScope(SupervisorJob())
```

All their exceptions will only be shown in logs; so, if you want to send them to a monitoring system, use CoroutineExceptionHandler.

```
private val exceptionHandler =
   CoroutineExceptionHandler { _, throwable ->
      FirebaseCrashlytics.getInstance()
         .recordException(throwable)
   }

val analyticsScope = CoroutineScope(
   SupervisorJob() + exceptionHandler
)
```

Another common customization is setting a different dispatcher. For instance, use Dispatchers.IO if you might have blocking calls on this scope, or use Dispatchers.Main if you might want to modify the main view on Android (if we set Dispatchers.Main, testing on Android is easier).

```
val analyticsScope = CoroutineScope(
   SupervisorJob() + Dispatchers.IO
)
```

Summary

I hope that after this chapter you will know how to construct scopes in most typical situations. This is important when using coroutines in real-life projects. This is enough for many small and simple applications, but for those that are more serious we still need to cover two more topics: proper synchronization and testing.

The problem with shared state

Before we start, take a look at the UserDownloader class below. It allows us to fetch a user by id or to get all the users that were downloaded before. What is wrong with this implementation?

```kotlin
class UserDownloader(
    private val api: NetworkService
) {
    private val users = mutableListOf<User>()

    fun downloaded(): List<User> = users.toList()

    suspend fun fetchUser(id: Int) {
        val newUser = api.fetchUser(id)
        users.add(newUser)
    }
}
```

Notice the use of the defensive copy toList. This is done to avoid a conflict between reading the object returned by downloaded and adding an element to the mutable list. We could also represent users using the read-only list (List<User>) and the read-write property (var). Then, we would not need to make a defensive copy, and downloaded would not need to be protected at all, but we would decrease the performance of adding elements to the collection. I personally prefer the second approach, but I decided to show the one using a mutable collection as I see it more often in real-life projects.

The above implementation is not prepared for concurrent use. Each fetchUser call modifies users. This is fine as long as this function is not started on more than one thread at the same time. Since it can be started on more than one thread at the same time, we say users is a shared state, therefore it needs to be secured. This is because concurrent modifications can lead to conflicts. This problem is presented below:

```
class FakeNetworkService : NetworkService {
    override suspend fun fetchUser(id: Int): User {
        delay(2)
        return User("User$id")
    }
}

suspend fun main() {
    val downloader = UserDownloader(FakeNetworkService())
    coroutineScope {
        repeat(1_000_000) {
            launch {
                downloader.fetchUser(it)
            }
        }
    }
    print(downloader.downloaded().size) // ~998242
}
```

Because there are multiple threads interacting with the same instance, the above code will print a number smaller than 1,000,000 (like 998,242 for example), or it might throw an exception.

```
Exception in thread "main"
java.lang.ArrayIndexOutOfBoundsException: 22
 at java.util.ArrayList.add(ArrayList.java:463)
 ...
```

This is a typical problem with shared state modifications. To see it more clearly, I will present a simpler example: multiple threads incrementing an integer. I am using massiveRun to call an operation 1,000 times on 1,000 coroutines using Dispatchers.Default. After these operations, the number should be 1,000,000 (1,000 * 1,000). However, without any synchronization the real result will be smaller because of the conflicts.

```
var counter = 0

fun main() = runBlocking {
    massiveRun {
        counter++
    }
    println(counter) // ~567231
}

suspend fun massiveRun(action: suspend () -> Unit) =
    withContext(Dispatchers.Default) {
        repeat(1000) {
            launch {
                repeat(1000) { action() }
            }
        }
    }
```

To understand why the result is not 1,000,000, imagine a scenario in which two threads try to increment the same number at the same time. Let's say that the initial value is 0. The first thread takes the current value 0, and then the processor decides to switch to the second thread. The second thread takes 0 as well, increments it to 1, and stores it in the variable. We switch to the first thread where it has finished: it has 0, so it increments it to 1 and stores it. As a result, the variable is 1 but it should be 2. This is how some operations are lost.

Blocking synchronization

The problem above can be solved using classic tools we know from Java, like `synchronized` block or synchronized collections.

```
var counter = 0

fun main() = runBlocking {
    val lock = Any()
    massiveRun {
        synchronized(lock) { // We are blocking threads!
            counter++
        }
    }
    println("Counter = $counter") // 1000000
}
```

This solution works, but there are a few problems. The biggest one is, that inside synchronized block you cannot use suspending functions. The second one is, that this block is blocking threads when a coroutine is waiting for its turn. I hope that after the chapter about dispatchers you understand that we do not want to block threads. What if it is the main thread? What if we only have a limited pool of threads? Why waste these resources? We should use coroutine-specific tools instead. Ones that do not block but instead suspend or avoid conflict. So, let's set aside this solution and explore some others.

Atomics

There is another Java solution that can help us in some simple cases. Java has a set of atomic values. All their operations are fast and guaranteed to be "thread-safe". They are called atomic. Their operations are implemented at a low level without locks, so this solution is efficient and appropriate for us. There are different atomic values we can use. For our case, we can use AtomicInteger.

```
ır counter = Atomic
            © AtomicInteger (java.util.concurrent.atomic)
  = runBlo © AtomicBoolean (java.util.concurrent.atomic)
 'eRun {    © AtomicIntegerArray (java.util.concurrent.atomic)
ıunter.inc © AtomicIntegerFieldUpdater <T> (java.util.concurrent.atomic)
            © AtomicLong (java.util.concurrent.atomic)
            © AtomicLongArray (java.util.concurrent.atomic)
.n("Counte © AtomicLongFieldUpdater<T> (java.util.concurrent.atomic)
            © AtomicMarkableReference<V> (java.util.concurrent.atomic)
            © AtomicReference<V> (java.util.concurrent.atomic)
            © AtomicReferenceArray <E> (java.util.concurrent.atomic)
            © AtomicReferenceFieldUpdater<T, V> (java.util.concurrent.at…
            © AtomicStampedReference<V> (java.util.concurrent.atomic)
```

```kotlin
private var counter = AtomicInteger()

fun main() = runBlocking {
    massiveRun {
        counter.incrementAndGet()
    }
    println(counter.get()) // 1000000
}
```

It works perfectly here, but the utility of atomic values is generally
very limited, therefore we need to be careful: just knowing a single
operation will be atomic does not help us when we have a bundle of
operations.

```kotlin
private var counter = AtomicInteger()

fun main() = runBlocking {
    massiveRun {
        counter.set(counter.get() + 1)
    }
    println(counter.get()) // ~430467
}
```

To secure our UserDownloader, we could use the AtomicReference
wrapping around the read-only list of users. We can use the
getAndUpdate atomic function to update its value without conflicts.

```
class UserDownloader(
    private val api: NetworkService
) {
    private val users = AtomicReference(listOf<User>())

    fun downloaded(): List<User> = users.get()

    suspend fun fetchUser(id: Int) {
        val newUser = api.fetchUser(id)
        users.getAndUpdate { it + newUser }
    }
}
```

We often use atomics to secure a single primitive or a single reference, but for more complicated cases we still need better tools.

A dispatcher limited to a single thread

We saw a dispatcher with parallelism limited to a single thread in the *Dispatchers*[47] chapter. This is the easiest solution for most problems with shared states.

```
val dispatcher = Dispatchers.IO
    .limitedParallelism(1)

var counter = 0

fun main() = runBlocking {
    massiveRun {
        withContext(dispatcher) {
            counter++
        }
    }
    println(counter) // 1000000
}
```

In practice, this approach can be used in two ways. The first approach is known as *coarse-grained thread confinement*. This is

---

[47]https://kt.academy/article/cc-dispatchers

an easy approach whereby we just wrap the whole function with `withContext`, with a dispatcher limited to a single thread. This solution is easy and eliminates conflicts, but the problem is that we lose the multithreading capabilities of the whole function. Let's take a look at the example below. `api.fetchUser(id)` could be started concurrently on many threads, but its body will be running on a dispatcher that is limited to a single thread. As a result, this function execution could slow down when we invoke functions that are blocking or CPU-intensive.

```kotlin
class UserDownloader(
    private val api: NetworkService
) {
    private val users = mutableListOf<User>()
    private val dispatcher = Dispatchers.IO
        .limitedParallelism(1)

    suspend fun downloaded(): List<User> =
        withContext(dispatcher) {
            users.toList()
        }

    suspend fun fetchUser(id: Int) = withContext(dispatcher) {
        val newUser = api.fetchUser(id)
        users += newUser
    }
}
```

The second approach is known as *fine-grained thread confinement*. In this approach, we wrap only those statements which modify the state. In our example, these are all the lines where `users` is used. This approach is more demanding, but it offers us better performance if the functions excluded from our critical section (like `fetchUser` in our example) are blocking or CPU-intensive. If they are just plain suspending functions, the performance improvement is unlikely to be seen.

```kotlin
class UserDownloader(
    private val api: NetworkService
) {
    private val users = mutableListOf<User>()
    private val dispatcher = Dispatchers.IO
        .limitedParallelism(1)

    suspend fun downloaded(): List<User> =
        withContext(dispatcher) {
            users.toList()
        }

    suspend fun fetchUser(id: Int) {
        val newUser = api.fetchUser(id)
        withContext(dispatcher) {
            users += newUser
        }
    }
}
```

In most cases, using a dispatcher with a single thread is not only easy, but also efficient, thanks to the fact that standard dispatchers share the same pool of threads.

Mutex

The last popular approach is to use a Mutex. You can imagine it as a room with a single key (or maybe a toilet at a cafeteria). Its most important function is lock. When the first coroutine calls it, it kind of takes the key and passes through lock without suspension. If another coroutine then calls lock, it will be suspended until the first coroutine calls unlock (like a person waiting for a key to the toilet[48]). If another coroutine reaches the lock function, it is suspended and

---

[48]To avoid giving a false impression of my home country, asking for the key to a toilet is something I mainly experience outside of Poland. For instance, in Poland practically every petrol station has a toilet available for everyone, no key required (and they are generally clean and tidy). However, in many other European countries, toilets are better protected from people who might try to use them without buying anything.

put in a queue, just after the second coroutine. When the first coroutine finally calls the unlock function, it gives back the key, so the
second coroutine (the first one in the queue) is now resumed and can
finally pass through the lock function. Thus, only one coroutine will
be between lock and unlock.

```kotlin
suspend fun main() = coroutineScope {
    repeat(5) {
        launch {
            delayAndPrint()
        }
    }
}

val mutex = Mutex()

suspend fun delayAndPrint() {
    mutex.lock()
    delay(1000)
    println("Done")
    mutex.unlock()
}
// (1 sec)
// Done
// (1 sec)
// Done
// (1 sec)
// Done
// (1 sec)
// Done
// (1 sec)
// Done
```

Using lock and unlock directly is risky, as any exception (or prema-
ture return) in between would lead to the key never being given back
(unlock never been called), and as a result, no other coroutines would
be able to pass through the lock. This is a serious problem known
as a deadlock (imagine a toilet that cannot be used because someone
was in a hurry and forgot to give back the key). So, instead we can
use the withLock function, which starts with lock but calls unlock on

the finally block so that any exceptions thrown inside the block will successfully release the lock. In use, it is similar to a synchronized block.

```
val mutex = Mutex()

var counter = 0

fun main() = runBlocking {
    massiveRun {
        mutex.withLock {
            counter++
        }
    }
    println(counter) // 1000000
}
```

The important advantage of mutex over a synchronized block is that we suspend a coroutine instead of blocking a thread. This is a safer and lighter approach. Compared to using a dispatcher with parallelism limited to a single thread, mutex is lighter, and in some cases it might offer better performance. On the other hand, it is also harder to use it properly. It has one important danger: a coroutine cannot get past the lock twice (maybe the key stays in the door, so another door requiring the same key would be impossible to get past). Execution of the code below will result in a program state called deadlock - it will be blocked forever.

```
suspend fun main() {
    val mutex = Mutex()
    println("Started")
    mutex.withLock {
        mutex.withLock {
            println("Will never be printed")
        }
    }
}
// Started
// (runs forever)
```

The second problem with mutex is that it is not unlocked when a coroutine is suspended. Take a look at the code below. It takes over 5 seconds because mutex is still locked during delay.

```kotlin
class MessagesRepository {
    private val messages = mutableListOf<String>()
    private val mutex = Mutex()

    suspend fun add(message: String) = mutex.withLock {
        delay(1000) // we simulate network call
        messages.add(message)
    }
}

suspend fun main() {
    val repo = MessagesRepository()

    val timeMillis = measureTimeMillis {
        coroutineScope {
            repeat(5) {
                launch {
                    repo.add("Message$it")
                }
            }
        }
    }
    println(timeMillis) // ~5120
}
```

When we use a dispatcher that is limited to a single thread, we don't have such a problem. When a delay or a network call suspends a coroutine, the thread can be used by other coroutines.

```kotlin
class MessagesRepository {
    private val messages = mutableListOf<String>()
    private val dispatcher = Dispatchers.IO
        .limitedParallelism(1)

    suspend fun add(message: String) =
        withContext(dispatcher) {
            delay(1000) // we simulate network call
            messages.add(message)
        }
}

suspend fun main() {
    val repo = MessagesRepository()

    val timeMillis = measureTimeMillis {
        coroutineScope {
            repeat(5) {
                launch {
                    repo.add("Message$it")
                }
            }
        }
    }
    println(timeMillis) // 1058
}
```

This is why we avoid using mutex to wrap whole functions (coarse-grained approach). When we use it at all, we need to do so with great care to avoid locking twice and calling suspending functions.

```kotlin
class MongoUserRepository(
    //...
) : UserRepository {
    private val mutex = Mutex()

    override suspend fun updateUser(
        userId: String,
        userUpdate: UserUpdate
```

```kotlin
): Unit = mutex.withLock {
    // Yes, update should happen on db,
    // not via multiple functions,
    // this is just an example.
    val currentUser = getUser(userId) // Deadlock!
    deleteUser(userId) // Deadlock!
    addUser(currentUser.updated(userUpdate)) // Deadlock!
}

override suspend fun getUser(
    userId: String
): User = mutex.withLock {
    // ...
}

override suspend fun deleteUser(
    userId: String
): Unit = mutex.withLock {
    // ...
}

override suspend fun addUser(
    user: User
): User = mutex.withLock {
    // ...
}
}
```

Fine-grained thread confinement (wrapping only the place where we modify the shared state) would help, but in the above example I would prefer to use a dispatcher that is limited to a single thread.

Semaphore

If we mentioned Mutex, we should also mention Semaphore, which works in similar way, but can have more than one permit. Regarding Mutex, we speak of a single lock, so it has functions lock, unlock and withLock. Regarding Semaphore, we speak of permits, so it has functions acquire, release and withPermit.

```kotlin
suspend fun main() = coroutineScope {
    val semaphore = Semaphore(2)

    repeat(5) {
        launch {
            semaphore.withPermit {
                delay(1000)
                print(it)
            }
        }
    }
}
// 01
// (1 sec)
// 23
// (1 sec)
// 4
```

Semaphore with more than one permit does not help us with the problem of shared state, but it can be used to limit the number of concurrent requests, so to implement *rate limiting*.

```kotlin
class LimitedNetworkUserRepository(
    private val api: UserApi
) {
    // We limit to 10 concurrent requests
    private val semaphore = Semaphore(10)

    suspend fun requestUser(userId: String) =
        semaphore.withPermit {
            api.requestUser(userId)
        }
}
```

Summary

There are many ways in which coroutines can be orchestrated to avoid conflicts when modifying a shared state. The most practical solution is to modify a shared state in a dispatcher that is limited to a single thread. This can be a *fine-grained thread confinement* that only wraps concrete places where synchronization is needed; alternatively, it can be a *coarse-grained thread confinement* that wraps the whole function. The second approach is easier, but it might be slower. We might also use atomic values or a mutex.

Testing Kotlin Coroutines

Testing suspending functions in most cases is not different from testing normal functions. Take a look at the `fetchUserData` below from `FetchUserUseCase`. Checking whether it shows data as expected can be easily achieved thanks to a few fakes[49] (or mocks[50]) and simple assertions.

```kotlin
class FetchUserUseCase(
    private val repo: UserDataRepository,
) {

    suspend fun fetchUserData(): User = coroutineScope {
        val name = async { repo.getName() }
        val friends = async { repo.getFriends() }
        val profile = async { repo.getProfile() }
        User(
            name = name.await(),
            friends = friends.await(),
            profile = profile.await()
        )
    }
}

class FetchUserDataTest {

    @Test
    fun `should construct user`() = runBlocking {
        // given
        val repo = FakeUserDataRepository()
        val useCase = FetchUserUseCase(repo)
```

---

[49]A fake is a class that implements an interface but contains fixed data and no logic. They are useful to mimic a concrete behavior for testing.

[50]Mocks are universal simulated objects that mimic the behavior of real objects in controlled ways. We generally create them using libraries, like MockK, which support mocking suspending functions. In the examples below, I decided to use fakes to avoid using an external library.

```
        // when
        val result = useCase.fetchUserData()

        // then
        val expectedUser = User(
            name = "Ben",
            friends = listOf(Friend("some-friend-id-1")),
            profile = Profile("Example description")
        )
        assertEquals(expectedUser, result)
    }

    class FakeUserDataRepository : UserDataRepository {
        override suspend fun getName(): String = "Ben"

        override suspend fun getFriends(): List<Friend> =
            listOf(Friend("some-friend-id-1"))

        override suspend fun getProfile(): Profile =
            Profile("Example description")
    }
}
```

> My method for testing logic should not be used as a reference. There are many conflicting ideas for how tests should look. I've used fakes here instead of mocks so as not to introduce any external library (I also personally prefer them). I've also tried to keep all tests minimalistic to make them easier to read.

Similarly, in many other cases, if we are interested in what the suspending function does, we practically need nothing else but runBlocking and classic tools for asserting. This is what unit tests look like in many projects. Here are a few unit tests from Kt. Academy backend:

```
class UserTests : KtAcademyFacadeTest() {

    @Test
    fun `should modify user details`() = runBlocking {
        // given
        thereIsUser(aUserToken, aUserId)

        // when
        facade.updateUserSelf(
            aUserToken,
            PatchUserSelfRequest(
                bio = aUserBio,
                bioPl = aUserBioPl,
                publicKey = aUserPublicKey,
                customImageUrl = aCustomImageUrl
            )
        )

        // then
        with(findUser(aUserId)) {
            assertEquals(aUserBio, bio)
            assertEquals(aUserBioPl, bioPl)
            assertEquals(aUserPublicKey, publicKey)
            assertEquals(aCustomImageUrl, customImageUrl)
        }
    }

    //...
}
```

Integration tests can be implemented in the same way. We just use `runBlocking`, and there is nearly no difference between testing how suspending and blocking functions behave.

Testing time dependencies

The difference arises when we want to start testing time dependencies. For example, think of the following functions:

```
suspend fun produceCurrentUserSeq(): User {
    val profile = repo.getProfile()
    val friends = repo.getFriends()
    return User(profile, friends)
}


suspend fun produceCurrentUserSym(): User = coroutineScope {
    val profile = async { repo.getProfile() }
    val friends = async { repo.getFriends() }
    User(profile.await(), friends.await())
}
```

Both functions produce the same result; the difference is that the first one does it sequentially, while the second one does it simultaneously. The difference is that if fetching the profile and the friends takes 1 second each, then the first function would require around 2 seconds, whereas the first would require only 1. How would you test this?

Notice that the difference arises only when execution of getProfile and getFriends truly takes some time. If they are immediate, both ways of producing the user are indistinguishable. So, we might help ourselves by delaying fake functions using delay to simulate a delayed data loading scenario:

```
class FakeDelayedUserDataRepository : UserDataRepository {

    override suspend fun getProfile(): Profile {
        delay(1000)
        return Profile("Example description")
    }

    override suspend fun getFriends(): List<Friend> {
        delay(1000)
        return listOf(Friend("some-friend-id-1"))
    }
}
```

Now, the difference will be visible in unit tests: the produceCurrentUserSeq call will take around 1 second, and the produceCurrentUserSym call will take around 2 seconds. The problem is that we do not want a single unit test to take so much time. We typically have thousands of unit tests in our projects, and we want all of them to execute as quickly as possible. How to have your cake and eat it too? For that, we need to operate in simulated time. Here comes the kotlinx-coroutines-test library to the rescue with its StandardTestDispatcher.

> This chapter presents the kotlinx-coroutines-test functions and classes introduced in version 1.6. If you use an older version of this library, in most cases it should be enough to use runBlockingTest instead of runTest, TestCoroutineDispatcher instead of StandardTestDispatcher, and TestCoroutineScope instead of TestScope. Also, advanceTimeBy in older versions is like advanceTimeBy and runCurrent in versions newer than 1.6. The detailed differences are described in the migration guide at https://github.com/Kotlin/kotlinx.coroutines/blob/master/kotlinx-coroutines-test/MIGRATION.md[51].

TestCoroutineScheduler and StandardTestDispatcher

When we call delay, our coroutine is suspended and resumed after a set time. This behavior can be altered thanks to TestCoroutineScheduler from kotlinx-coroutines-test, which makes delay operate in virtual time, which is fully simulated and does not depend on real time.

```
fun main() {
    val scheduler = TestCoroutineScheduler()

    println(scheduler.currentTime) // 0
    scheduler.advanceTimeBy(1_000)
    println(scheduler.currentTime) // 1000
    scheduler.advanceTimeBy(1_000)
    println(scheduler.currentTime) // 2000
}
```

---

[51]https://github.com/Kotlin/kotlinx.coroutines/blob/master/kotlinx-coroutines-test/MIGRATION.md

TestCoroutineScheduler as well as StandardTestDispatcher, TestScope and runTest are still experimental.

To use `TestCoroutineScheduler` on coroutines, we should use a dispatcher that supports it. The standard option is `StandardTestDispatcher`. Unlike most dispatchers, it is not used just to decide on which thread a coroutine should run. Coroutines started with such a dispatcher will not run until we advance virtual time. The most typical way to do this is by using `advanceUntilIdle`, which advances virtual time and invokes all the operations that would be called during that time if this were real time.

```kotlin
fun main() {
    val scheduler = TestCoroutineScheduler()
    val testDispatcher = StandardTestDispatcher(scheduler)

    CoroutineScope(testDispatcher).launch {
        println("Some work 1")
        delay(1000)
        println("Some work 2")
        delay(1000)
        println("Coroutine done")
    }

    println("[${scheduler.currentTime}] Before")
    scheduler.advanceUntilIdle()
    println("[${scheduler.currentTime}] After")
}
// [0] Before
// Some work 1
// Some work 2
// Coroutine done
// [2000] After
```

StandardTestDispatcher creates TestCoroutineScheduler by default, so we do not need to do so explicitly. We can access it with the `scheduler` property.

```
fun main() {
    val dispatcher = StandardTestDispatcher()

    CoroutineScope(dispatcher).launch {
        println("Some work 1")
        delay(1000)
        println("Some work 2")
        delay(1000)
        println("Coroutine done")
    }

    println("[${dispatcher.scheduler.currentTime}] Before")
    dispatcher.scheduler.advanceUntilIdle()
    println("[${dispatcher.scheduler.currentTime}] After")
}
// [0] Before
// Some work 1
// Some work 2
// Coroutine done
// [2000] After
```

It is important to notice that StandardTestDispatcher does not advance time by itself. We need to do this, otherwise our coroutine will never be resumed.

```
fun main() {
    val testDispatcher = StandardTestDispatcher()

    runBlocking(testDispatcher) {
        delay(1)
        println("Coroutine done")
    }
}
// (code runs forever)
```

Another way to push time is using advanceTimeBy with a concrete number of milliseconds. This function advances time and executes all operations that happened in the meantime. This means that if we push by 2 milliseconds, everything that was delayed by less than that

time will be resumed. To resume operations scheduled exactly at the
second millisecond, we need to additionally invoke the `runCurrent`
function.

```kotlin
fun main() {
    val testDispatcher = StandardTestDispatcher()

    CoroutineScope(testDispatcher).launch {
        delay(1)
        println("Done1")
    }
    CoroutineScope(testDispatcher).launch {
        delay(2)
        println("Done2")
    }
    testDispatcher.scheduler.advanceTimeBy(2) // Done
    testDispatcher.scheduler.runCurrent() // Done2
}
```

Here is a bigger example of using `advanceTimeBy` together with
`runCurrent`.

```kotlin
fun main() {
    val testDispatcher = StandardTestDispatcher()

    CoroutineScope(testDispatcher).launch {
        delay(2)
        print("Done")
    }

    CoroutineScope(testDispatcher).launch {
        delay(4)
        print("Done2")
    }

    CoroutineScope(testDispatcher).launch {
        delay(6)
        print("Done3")
    }
```

```
    for (i in 1..5) {
        print(".")
        testDispatcher.scheduler.advanceTimeBy(1)
        testDispatcher.scheduler.runCurrent()
    }
}
// ..Done..Done2.
```

How does it work under the hood? When `delay` is called, it checks if the dispatcher (class with `ContinuationInterceptor` key) implements the `Delay` interface (`StandardTestDispatcher` does). For such dispatchers, it calls their `scheduleResumeAfterDelay` function instead of the one from the `DefaultDelay`, which waits in real time.

To see that virtual time is truly independent of real time, see the example below. Adding `Thread.sleep` will not influence the coroutine with `StandardTestDispatcher`. Note also that the call to `advanceUntilIdle` takes only a few milliseconds, so it does not wait for any real time. It immediately pushes the virtual time and executes coroutine operations.

```
fun main() {
    val dispatcher = StandardTestDispatcher()

    CoroutineScope(dispatcher).launch {
        delay(1000)
        println("Coroutine done")
    }

    Thread.sleep(Random.nextLong(2000)) // Does not matter
    // how much time we wait here, it will not influence
    // the result

    val time = measureTimeMillis {
        println("[${dispatcher.scheduler.currentTime}] Before")
        dispatcher.scheduler.advanceUntilIdle()
        println("[${dispatcher.scheduler.currentTime}] After")
```

```
    }
    println("Took $time ms")
}
// [0] Before
// Coroutine done
// [1000] After
// Took 15 ms (or other small number)
```

In the previous examples, we were using StandardTestDispatcher
and wrapping it with a scope. Instead, we could use TestScope,
which does the same (and it collects all exceptions with
CoroutineExceptionHandler). The trick is that on this scope we
can also use functions like advanceUntilIdle, advanceTimeBy, or the
currentTime property , all of which are delegated to the scheduler
used by this scope. This is very convenient.

```
fun main() {
    val scope = TestScope()

    scope.launch {
        delay(1000)
        println("First done")
        delay(1000)
        println("Coroutine done")
    }

    println("[${scope.currentTime}] Before") // [0] Before
    scope.advanceTimeBy(1000)
    scope.runCurrent() // First done
    println("[${scope.currentTime}] Middle") // [1000] Middle
    scope.advanceUntilIdle() // Coroutine done
    println("[${scope.currentTime}] After") // [2000] After
}
```

We will later see that StandardTestDispatcher is often used
directly on Android to test ViewModels, Presenters, Fragments,
etc. We could also use it to test the produceCurrentUserSeq and
produceCurrentUserSym functions by starting them in a coroutine,
advancing time until idle, and checking how much simulated time
they took. However, this would be quite complicated; instead, we
should use runTest, which is designed for such purposes.

runTest

runTest is the most commonly used function from kotlinx-coroutines-test. It starts a coroutine with TestScope and immediately advances it until idle. Within its coroutine, the scope is of type TestScope, so we can check currentTime at any point. Therefore, we can check how time flows in our coroutines, while our tests take milliseconds.

```
class TestTest {

    @Test
    fun test1() = runTest {
        assertEquals(0, currentTime)
        delay(1000)
        assertEquals(1000, currentTime)
    }

    @Test
    fun test2() = runTest {
        assertEquals(0, currentTime)
        coroutineScope {
            launch { delay(1000) }
            launch { delay(1500) }
            launch { delay(2000) }
        }
        assertEquals(2000, currentTime)
    }
}
```

Let's get back to our functions, where we loaded user data sequentially and simultaneously. With runTest, testing them is easy. Assuming that our fake repository needs 1 second for each function call, sequential processing should take 2 seconds, and simultaneous processing should take only 1. Thanks to the fact we are using virtual time, our tests are immediate, and the values of currentTime are precise.

```kotlin
@Test
fun `Should produce user sequentially`() = runTest {
    // given
    val userDataRepository = FakeDelayedUserDataRepository()
    val useCase = ProduceUserUseCase(userDataRepository)

    // when
    useCase.produceCurrentUserSeq()

    // then
    assertEquals(2000, currentTime)
}

@Test
fun `Should produce user simultaneously`() = runTest {
    // given
    val userDataRepository = FakeDelayedUserDataRepository()
    val useCase = ProduceUserUseCase(userDataRepository)

    // when
    useCase.produceCurrentUserSym()

    // then
    assertEquals(1000, currentTime)
}
```

Since it is an important use case, let's see a full example of testing a
sequential function with all required classes and interfaces:

```kotlin
class FetchUserUseCase(
    private val repo: UserDataRepository,
) {

    suspend fun fetchUserData(): User = coroutineScope {
        val name = async { repo.getName() }
        val friends = async { repo.getFriends() }
        val profile = async { repo.getProfile() }
        User(
            name = name.await(),
```

```
            friends = friends.await(),
            profile = profile.await()
        )
    }
}

class FetchUserDataTest {

    @Test
    fun `should load data concurrently`() = runTest {
        // given
        val userRepo = FakeUserDataRepository()
        val useCase = FetchUserUseCase(userRepo)

        // when
        useCase.fetchUserData()

        // then
        assertEquals(1000, currentTime)
    }

    @Test
    fun `should construct user`() = runTest {
        // given
        val userRepo = FakeUserDataRepository()
        val useCase = FetchUserUseCase(userRepo)

        // when
        val result = useCase.fetchUserData()

        // then
        val expectedUser = User(
            name = "Ben",
            friends = listOf(Friend("some-friend-id-1")),
            profile = Profile("Example description")
        )
        assertEquals(expectedUser, result)
    }
```

```kotlin
class FakeUserDataRepository : UserDataRepository {
    override suspend fun getName(): String {
        delay(1000)
        return "Ben"
    }

    override suspend fun getFriends(): List<Friend> {
        delay(1000)
        return listOf(Friend("some-friend-id-1"))
    }

    override suspend fun getProfile(): Profile {
        delay(1000)
        return Profile("Example description")
    }
}
}

interface UserDataRepository {
    suspend fun getName(): String
    suspend fun getFriends(): List<Friend>
    suspend fun getProfile(): Profile
}

data class User(
    val name: String,
    val friends: List<Friend>,
    val profile: Profile
)

data class Friend(val id: String)
data class Profile(val description: String)
```

runTest includes TestScope, that includes StandardTestDispatcher, that includes TestCoroutineScheduler.

Background scope

The runTest function creates a scope; like all such functions, it awaits the completion of its children. This means that if you start a process that never ends, your test will never stop.

```kotlin
@Test
fun `should increment counter`() = runTest {
    var i = 0
    launch {
        while (true) {
            delay(1000)
            i++
        }
    }

    delay(1001)
    assertEquals(1, i)
    delay(1000)
    assertEquals(2, i)

    // Test would pass if we added
```

```
    // coroutineContext.job.cancelChildren()
}
```

For such situations, runTest offers backgroundScope. This is a scope
that also operates on virtual time, but runTest will not await its
completion. This is why the test below passes without any problems.
We use backgroundScope to start all the processes we don't want our
test to wait for.

```
@Test
fun `should increment counter`() = runTest {
    var i = 0
    backgroundScope.launch {
        while (true) {
            delay(1000)
            i++
        }
    }


    delay(1001)
    assertEquals(1, i)
    delay(1000)
    assertEquals(2, i)
}
```

Testing cancellation and context passing

If you want to test whether a certain function respects structured
concurrency, the easiest way is to capture the context from a suspending function, then check if it contains the expected value or if its
job has the appropriate state. As an example, consider the mapAsync
function, which I explain in more detail in the *Recipes* chapter.

```
suspend fun <T, R> Iterable<T>.mapAsync(
    transformation: suspend (T) -> R
): List<R> = coroutineScope {
    this@mapAsync.map { async { transformation(it) } }
        .awaitAll()
}
```

This function should map elements asynchronously while preserving their order. This behavior can be verified by the following test:

```
@Test
fun `should map async and keep elements order`() = runTest {
    val transforms = listOf(
        suspend { delay(3000); "A" },
        suspend { delay(2000); "B" },
        suspend { delay(4000); "C" },
        suspend { delay(1000); "D" },
    )

    val res = transforms.mapAsync { it() }
    assertEquals(listOf("A", "B", "C", "D"), res)
    assertEquals(4000, currentTime)
}
```

But this is not all. We expect a properly implemented suspending function to respect structured concurrency.

The easiest way to check this is by specifying some context, like CoroutineName, for the parent coroutine, then check that it is still the same in the transformation function.

To capture the context of a suspending function, we can use the currentCoroutineContext function or the coroutineContext property. In lambda expressions nested in coroutine builders or scope functions, we should use the currentCoroutineContext function because the coroutineContext property from CoroutineScope has priority over the property that provides the current coroutine context.

```
@Test
fun `should support context propagation`() = runTest {
    var ctx: CoroutineContext? = null

    val name1 = CoroutineName("Name 1")
    withContext(name1) {
        listOf("A").mapAsync {
            ctx = currentCoroutineContext()
            it
        }
        assertEquals(name1, ctx?.get(CoroutineName))
    }

    val name2 = CoroutineName("Some name 2")
    withContext(name2) {
        listOf(1, 2, 3).mapAsync {
            ctx = currentCoroutineContext()
            it
        }
        assertEquals(name2, ctx?.get(CoroutineName))
    }
}
```

The easiest way to test cancellation is by capturing the inner function job and verifying its cancellation after the cancellation of the outer coroutine.

```
@Test
fun `should support cancellation`() = runTest {
    var job: Job? = null

    val parentJob = launch {
        listOf("A").mapAsync {
            job = currentCoroutineContext().job
            delay(Long.MAX_VALUE)
        }
    }
```

```
    delay(1000)
    parentJob.cancel()
    assertEquals(true, job?.isCancelled)
}
```

I don't think such tests are required in most applications, but I find them useful in libraries. It's not so obvious that structured concurrency is respected. Both the tests above would fail if `async` were started on an outer scope.

```
// Incorrect implementation, that would make above tests fail
suspend fun <T, R> Iterable<T>.mapAsync(
    transformation: suspend (T) -> R
): List<R> =
    this@mapAsync
        .map { GlobalScope.async { transformation(it) } }
        .awaitAll()
```

UnconfinedTestDispatcher

Except for `StandardTestDispatcher` we also have `UnconfinedTestDispatcher`. The biggest difference is that `StandardTestDispatcher` does not invoke any operations until we use its scheduler. `UnconfinedTestDispatcher` immediately invokes all the operations before the first delay on started coroutines, which is why the code below prints "C".

```
fun main() {
    CoroutineScope(StandardTestDispatcher()).launch {
        print("A")
        delay(1)
        print("B")
    }
    CoroutineScope(UnconfinedTestDispatcher()).launch {
        print("C")
        delay(1)
        print("D")
    }
}
// C
```

The `runTest` function was introduced in version 1.6 of `kotlinx-coroutines-test`. Previously, we used `runBlockingTest`, whose behavior is much closer to `runTest` using `UnconfinedTestDispatcher`. So, if want to directly migrate from `runBlockingTest` to `runTest`, this is how our tests might look:

```
@Test
fun testName() = runTest(UnconfinedTestDispatcher()) {
    //...
}
```

Using mocks

Using `delay` in fakes is easy but not very explicit. Many developers prefer to call `delay` in the test function. One way to do this is using mocks[52]:

```
@Test
fun `should load data concurrently`() = runTest {
    // given
    val userRepo = mockk<UserDataRepository>()
    coEvery { userRepo.getName() } coAnswers {
        delay(600)
        aName
    }
    coEvery { userRepo.getFriends() } coAnswers {
        delay(700)
        someFriends
    }
    coEvery { userRepo.getProfile() } coAnswers {
        delay(800)
        aProfile
    }
```

---

[52]Not everyone likes mocking. On one hand, mocking libraries have plenty of powerful features. On the other hand, think of the following situation: you have thousands of tests, and you change an interface of a repository that is used by all of them. If you use fakes, it is typically enough to update only a few classes. This is a big problem, which is why I generally prefer to use fakes.

```
val useCase = FetchUserUseCase(userRepo)

// when
useCase.fetchUserData()

// then
assertEquals(800, currentTime)
}
```

In the above example, I've used the MockK[53] library.

Testing functions that change a dispatcher

In the **Dispatchers** chapter, we covered typical cases where we set concrete dispatchers. For example, we use Dispatcher.IO (or a custom dispatcher) for blocking calls, or Dispatchers.Default for CPU-intensive calls. Such functions rarely need to be simultaneous, so typically it is enough to test them with runBlocking. This case is easy and practically indistinguishable from testing blocking functions. For example, think of the following function:

```
suspend fun readSave(name: String): GameState =
    withContext(Dispatchers.IO) {
        reader.readCsvBlocking(name, GameState::class.java)
    }

suspend fun calculateModel() =
    withContext(Dispatchers.Default) {
        model.fit(
            dataset = newTrain,
            epochs = 10,
            batchSize = 100,
            verbose = false
        )
    }
```

We could test the behavior of such functions in tests wrapped with runBlocking, but how about checking if these functions truly do

---

[53]https://mockk.io/

change the dispatcher? This can also be done if we mock the functions we call, and inside we capture the name of the used thread.

```
@Test
fun `should change dispatcher`() = runBlocking {
    // given
    val csvReader = mockk<CsvReader>()
    val startThreadName = "MyName"
    var usedThreadName: String? = null
    every {
        csvReader.readCsvBlocking(
            aFileName,
            GameState::class.java
        )
    } coAnswers {
        usedThreadName = Thread.currentThread().name
        aGameState
    }
    val saveReader = SaveReader(csvReader)

    // when
    withContext(newSingleThreadContext(startThreadName)) {
        saveReader.readSave(aFileName)
    }

    // then
    assertNotNull(usedThreadName)
    val expectedPrefix = "DefaultDispatcher-worker-"
    assert(usedThreadName!!.startsWith(expectedPrefix))
}
```

In the above function, I couldn't use fakes because CsvReader is a class, so I used mocks.

Remember,   that   Dispatchers.Default   and Dispatchers.IO share the same pool of threads.

However, in rare cases we might want to test time dependencies in functions that do change the dispatcher. This is a tricky case because the new dispatcher replaces our StandardTestDispatcher, so we stop operating in virtual time. To make this clear, let's wrap the fetchUserData function with withContext(Dispatchers.IO).

```
suspend fun fetchUserData() = withContext(Dispatchers.IO) {
    val name = async { userRepo.getName() }
    val friends = async { userRepo.getFriends() }
    val profile = async { userRepo.getProfile() }
    User(
        name = name.await(),
        friends = friends.await(),
        profile = profile.await()
    )
}
```

Now all our previously implemented tests will wait in real time, and currentTime will keep returning 0. The easiest way to prevent this is by injecting the dispatcher via a constructor and replacing it in unit tests.

```
class FetchUserUseCase(
    private val userRepo: UserDataRepository,
    private val ioDispatcher: CoroutineDispatcher =
        Dispatchers.IO
) {

    suspend fun fetchUserData() = withContext(ioDispatcher) {
        val name = async { userRepo.getName() }
        val friends = async { userRepo.getFriends() }
        val profile = async { userRepo.getProfile() }
        User(
            name = name.await(),
            friends = friends.await(),
            profile = profile.await()
        )
    }
}
```

Now, instead of providing Dispatchers.IO in unit tests, we should use StandardTestDispatcher from runTest. We can get it from coroutineContext using the ContinuationInterceptor key.

```
val testDispatcher = this
    .coroutineContext[ContinuationInterceptor]
    as CoroutineDispatcher

val useCase = FetchUserUseCase(
    userRepo = userRepo,
    ioDispatcher = testDispatcher,
)
```

Another possibility is to cast ioDispatcher as CoroutineContext, and replace it in unit tests with EmptyCoroutineContext. The final behavior will be the same: the function will never change the dispatcher.

```
val useCase = FetchUserUseCase(
    userRepo = userRepo,
    ioDispatcher = EmptyCoroutineContext,
)
```

Testing what happens during function execution

Imagine a function which during its execution first shows a progress bar and later hides it.

```
suspend fun sendUserData() {
    val userData = database.getUserData()
    progressBarVisible.value = true
    userRepository.sendUserData(userData)
    progressBarVisible.value = false
}
```

If we only check the final result, we cannot verify that the progress bar changed its state during function execution. The trick that is helpful in such cases is to start this function in a new coroutine and control virtual time from outside. Notice that runTest creates a coroutine with the StandardTestDispatcher dispatcher and advances its time until idle (using the advanceUntilIdle function). This means that its children's time will start once the parent starts waiting for them, so once its body is finished. Before that, we can advance virtual time by ourselves.

```
@Test
fun `should show progress bar when sending data`() = runTest {
    // given
    val database = FakeDatabase()
    val vm = UserViewModel(database)

    // when
    launch {
        vm.sendUserData()
    }

    // then
    assertEquals(false, vm.progressBarVisible.value)

    // when
    advanceTimeBy(1000)

    // then
    assertEquals(false, vm.progressBarVisible.value)

    // when
    runCurrent()

    // then
    assertEquals(true, vm.progressBarVisible.value)

    // when
    advanceUntilIdle()

    // then
    assertEquals(false, vm.progressBarVisible.value)
}
```

Notice that, thanks to `runCurrent`, we can precisely check when some value changes.

A similar effect could be achieved if we used `delay`. This is like having two independent processes: one is doing things, while the other is checking if the first one is behaving properly.

```
@Test
fun `should show progress bar when sending data`() =
    runTest {
        val database = FakeDatabase()
        val vm = UserViewModel(database)
        launch {
            vm.showUserData()
        }

        // then
        assertEquals(false, vm.progressBarVisible.value)
        delay(1000)
        assertEquals(true, vm.progressBarVisible.value)
        delay(1000)
        assertEquals(false, vm.progressBarVisible.value)
    }
```

Using explicit functions like advanceTimeBy is considered more readable than using delay.

Testing functions that launch new coroutines

Coroutines need to start somewhere. On the backend, they are often started by the framework we use (for instance Spring or Ktor), but sometimes we might also need to construct a scope ourselves and launch coroutines on it.

```
@Scheduled(fixedRate = 5000)
fun sendNotifications() {
    notificationsScope.launch {
        val notifications = notificationsRepository
            .notificationsToSend()
        for (notification in notifications) {
            launch {
                notificationsService.send(notification)
                notificationsRepository
                    .markAsSent(notification.id)
            }
        }
    }
}
```

```
    }
}
```

How can we test `sendNotifications` if the notifications are truly sent concurrently? Again, in unit tests we need to use `StandardTestDispatcher` as part of our scope. We should also add some delays to `send` and `markAsSent`.

```
@Test
fun testSendNotifications() {
    // given
    val notifications = List(100) { Notification(it) }
    val repo = FakeNotificationsRepository(
        delayMillis = 200,
        notifications = notifications,
    )
    val service = FakeNotificationsService(
        delayMillis = 300,
    )
    val testScope = TestScope()
    val sender = NotificationsSender(
        notificationsRepository = repo,
        notificationsService = service,
        notificationsScope = testScope
    )

    // when
    sender.sendNotifications()
    testScope.advanceUntilIdle()

    // then all notifications are sent and marked
    assertEquals(
        notifications.toSet(),
        service.notificationsSent.toSet()
    )
    assertEquals(
        notifications.map { it.id }.toSet(),
        repo.notificationsMarkedAsSent.toSet()
    )
```

```
// and notifications are sent concurrently
assertEquals(700, testScope.currentTime)
}
```

Notice that `runBlocking` is not needed in the code above. Both `sendNotifications` and `advanceUntilIdle` are regular functions.

Replacing the main dispatcher

There is no main function in unit tests. This means that if we try to use it, our tests will fail with the "Module with the Main dispatcher is missing" exception. On the other hand, injecting the Main thread every time would be demanding, so the "kotlinx-coroutines-test" library provides the `setMain` extension function on `Dispatchers` instead.

We often define main in a setup function (function with `@Before` or `@BeforeEach`) in a base class extended by all unit tests. As a result, we are always sure we can run our coroutines on `Dispatchers.Main`. We should also reset the main dispatcher to the initial state with `Dispatchers.resetMain()`.

Testing Android functions that launch coroutines

On Android, we typically start coroutines in ViewModels, Presenters, Fragments, or Activities. These are very important classes, and we should test them. Think of the `MainViewModel` implementation below:

```
class MainViewModel(
    private val userRepo: UserRepository,
    private val newsRepo: NewsRepository,
) : BaseViewModel() {

    private val _userName: MutableLiveData<String> =
        MutableLiveData()
    val userName: LiveData<String> = _userName

    private val _news: MutableLiveData<List<News>> =
```

```
    MutableLiveData()
val news: LiveData<List<News>> = _news

private val _progressVisible: MutableLiveData<Boolean> =
    MutableLiveData()
val progressVisible: LiveData<Boolean> =
    _progressVisible

fun onCreate() {
    viewModelScope.launch {
        val user = userRepo.getUser()
        _userName.value = user.name
    }
    viewModelScope.launch {
        _progressVisible.value = true
        val news = newsRepo.getNews()
            .sortedByDescending { it.date }
        _news.value = news
        _progressVisible.value = false
    }
}
}
```

Instead of `viewModelScope`, there might be our own scope, and instead of ViewModel, it might be Presenter, Activity, or some other class. It does not matter for our example. As in every class that starts coroutines, we should use `StandardTestDispatcher` as a part of the scope. Previously, we needed to inject a different scope with a dependency injection, but now there is a simpler way: on Android, we use `Dispatchers.Main` as the default dispatcher, and we can replace it with `StandardTestDispatcher` thanks to the `Dispatchers.setMain` function:

```
private lateinit var testDispatcher

@Before
fun setUp() {
    testDispatcher = StandardTestDispatcher()
    Dispatchers.setMain(testDispatcher)
}

@After
fun tearDown() {
    Dispatchers.resetMain()
}
```

After setting the Main dispatcher this way, onCreate coroutines will
be running on testDispatcher, so we can control their time. We can
use the advanceTimeBy function to pretend that a certain amount of
time has passed. We can also use advanceUntilIdle to resume all
coroutines until they are done.

```
class MainViewModelTests {
    private lateinit var scheduler: TestCoroutineScheduler
    private lateinit var viewModel: MainViewModel

    @BeforeEach
    fun setUp() {
        scheduler = TestCoroutineScheduler()
        Dispatchers.setMain(StandardTestDispatcher(scheduler))
        viewModel = MainViewModel(
            userRepo = FakeUserRepository(aName),
            newsRepo = FakeNewsRepository(someNews)
        )
    }

    @AfterEach
    fun tearDown() {
        Dispatchers.resetMain()
        viewModel.onCleared()
    }
```

```kotlin
@Test
fun `should show user name and sorted news`() {
    // when
    viewModel.onCreate()
    scheduler.advanceUntilIdle()

    // then
    assertEquals(aName, viewModel.userName.value)
    val someNewsSorted =
        listOf(News(date1), News(date2), News(date3))
    assertEquals(someNewsSorted, viewModel.news.value)
}

@Test
fun `should show progress bar when loading news`() {
    // given
    assertEquals(null, viewModel.progressVisible.value)

    // when
    viewModel.onCreate()

    // then
    assertEquals(false, viewModel.progressVisible.value)

    // when
    scheduler.runCurrent()

    // then
    assertEquals(true, viewModel.progressVisible.value)

    // when
    scheduler.advanceTimeBy(200)

    // then
    assertEquals(true, viewModel.progressVisible.value)

    // when
    scheduler.runCurrent()
```

```kotlin
        // then
        assertEquals(false, viewModel.progressVisible.value)
    }

    @Test
    fun `user and news are called concurrently`() {
        // when
        viewModel.onCreate()
        scheduler.advanceUntilIdle()

        // then
        assertEquals(300, testDispatcher.currentTime)
    }

    class FakeUserRepository(
        private val name: String
    ) : UserRepository {
        override suspend fun getUser(): UserData {
            delay(300)
            return UserData(name)
        }
    }

    class FakeNewsRepository(
        private val news: List<News>
    ) : NewsRepository {
        override suspend fun getNews(): List<News> {
            delay(200)
            return news
        }
    }
}
```

Setting a test dispatcher with a rule

JUnit 4 allows us to use rules. These are classes that contain logic that should be invoked on some test class lifecycle events. For instance, a rule can define what to do before and after all tests, therefore it can be used in our case to set our test dispatcher and clean it up later. Here is a good implementation of such a rule:

```
class MainCoroutineRule : TestWatcher() {
    lateinit var scheduler: TestCoroutineScheduler
        private set
    lateinit var dispatcher: TestDispatcher
        private set

    override fun starting(description: Description) {
        scheduler = TestCoroutineScheduler()
        dispatcher = StandardTestDispatcher(scheduler)
        Dispatchers.setMain(dispatcher)
    }

    override fun finished(description: Description) {
        Dispatchers.resetMain()
    }
}
```

This rule needs to extend `TestWatcher`, which provides test life-cycle methods, like `starting` and `finished`, which we override. It composes `TestCoroutineScheduler` and `TestDispatcher`. Before each test in a class using this rule, `TestDispatcher` will be set as Main. After each test, the Main dispatcher will be reset. We can access the scheduler with the `scheduler` property of this rule.

```
class MainViewModelTests {
    @get:Rule
    var mainCoroutineRule = MainCoroutineRule()

    // ...

    @Test
    fun `should show user name and sorted news`() {
        // when
        viewModel.onCreate()
        mainCoroutineRule.scheduler.advanceUntilIdle()

        // then
```

```
        assertEquals(aName, viewModel.userName.value)
        val someNewsSorted =
            listOf(News(date1), News(date2), News(date3))
        assertEquals(someNewsSorted, viewModel.news.value)
    }

    @Test
    fun `should show progress bar when loading news`() {
        // given
        assertEquals(null, viewModel.progressVisible.value)

        // when
        viewModel.onCreate()

        // then
        assertEquals(true, viewModel.progressVisible.value)

        // when
        mainCoroutineRule.scheduler.advanceTimeBy(200)

        // then
        assertEquals(false, viewModel.progressVisible.value)
    }

    @Test
    fun `user and news are called concurrently`() {
        // when
        viewModel.onCreate()

        mainCoroutineRule.scheduler.advanceUntilIdle()

        // then
        assertEquals(300, mainCoroutineRule.currentTime)
    }
}
```

If you want to call `advanceUntilIdle`, `advanceTimeBy`, `runCurrent` and `currentTime` directly on `MainCoroutineRule`, you can define them as extension functions and properties.

This way of testing Kotlin coroutines is fairly common on Android. It is even explained in Google's Codelabs materials (Advanced Android in Kotlin 05.3: Testing Coroutines and Jetpack integrations[54]) (currently, for older `kotlinx-coroutines-test` API).

It is similar with JUnit 5, where we can define an extension:

```
@ExperimentalCoroutinesApi
class MainCoroutineExtension :
    BeforeEachCallback, AfterEachCallback {

    lateinit var scheduler: TestCoroutineScheduler
        private set
    lateinit var dispatcher: TestDispatcher
        private set

    override fun beforeEach(context: ExtensionContext?) {
        scheduler = TestCoroutineScheduler()
        dispatcher = StandardTestDispatcher(scheduler)
        Dispatchers.setMain(dispatcher)
    }

    override fun afterEach(context: ExtensionContext?) {
        Dispatchers.resetMain()
    }
}
```

Using `MainCoroutineExtension` is nearly identical to using the `MainCoroutineRule` rule. The difference is that instead of `@get:Rule` annotation, we need to use `@JvmField` and `@RegisterExtension`.

```
@JvmField
@RegisterExtension
var mainCoroutineExtension = MainCoroutineExtension()
```

---

[54]https://developer.android.com/codelabs/advanced-android-kotlin-training-testing-survey#3

Summary

In this chapter, we've discussed the most important use cases for testing Kotlin coroutines. There are some tricks we need to know, but in the end our tests can be very elegant and everything can be tested quite easily. I hope you feel inspired to write good tests in your applications using Kotlin Coroutines.

Part 3: Channel and Flow

In my workshops, many attendees are eager to finally hear about Flow - also known as coroutines' reactive streams. We are finally getting there: in this chapter, we will learn about Channel and Flow, both of which are useful tools that are worth knowing. We will start with Channel, as it is a bit more of a basic concept, then we will get deeply into Flow.

Channel

The Channel API was added as an inter-coroutine communication primitive. Many imagine a channel as a pipe, but I prefer a different metaphor. Are you familiar with public bookcases for exchanging books? One person needs to bring a book for another person to find it. This is very similar to how `Channel` from `kotlinx.coroutines` works.

Channel supports any number of senders and receivers, and every value that is sent to a channel is received only once.

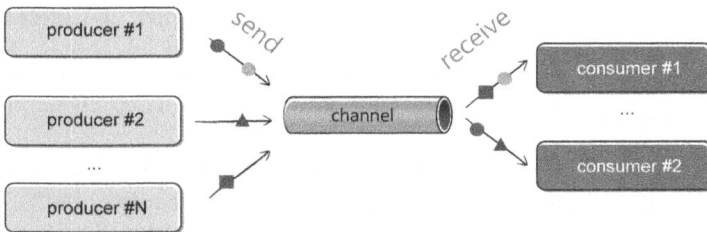

Channel is an interface that implements two other interfaces:

- SendChannel, which is used to send elements (adding elements) and to close the channel;
- ReceiveChannel, which receives (or takes)the elements.

```
interface SendChannel<in E> {
    suspend fun send(element: E)
    fun close(): Boolean
    //...
}

interface ReceiveChannel<out E> {
    suspend fun receive(): E
    fun cancel(cause: CancellationException? = null)
    // ...
}

interface Channel<E> : SendChannel<E>, ReceiveChannel<E>
```

Thanks to this distinction, we can expose just ReceiveChannel or SendChannel in order to restrict the channel entry points.

You might notice that both send and receive are suspending functions. This is an essential feature:

- When we try to receive and there are no elements in the channel, the coroutine is suspended until the element is available. Like in our metaphorical bookshelf, when someone goes to the shelf to find a book but the bookshelf is empty, that person needs to suspend until someone puts an element there.

- On the other hand, send will be suspended when the channel reaches its capacity. We will soon see that most channels have limited capacity. Like in our metaphorical bookshelf, when someone tries to put a book on a shelf but it is full, that person needs to suspend until someone takes a book and makes space.

  If you need to send or receive from a non-suspending function, you can use trySend and tryReceive. Both operations are immediate and return ChannelResult, which contains information about the success or failure of the operation, as well as its result. Use trySend and tryReceive only for channels with limited capacity because they will not work for the rendezvous channel.

A channel might have any number of senders and receivers. However, the most common situation is when there is one coroutine on both sides of the channel.

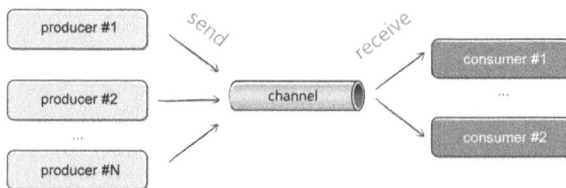

To see the simplest example of a channel, we need to have a producer (sender) and a consumer (receiver) in separate coroutines. The producer will send elements, and the consumer will receive them. This is how it can be implemented:

```
suspend fun main(): Unit = coroutineScope {
    val channel = Channel<Int>()
    launch {
        repeat(5) { index ->
            delay(1000)
            println("Producing next one")
            channel.send(index * 2)
        }
    }

    launch {
        repeat(5) {
            val received = channel.receive()
            println(received)
        }
    }
}
// (1 sec)
// Producing next one
// 0
// (1 sec)
// Producing next one
// 2
// (1 sec)
// Producing next one
// 4
// (1 sec)
// Producing next one
// 6
// (1 sec)
// Producing next one
// 8
```

Such an implementation is far from perfect. First, the receiver needs to know how many elements will be sent; however, this is rarely the case, so we would prefer to listen for as long as the sender is willing to send. To receive elements on the channel until it is closed, we could use a for-loop or consumeEach function[55].

```kotlin
suspend fun main(): Unit = coroutineScope {
    val channel = Channel<Int>()
    launch {
        repeat(5) { index ->
            println("Producing next one")
            delay(1000)
            channel.send(index * 2)
        }
        channel.close()
    }

    launch {
        for (element in channel) {
            println(element)
        }
        // or
        // channel.consumeEach { element ->
        //     println(element)
        // }
    }
}
```

The common problem with this way of sending elements is that it is easy to forget to close the channel, especially in the case of exceptions. If one coroutine stops producing because of an exception, the other will wait for elements forever. It is much more convenient to use the produce function, which is a coroutine builder that returns ReceiveChannel.

---

[55]The consumeEach function uses a for-loop under the hood, but it also cancels the channel once it has consumed all its elements (so, once it is closed).

```
// This function produces a channel with
// next positive integers from 0 to `max`
fun CoroutineScope.produceNumbers(
   max: Int
): ReceiveChannel<Int> = produce {
      var x = 0
      while (x < 5) send(x++)
   }
```

The produce function closes the channel whenever the builder coroutine ends in any way (finished, stopped, cancelled). Thanks to this,
we will never forget to call close. The produce builder is a very
popular way to create a channel, and for good reason: it offers a lot
of safety and convenience.

```
suspend fun main(): Unit = coroutineScope {
   val channel = produce {
      repeat(5) { index ->
         println("Producing next one")
         delay(1000)
         send(index * 2)
      }
   }

   for (element in channel) {
      println(element)
   }
}
```

Channel types

Depending on the capacity size we set, we distinguish four types of
channels:

- **Unlimited** - channel with capacity Channel.UNLIMITED that has
  an unlimited capacity buffer, and send never suspends.
- **Buffered**   -   channel   with   concrete   capacity
  size   or   Channel.BUFFERED   (which   is   64   by   default   and   can   be   overridden   by   setting   the
  kotlinx.coroutines.channels.defaultBuffer   system
  property in JVM).

- **Rendezvous**[56] (default) - channel with capacity 0 or `Channel.RENDEZVOUS` (which is equal to 0), meaning that an exchange can happen only if sender and receiver meet (so it is like a book exchange spot, instead of a bookshelf).
- **Conflated** - channel with capacity `Channel.CONFLATED` which has a buffer of size 1, and each new element replaces the previous one.

Let's now see these capacities in action. We can set them directly on `Channel`, but we can also set them when we call the `produce` function.

We will make our producer fast and our receiver slow. With unlimited capacity, the channel should accept all the elements and then let them be received one after another.

```
suspend fun main(): Unit = coroutineScope {
    val channel = produce(capacity = Channel.UNLIMITED) {
        repeat(5) { index ->
            send(index * 2)
            delay(100)
            println("Sent")
        }
    }

    delay(1000)
    for (element in channel) {
        println(element)
        delay(1000)
    }
}

// Sent
// (0.1 sec)
// Sent
// (0.1 sec)
// Sent
```

---

[56]The origin is the French word "rendez-vous", which commonly means "appointment". This beautiful word has crossed borders: in English, there is the less popular word "rendezvous"; in Polish, there is the word "randka", which means a date (a romantic appointment).

```
// (0.1 sec)
// Sent
// (0.1 sec)
// Sent
// (1 - 4 * 0.1 = 0.6 sec)
// 0
// (1 sec)
// 2
// (1 sec)
// 4
// (1 sec)
// 6
// (1 sec)
// 8
// (1 sec)
```

With a capacity of concrete size, we will first produce until the buffer is full, after which the producer will need to start waiting for the receiver.

```
suspend fun main(): Unit = coroutineScope {
    val channel = produce(capacity = 3) {
        repeat(5) { index ->
            send(index * 2)
            delay(100)
            println("Sent")
        }
    }

    delay(1000)
    for (element in channel) {
        println(element)
        delay(1000)
    }
}

// Sent
// (0.1 sec)
// Sent
```

```
// (0.1 sec)
// Sent
// (1 - 2 * 0.1 = 0.8 sec)
// 0
// Sent
// (1 sec)
// 2
// Sent
// (1 sec)
// 4
// (1 sec)
// 6
// (1 sec)
// 8
// (1 sec)
```

With a channel of default (or `Channel.RENDEZVOUS`) capacity, the producer will always wait for a receiver.

```
suspend fun main(): Unit = coroutineScope {
    val channel = produce {
        // or produce(capacity = Channel.RENDEZVOUS) {
        repeat(5) { index ->
            send(index * 2)
            delay(100)
            println("Sent")
        }
    }

    delay(1000)
    for (element in channel) {
        println(element)
        delay(1000)
    }
}

// 0
// Sent
// (1 sec)
```

```
// 2
// Sent
// (1 sec)
// 4
// Sent
// (1 sec)
// 6
// Sent
// (1 sec)
// 8
// Sent
// (1 sec)
```

Finally, we will not be storing past elements when using the Channel.CONFLATED capacity. New elements will replace the previous ones, so we will be able to receive only the last one, therefore we lose elements that were sent earlier.

```kotlin
suspend fun main(): Unit = coroutineScope {
    val channel = produce(capacity = Channel.CONFLATED) {
        repeat(5) { index ->
            send(index * 2)
            delay(100)
            println("Sent")
        }
    }

    delay(1000)
    for (element in channel) {
        println(element)
        delay(1000)
    }
}

// Sent
// (0.1 sec)
// Sent
// (0.1 sec)
// Sent
```

```
// (0.1 sec)
// Sent
// (0.1 sec)
// Sent
// (1 - 4 * 0.1 = 0.6 sec)
// 8
```

On buffer overflow

To customize channels further, we can control what happens when the buffer is full (onBufferOverflow parameter). There are the following options:

- SUSPEND (default) - when the buffer is full, suspend on the send method.
- DROP_OLDEST - when the buffer is full, drop the oldest element.
- DROP_LATEST - when the buffer is full, drop the latest element.

As you might guess, the channel capacity Channel.CONFLATED is the same as setting the capacity to 1 and onBufferOverflow to DROP_-OLDEST. Currently, the produce function does not allow us to set custom onBufferOverflow, so to set it we need to define a channel using the function Channel[57].

```
suspend fun main(): Unit = coroutineScope {
    val channel = Channel<Int>(
        capacity = 2,
        onBufferOverflow = BufferOverflow.DROP_OLDEST
    )

    launch {
        repeat(5) { index ->
            channel.send(index * 2)
            delay(100)
            println("Sent")
        }
        channel.close()
```

---

[57]Channel is an interface, so Channel() is a call of a function that is pretending to be a constructor.

```
    }

    delay(1000)
    for (element in channel) {
        println(element)
        delay(1000)
    }
}

// Sent
// (0.1 sec)
// Sent
// (0.1 sec)
// Sent
// (0.1 sec)
// Sent
// (0.1 sec)
// Sent
// (1 - 4 * 0.1 = 0.6 sec)
// 6
// (1 sec)
// 8
```

On undelivered element handler

One more Channel function parameter which we should know about
is onUndeliveredElement. It is called when an element couldn't be
handled for some reason. Most often this means that a channel was
closed or cancelled, but it might also happen when send, receive,
receiveOrNull, or hasNext throw an error. We generally use it to
close resources that are sent by this channel.

```
val channel = Channel<Resource>(capacity) { resource ->
    resource.close()
}
// or
// val channel = Channel<Resource>(
//        capacity,
//        onUndeliveredElement = { resource ->
//            resource.close()
//        }
// )

// Producer code
val resourceToSend = openResource()
channel.send(resourceToSend)

// Consumer code
val resourceReceived = channel.receive()
try {
    // work with received resource
} finally {
    resourceReceived.close()
}
```

Fan-out

Multiple coroutines can receive from a single channel; however, to receive them properly we should use a for-loop (consumeEach is not safe to use from multiple coroutines).

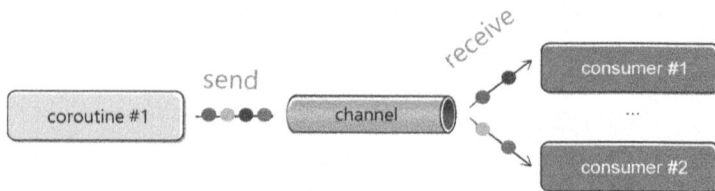

```kotlin
fun CoroutineScope.produceNumbers() = produce {
    repeat(10) {
        delay(100)
        send(it)
    }
}

fun CoroutineScope.launchProcessor(
    id: Int,
    channel: ReceiveChannel<Int>
) = launch {
    for (msg in channel) {
        println("#$id received $msg")
    }
}

suspend fun main(): Unit = coroutineScope {
    val channel = produceNumbers()
    repeat(3) { id ->
        delay(10)
        launchProcessor(id, channel)
    }
}

// #0 received 0
// #1 received 1
// #2 received 2
// #0 received 3
// #1 received 4
// #2 received 5
// #0 received 6
// ...
```

The elements are distributed fairly. The channel has a FIFO (first-in-first-out) queue of coroutines waiting for an element. This is why in the above example you can see that the elements are received by the next coroutines (0, 1, 2, 0, 1, 2, etc).

To better understand why, imagine kids in a kindergarten queuing for candies. Once they get some, they immediately eat them and go to the last position in the queue. Such distribution is fair (assuming the number of candies is a multiple of the number of kids, and assuming their parents are fine with their children eating candies).

Fan-in

Multiple coroutines can send to a single channel. In the below example, you can see two coroutines sending elements to the same channel.

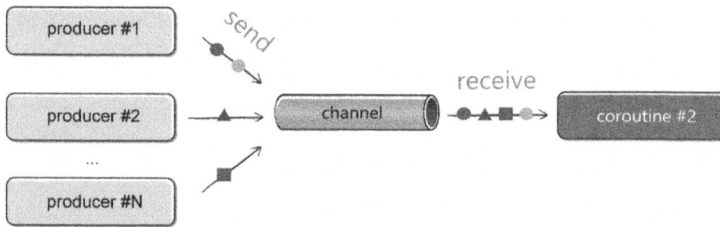

```kotlin
suspend fun sendString(
    channel: SendChannel<String>,
    text: String,
    time: Long
) {
    while (true) {
        delay(time)
        channel.send(text)
    }
}

fun main() = runBlocking {
    val channel = Channel<String>()
    launch { sendString(channel, "foo", 200L) }
    launch { sendString(channel, "BAR!", 500L) }
    repeat(50) {
        println(channel.receive())
    }
```

```
    coroutineContext.cancelChildren()
}
// (200 ms)
// foo
// (200 ms)
// foo
// (100 ms)
// BAR!
// (100 ms)
// foo
// (200 ms)
// ...
```

Sometimes, we need to merge multiple channels into one. For that, you might find the following function useful as it merges multiple channels using the produce function:

```
fun <T> CoroutineScope.fanIn(
    channels: List<ReceiveChannel<T>>
): ReceiveChannel<T> = produce {
    for (channel in channels) {
        launch {
            for (elem in channel) {
                send(elem)
            }
        }
    }
}
```

Pipelines

Sometimes we set two channels such that one produces elements based on those received from another. In such cases, we call it a pipeline.

```
// A channel of number from 1 to 3
fun CoroutineScope.numbers(): ReceiveChannel<Int> =
    produce {
        repeat(3) { num ->
            send(num + 1)
        }
    }

fun CoroutineScope.square(numbers: ReceiveChannel<Int>) =
    produce {
        for (num in numbers) {
            send(num * num)
        }
    }

suspend fun main() = coroutineScope {
    val numbers = numbers()
    val squared = square(numbers)
    for (num in squared) {
        println(num)
    }
}
// 1
// 4
// 9
```

Channels as a communication primitive

Channels are useful when different coroutines need to communicate with each other. They guarantee no conflicts (i.e., no problem with the shared state) and fairness.

To see them in action, imagine that different baristas are making coffees. Each barista should be a separate coroutine working independently. Different coffee types take different amounts of time to prepare, but we want to handle orders in the order they appear. The easiest way to solve this problem is by sending both the orders and the resulting coffees in channels. A barista can be defined using the produce builder:

```
suspend fun CoroutineScope.serveOrders(
    orders: ReceiveChannel<Order>,
    baristaName: String
): ReceiveChannel<CoffeeResult> = produce {
    for (order in orders) {
        val coffee = prepareCoffee(order.type)
        send(
            CoffeeResult(
                coffee = coffee,
                customer = order.customer,
                baristaName = baristaName
            )
        )
    }
}
```

When we set up a pipeline, we can use the previously defined fanIn function to merge the results produced by the different baristas into one:

```
val coffeeResults = fanIn(
    serveOrders(ordersChannel, "Alex"),
    serveOrders(ordersChannel, "Bob"),
    serveOrders(ordersChannel, "Celine"),
)
```

You will find more practical examples in the next chapter.

Practical usage

A typical case in which we use channels is when values are produced on one side, and we want to process them on the other side. Examples include responding to user clicks, new notifications from a server, or updating search results over time (a good example is SkyScanner, which searches for the cheapest flights by querying multiple airline websites). However, in most of these cases it's better to use channelFlow or callbackFlow, both of which are a hybrid of Channel and Flow (we will explain them in the *Flow building* chapter).

SkyScanner displays better and better flight search results as more and more airlines respond.

In their pure form, I find channels useful in some more complex processing cases. For example, let's say that we are maintaining an online shop, like Amazon. Let's say that your service receives a big number of seller changes that might affect their offers. For each change, we need to first find a list of offers to update, and then we update them one after another.

Doing this the traditional way wouldn't be optimal. One seller might even have hundreds of thousands of offers. Doing it all in a single long process is not the best idea.

First, either an internal exception or a server restart might leave us not knowing where we stopped. Second, one big seller might block the server for a long time, thus leaving small sellers waiting for their changes to apply. Moreover, we should not send too many network requests at the same time so as to not overload the service that needs to handle them (and our network interface).

The solution to this problem might be to set up a pipeline. The first channel could contain the sellers to process, while the second one would contain the offers to be updated. These channels would have a buffer. The buffer in the second one could prevent our service from getting more offers when too many are already waiting. Thus, our server would be able to balance the number of offers we are updating at the same time.

We might also easily add some intermediate steps, like removing duplicates. By defining the number of coroutines that listen on each channel, we decide how many concurrent requests to the external service we wish to make. Manipulating these parameters gives us a lot of freedom. There are also many improvements that can be added quite easily, like persistence (for cases where the server is restarted) or element uniqueness (for cases where the seller made another change before the previous one was processed).

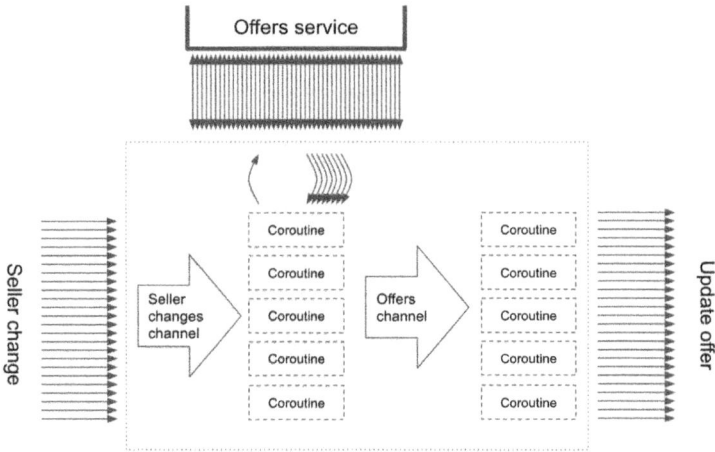

```
// A simplified implementation
suspend fun handleOfferUpdates() = coroutineScope {
    val sellerChannel = listenOnSellerChanges()

    val offerToUpdateChannel = produce(capacity = UNLIMITED) {
        repeat(NUMBER_OF_CONCURRENT_OFFER_SERVICE_REQUESTS) {
            launch {
                for (seller in sellerChannel) {
                    val offers = offerService
                        .requestOffers(seller.id)
                    offers.forEach { send(it) }
                }
            }
        }
    }

    repeat(NUMBER_OF_CONCURRENT_UPDATE_SENDERS) {
        launch {
            for (offer in offerToUpdateChannel) {
                sendOfferUpdate(offer)
            }
        }
    }
}
```

```
}
```

Summary

Channel is a powerful inter-coroutine communication primitive. It supports any number of senders and receivers, and every value that is sent to a channel is received once. We often create a channel using the `produce` builder. Channels can also be used to set up a pipeline where we control the number of coroutines working on some tasks. Nowadays, we most often use channels in connection with Flow, which will be presented later in the book.

Select

Coroutines provide the select function, which lets us await the result of the first coroutine that completes. It also offers the possibility of sending to the first channel that has space in the buffer or receiving from the first channel that has an available element. This lets us make races between coroutines or join results from multiple sources. Let's see it in practice.

> The select function is still experimental, even though this feature has been available since early Kotlin Coroutines releases. It is highly unlikely that select will be removed, but its API might still change. This feature will probably never be stabilized because there is little demand for it - it is actually used rather rarely, so I decided to keep this chapter as short as possible.

Selecting deferred values

Let's say that we want to request data from multiple sources, but we're only interested in the fastest response. The easiest way to achieve this is to start these requests in async processes; then, use the select function as an expression, and await different values inside it. Inside select, we can call onAwait on Deferred value, which specifies a possible select expression result. Inside its lambda expression, you can transform the value. In the example below, we just return an async result, so the select expression will complete once the first async task is completed, then it will return its result.

```
suspend fun requestData1(): String {
    delay(100_000)
    return "Data1"
}

suspend fun requestData2(): String {
    delay(1000)
    return "Data2"
}

val scope = CoroutineScope(SupervisorJob())
```

```
suspend fun askMultipleForData(): String {
    val defData1 = scope.async { requestData1() }
    val defData2 = scope.async { requestData2() }
    return select {
        defData1.onAwait { it }
        defData2.onAwait { it }
    }
}

suspend fun main(): Unit = coroutineScope {
    println(askMultipleForData())
}
// (1 sec)
// Data2
```

Notice that `async` in the example above needs to be started on an outside scope. This means that if you cancel the coroutine that started `askMultipleForData`, these async tasks will not be cancelled. This is a problem, but I don't know any better implementation. If we had used `coroutineScope`, then it would have awaited its children; so, for the implementation below, we'll still receive `Data2` as a result, but after 100 seconds instead of after one.

```
// ...

suspend fun askMultipleForData(): String {
    val defData1 = scope.async { requestData1() }
    val defData2 = scope.async { requestData2() }
    return select<String> {
        defData1.onAwait { it }
        defData2.onAwait { it }
    }
}

suspend fun main(): Unit = coroutineScope {
    println(askMultipleForData())
}
// (100 sec)
// Data2
```

A coroutine race can be implemented well using `async` and `select`, but it would require explicit scope cancellation. We could cancel those other coroutines in the `also` that is called once `select` has produced a value.

```
suspend fun askMultipleForData(): String = coroutineScope {
    select<String> {
        async { requestData1() }.onAwait { it }
        async { requestData2() }.onAwait { it }
    }.also { coroutineContext.cancelChildren() }
}

suspend fun main(): Unit = coroutineScope {
    println(askMultipleForData())
}
// (1 sec)
// Data2
```

The solution above is a bit complex, which is why many developers define a helper function or use an external library (like Splitties by Louis CAD) that includes the following `raceOf` function. Such a function can be defined in a couple of lines, as I will show in the *Recipes* chapter.

```
// Implementation using raceOf from Splitties library
suspend fun askMultipleForData(): String = raceOf({
    requestData1()
}, {
    requestData2()
})

suspend fun main(): Unit = coroutineScope {
    println(askMultipleForData())
}
// (1 sec)
// Data2
```

Selecting from channels

The `select` function can also be used with channels. These are the main functions that can be used inside it:

- onReceive - selected when this channel has a value. It receives this value (like the receive method) and uses it as an argument for its lambda expression. When onReceive is selected, select returns the result of its lambda expression.
- onReceiveCatching - selected when this channel has a value or is closed. It receives ChannelResult, which either represents a value or signals that this channel is closed, and it uses this value as an argument for its lambda expression. When onReceiveCatching is selected, select returns the result of its lambda expression.
- onSend - selected when this channel has space in the buffer. It sends a value to this channel (like the send method) and invokes its lambda expression with a reference to the channel. When onSend is selected, select returns Unit.

Let's see some practical applications. The select expression can be used with onReceive or onReceiveCatching to receive from multiple channels.

```kotlin
suspend fun CoroutineScope.produceString(
    s: String,
    time: Long
) = produce {
    while (true) {
        delay(time)
        send(s)
    }
}

fun main() = runBlocking {
    val fooChannel = produceString("foo", 210L)
    val barChannel = produceString("BAR", 500L)

    repeat(7) {
        select {
            fooChannel.onReceive {
                println("From fooChannel: $it")
            }
            barChannel.onReceive {
                println("From barChannel: $it")
```

```
            }
        }
    }

    coroutineContext.cancelChildren()
}
// From fooChannel: foo
// From fooChannel: foo
// From barChannel: BAR
// From fooChannel: foo
// From fooChannel: foo
// From barChannel: BAR
// From fooChannel: foo
```

The select function can be used with onSend to send to the first
channel that has space in the buffer.

```
fun main(): Unit = runBlocking {
    val c1 = Channel<Char>(capacity = 2)
    val c2 = Channel<Char>(capacity = 2)

    // Send values
    launch {
        for (c in 'A'..'H') {
            delay(400)
            select<Unit> {
                c1.onSend(c) { println("Sent $c to 1") }
                c2.onSend(c) { println("Sent $c to 2") }
            }
        }
    }

    // Receive values
    launch {
        while (true) {
            delay(1000)
            val c = select<String> {
                c1.onReceive { "$it from 1" }
                c2.onReceive { "$it from 2" }
```

```
            }
            println("Received $c")
        }
    }
}
// Sent A to 1
// Sent B to 1
// Received A from 1
// Sent C to 1
// Sent D to 2
// Received B from 1
// Sent E to 1
// Sent F to 2
// Received C from 1
// Sent G to 1
// Received E from 1
// Sent H to 1
// Received G from 1
// Received H from 1
// Received D from 2
// Received F from 2
```

Summary

select is a useful function that lets us await the result of the first coroutine that completes, or send to or receive from the first from multiple channels. It is mainly used to implement different patterns for operating on channels, but it can also be used to implement async coroutine races.

Hot and cold data sources

Kotlin Coroutines initially had only Channel, but creators noticed
that this was not enough. Channels are a *hot* stream of values, but
we often need a stream that is *cold*.

Provide abstraction for cold streams #254

Closed   elizarov opened this issue on 21 Feb 2018 · 116 comments

elizarov commented on 21 Feb 2018   Member 😊 ···

All the currently provided channel abstractions in `kotlinx.coroutines` are *hot*. The data is being produced regardless of the
presence of subscriber. This is good for data sources and applications that are inherently hot, like incoming network and UI-
events.

However, hot streams are not an ideal solution for cases where data stream is produced on demand. Consider, for example,

Understanding the difference between hot and cold streams of
data is useful software-craftsmanship knowledge because most
data sources you use daily fall into one of these two categories.
Collections (`List`, `Set`, etc.) are hot, while `Sequence` and Java `Stream`
are cold. `Channel` is hot, while `Flow` and RxJava streams (`Observable`,
`Single`, etc.) are cold[58].

Hot	Cold
Collections (List, Set)	Sequence, Stream
Channel	Flow, RxJava streams

Hot vs cold

Hot data streams are eager, produce elements independently of their
consumption, and store the elements. Cold data streams are lazy,
perform their operations on-demand, and store nothing.

We can observe these differences when we use lists (hot) and sequences (cold). Builders and operations on hot data streams start
immediately. On cold data streams, they are not started until the
elements are needed.

---

[58]This is true in general, but there are exceptions. Some functions
and builders, like `buffer` or `channelFlow`, introduce some hotness
into Flow. Also, `SharedFlow` and `StateFlow` are hot.

```
fun main() {
    val l = buildList {
        repeat(3) {
            add("User$it")
            println("L: Added User")
        }
    }

    val l2 = l.map {
        println("L: Processing")
        "Processed $it"
    }

    val s = sequence {
        repeat(3) {
            yield("User$it")
            println("S: Added User")
        }
    }

    val s2 = s.map {
        println("S: Processing")
        "Processed $it"
    }
}
// L: Added User
// L: Added User
// L: Added User
// L: Processing
// L: Processing
// L: Processing
//sampleEnd
```

As a result, cold data streams (like Sequence, Stream or Flow):

- can be infinite;
- do a minimal number of operations;
- use less memory (no need to allocate all the intermediate collections).

Sequence processing does fewer operations because it processes elements lazily. The way it works is very simple. Each intermediate operation (like map or filter) just decorates the previous sequence with a new operation. The terminal operation[59] does all the work. Think of the example below. In the case of a sequence, find asks the result of the map for the first element. It asks the sequence returned from the sequenceOf (returns 1), then maps it (to 1) and returns it to the filter. filter checks if this is an element that fulfills its criteria. If the element does not fulfill the criteria, filter asks again and again until the proper element is found.

This is very different from list processing, which at every intermediate step calculates and returns a fully processed collection. This is why the order of element processing is different and collection processing takes more memory and might require more operations (like in the example below).

```
fun m(i: Int): Int {
    print("m$i ")
    return i * i
}

fun f(i: Int): Boolean {
    print("f$i ")
    return i >= 10
}

fun main() {
    listOf(1, 2, 3, 4, 5, 6, 7, 8, 9, 10)
        .map { m(it) }
        .find { f(it) }
        .let { print(it) }
    // m1 m2 m3 m4 m5 m6 m7 m8 m9 m10 f1 f4 f9 f16 16

    println()

    sequenceOf(1, 2, 3, 4, 5, 6, 7, 8, 9, 10)
        .map { m(it) }
```

---

[59]An operation on a sequence that returns a different type. Typically find or toList.

```
        .find { f(it) }
        .let { print(it) }
    // m1 f1 m2 f4 m3 f9 m4 f16 16
}
```

This means that a list is a collection of elements, but a sequence is just a definition of how these elements should be calculated. Hot data streams:

- are always ready to be used (each operation can be a terminal operation);
- do not need to recalculate the result when used multiple times.

```
fun m(i: Int): Int {
    print("m$i ")
    return i * i
}

fun main() {
    val l = listOf(1, 2, 3, 4, 5, 6, 7, 8, 9, 10)
        .map { m(it) } // m1 m2 m3 m4 m5 m6 m7 m8 m9 m10

    println(l) // [1, 4, 9, 16, 25, 36, 49, 64, 81, 100]
    println(l.find { it > 10 }) // 16
    println(l.find { it > 10 }) // 16
    println(l.find { it > 10 }) // 16

    val s = sequenceOf(1, 2, 3, 4, 5, 6, 7, 8, 9, 10)
        .map { m(it) }

    println(s.toList())
    // [1, 4, 9, 16, 25, 36, 49, 64, 81, 100]
    println(s.find { it > 10 }) // m1 m2 m3 m4 16
    println(s.find { it > 10 }) // m1 m2 m3 m4 16
    println(s.find { it > 10 }) // m1 m2 m3 m4 16
}
```

Java Stream shares characteristics with Kotlin's Sequence. They are both cold streams of values.

Hot channels, cold flow

Time to get back to coroutines. The most typical way to create a flow is by using a builder, which is similar to the produce function. It is called flow.

```
val channel = produce {
    while (true) {
        val x = computeNextValue()
        send(x)
    }
}

val flow = flow {
    while (true) {
        val x = computeNextValue()
        emit(x)
    }
}
```

These builders are conceptually equivalent, but since the behavior of channel and flow is very different, there are also important differences between these two functions. Take a look at the example below. Channels are hot, so they immediately start calculating the values. This calculation starts in a separate coroutine. This is why produce needs to be a coroutine builder that is defined as an extension function on CoroutineScope. The calculation starts immediately, but since the default buffer size is 0 (rendezvous) it will soon be suspended until the receiver is ready in the example below. Note that there is a difference between stopping production when there is no receiver and producing on-demand. Channels, as hot data streams, produce elements independently of their consumption and then keep them. They do not care how many receivers there are. Since each element can be received only once, after the first receiver consumes all the elements, the second one will find a channel that is empty and closed already. This is why it will receive no elements at all.

```
private fun CoroutineScope.makeChannel() = produce {
    println("Channel started")
    for (i in 1..3) {
        delay(1000)
        send(i)
    }
}

suspend fun main() = coroutineScope {
    val channel = makeChannel()

    delay(1000)
    println("Calling channel...")
    for (value in channel) {
        println(value)
    }
    println("Consuming again...")
    for (value in channel) {
        println(value)
    }
}
// Channel started
// (1 sec)
// Calling channel...
// 1
// (1 sec)
// 2
// (1 sec)
// 3
// Consuming again...
```

The same processing using Flow is very different. Since it is a cold data source, the production happens on demand. This means that flow is not a builder and does no processing. It is only a definition of how elements should be produced that will be used when a terminal operation (like collect) is used. This is why the flow builder does not need a CoroutineScope. It will run in the scope from the terminal operation that executed it (it takes the scope from the suspending function's continuation, just like coroutineScope and other coroutine scope functions). Each terminal operation on a flow starts processing from scratch. Compare the examples above and below because they show the key differences between Channel and Flow.

```
private fun makeFlow() = flow {
    println("Flow started")
    for (i in 1..3) {
        delay(1000)
        emit(i)
    }
}

suspend fun main() = coroutineScope {
    val flow = makeFlow()

    delay(1000)
    println("Calling flow...")
    flow.collect { value -> println(value) }
    println("Consuming again...")
    flow.collect { value -> println(value) }
}
// (1 sec)
// Calling flow...
// Flow started
// (1 sec)
// 1
// (1 sec)
// 2
// (1 sec)
// 3
// Consuming again...
// Flow started
// (1 sec)
// 1
// (1 sec)
// 2
// (1 sec)
// 3
```

RxJava streams share most characteristics with Kotlin's Flow. Some even say that Flow could be called "RxCoroutines"[60].

Summary

Most data sources are either hot or cold:

- Hot data sources are eager. They produce elements as soon as possible and store them. They create elements independently of their consumption. These are collections (List, Set) and Channel.
- Cold data sources are lazy. They process elements on-demand on the terminal operation. All intermediate functions just define what should be done (most often using the Decorator pattern). They generally do not store elements and create them on demand. They do the minimal number of operations and can be infinite. Their creation and processing of elements is typically the same process as consumption. These elements are Sequence, Java Stream, Flow and RxJava streams (Observable, Single, etc).

This explains the essential difference between Channel and Flow. Now it is time to discuss all the different features supported by the latter.

---

[60]I heard this first from Alex Piotrowski during Kotlin/Everywhere Warsaw 21.11.2019, https://youtu.be/xV1XRakSoWI. Who knows, maybe he is the one who popularized this term.

Flow introduction

A flow represents a stream of values that are computed asynchronously. The Flow interface itself only allows the flowing elements to be collected, which means handling each element as it reaches the end of the flow (collect for Flow is like forEach for collections).

```
interface Flow<out T> {
    suspend fun collect(collector: FlowCollector<T>)
}
```

As you can see, collect is the only member function in Flow. All others are defined as extensions. This is similar to Iterable or Sequence, both of which only have iterator as a member function.

```
interface Iterable<out T> {
    operator fun iterator(): Iterator<T>
}
```

```
interface Sequence<out T> {
    operator fun iterator(): Iterator<T>
}
```

Comparing flow to other ways of representing values

The concept of Flow should be well known to those using RxJava[61] or Reactor[62], but others might need a better explanation. Imagine that you need a function to return more than a single value. When all these values are provided at the same time, we use a collection like List or Set.

```
fun allUsers(): List<User> =
    api.getAllUsers().map { it.toUser() }
```

The essence here is that List and Set represent a fully calculated collection. Since the process of calculating these values takes time, we need to wait for all the values before we can have them returned.

---

[61]https://github.com/ReactiveX/RxJava
[62]https://projectreactor.io/

```
fun getList(): List<Int> = List(3) {
    Thread.sleep(1000)
    "User$it"
}

fun main() {
    val list = getList()
    println("Function started")
    list.forEach { println(it) }
}
// (3 sec)
// Function started
// User0
// User1
// User2
```

If the elements are calculated one by one, we prefer to have the next elements as soon as they appear. One way of doing this is by using Sequence, which we've already learned about in the *Sequence builder* chapter.

```
fun getSequence(): Sequence<String> = sequence {
    repeat(3) {
        Thread.sleep(1000)
        yield("User$it")
    }
}

fun main() {
    val list = getSequence()
    println("Function started")
    list.forEach { println(it) }
}
// Function started
// (1 sec)
// User0
// (1 sec)
// User1
// (1 sec)
```

```
// User2
```

Sequences are perfect for representing a flow of values calculated on demand when calculating them might be CPU-intensive (like calculating complex results) or blocking (like reading files). However, it is essential to know that sequence terminal operations (like forEach) are not suspending, so any suspension inside a sequence builder means blocking the thread that waits for the value. This is why, in the scope of a sequence builder, you cannot use any suspending function except for those called on the SequenceScope receiver (yield and yieldAll).

```
fun getSequence(): Sequence<String> = sequence {
    repeat(3) {
        delay(1000) // Compilation error
        yield("User$it")
    }
}
```

This mechanism was introduced so sequences are not misused. Even if the above example could compile, it wouldn't be correct anyway because the terminal operation (like forEach) would be blocking the thread instead of the suspending coroutine, which could lead to unexpected thread-blocking. Consider that someone might want to use a sequence to fetch, in a paginated manner, a list of all the users from an HTTP endpoint until an empty page is received. The problem is, that any consumption of such a sequence would be blocking, because iterator function in Sequence is not suspend.

```
// Don't do that, we should use Flow instead of Sequence
fun allUsersSequence(
    api: UserApi
): Sequence<User> = sequence {
    var page = 0
    do {
        val users = api.takePage(page++) // suspending,
        // so compilation error
        yieldAll(users)
    } while (!users.isNullOrEmpty())
}
```

This is not what sequences should be used for. Sequences are prefect for sources of data whose size might be big (or infinite) and elements might be heavy, so we want to calculate or read them on demand, lazily.

```kotlin
val fibonacci: Sequence<BigInteger> = sequence {
    var first = 0.toBigInteger()
    var second = 1.toBigInteger()
    while (true) {
        yield(first)
        val temp = first
        first += second
        second = temp
    }
}


fun countCharactersInFile(path: String): Int =
    File(path).useLines { lines ->
        lines.sumBy { it.length }
    }
```

I hope you already have some idea that thread blocking can be very dangerous and lead to unexpected situations. To make this crystal clear, take a look at the example below. We use Sequence, so its forEach is a blocking operation. This is why a coroutine started on the same thread with launch will wait, so one coroutine's execution blocks another's.

```kotlin
fun getSequence(): Sequence<String> = sequence {
    repeat(3) {
        Thread.sleep(1000)
        // the same result as if there were delay(1000) here
        yield("User$it")
    }
}


suspend fun main() {
    withContext(newSingleThreadContext("main")) {
        launch {
```

```
        repeat(3) {
            delay(100)
            println("Processing on coroutine")
        }
    }

    val list = getSequence()
    list.forEach { println(it) }
    }
}
// (1 sec)
// User0
// (1 sec)
// User1
// (1 sec)
// User2
// Processing on coroutine
// (0.1 sec)
// Processing on coroutine
// (0.1 sec)
// Processing on coroutine
```

This is a case where we should use Flow instead of Sequence. Such an approach fully supports coroutines in its operations. Its builder and operations are suspending functions, and it supports structured concurrency and proper exception handling. We will explain all this in the next chapters, but for now let's see how it helps with this case.

```
fun getFlow(): Flow<String> = flow {
    repeat(3) {
        delay(1000)
        emit("User$it")
    }
}

suspend fun main() {
    withContext(newSingleThreadContext("main")) {
        launch {
            repeat(3) {
```

```
                delay(100)
                println("Processing on coroutine")
            }
        }

        val list = getFlow()
        list.collect { println(it) }
    }
}
// (0.1 sec)
// Processing on coroutine
// (0.1 sec)
// Processing on coroutine
// (0.1 sec)
// Processing on coroutine
// (1 - 3 * 0.1 = 0.7 sec)
// User0
// (1 sec)
// User1
// (1 sec)
// User2
```

Flow should be used for streams of data that need to use coroutines. For example, it can be used to produce a stream of users that are fetched from an API page by page. Notice that the caller of this function can handle the next pages as they come and decide how many pages will be fetched. For instance, if we call allUsersFlow(api).first(), we will fetch only the first page; if we call allUsersFlow(api).toList(), we will fetch all of them; if we call allUsersFlow(api).find { it.id == id }, we will fetch pages until we find the one we're looking for.

```
fun allUsersFlow(
    api: UserApi
): Flow<User> = flow {
    var page = 0
    do {
        val users = api.takePage(page++) // suspending
        emitAll(users)
```

```
    } while (!users.isNullOrEmpty())
}
```

The characteristics of Flow

Flow's terminal operations (like `collect`) suspend a coroutine instead of blocking a thread. They also support other coroutine functionalities, such as respecting the coroutine context and handling exceptions. Flow processing can be cancelled, and structured concurrency is supported out of the box. The `flow` builder is not suspending and does not require any scope. It is the terminal operation that is suspending and builds a relation to its parent coroutine (similar to the `coroutineScope` function).

The below example shows how `CoroutineName` context is passed from `collect` to the lambda expression in the `flow` builder. It also shows that `launch` cancellation also leads to proper flow processing cancellation.

```
// Notice, that this function is not suspending
// and does not need CoroutineScope
fun usersFlow(): Flow<String> = flow {
    repeat(3) {
        delay(1000)
        val ctx = currentCoroutineContext()
        val name = ctx[CoroutineName]?.name
        emit("User$it in $name")
    }
}

suspend fun main() {
    val users = usersFlow()

    withContext(CoroutineName("Name")) {
        val job = launch {
            // collect is suspending
            users.collect { println(it) }
        }

        launch {
```

```
        delay(2100)
        println("I got enough")
        job.cancel()
    }
  }
}
// (1 sec)
// User0 in Name
// (1 sec)
// User1 in Name
// (0.1 sec)
// I got enough
```

Flow nomenclature

Every flow consists of a few elements:

- Flow needs to start somewhere. It often starts with a flow builder, conversion from a different object, or from some helper function. The most important option will be explained in the next chapter, Flow building.
- The last operation on the flow is called the **terminal operation**, which is very important as it is often the only one that is suspending or requires a scope. The typical terminal operation is collect, either with or without a lambda expression. However, there are also other terminal operations. Some of them will be explained in the Flow processing chapter.
- Between the start operation and the terminal operation, we might have **intermediate operations**, each of which modifies the flow in some way. We will learn about different intermediate operations in the Flow lifecycle and Flow processing chapters.

```
suspend fun main() {
    flow { emit( value: "Message 1") } ◄─────── Flow builder
        .onEach { println(it) }
        .onStart { println("Do something before") }        Intermediate
        .onCompletion { println("Do something after") }    operations
        .catch { emit( value: "Error") }
        .collect { println("Collected $it") }  ◄─────── Terminal operation
}
```

Real-life use cases

Practice shows that we more often need a flow instead of a channel.
If you request a stream of data, you typically want to request it on-
demand. If you need to observe something, such as changes in your
database or events from UI widgets or sensors, you likely want these
events to be received by each observer. You also need to stop listening
when no one is observing. This is why, for all these cases, using a flow
is preferred over using a channel (although in some cases we will use
a hybrid of these two).

The most typical usages of flow include:

  • receiving or sending messages that are communicated
    through Server-Sent Events, such as WebSockets, RSocket,
    notifications, etc.;
  • observing user actions, such as text changes or clicks;
  • receiving updates from sensors or other information about a
    device, such as its location or orientation;
  • observing changes in databases.

Here is how we can observe changes in an SQL database using the
Room library:

```
@Dao
interface MyDao {
    @Query("SELECT * FROM somedata_table")
    fun getData(): Flow<List<SomeData>>
}
```

Let's see some examples of how we might use a flow to handle a stream of responses from an API. I will start with the one I recently worked on. Consider trading workstation, like Bloomberg or Scanz, that always shows you the current state of the market. Since market changes constantly, those programs update many times per second. This is a perfect use case for a flow, both on the backend and on the client.

A more everyday example might be a chat, or a client providing realtime suggestions for a search. For example, when we search for the best flight on SkyScanner[63], some offers arrive quickly, but then more arrive over time; therefore, you see better and better results. This is also a great case for a flow.

---

[63]https://www.skyscanner.pl/

On SkyScanner we can see better and better flight search results as airlines respond to your offer request.

In addition to these situations, a flow is also a useful tool for different concurrent processing cases. For example, imagine that you have a list of sellers, for each of which you need to fetch their offers. We've already learned that we can do this using `async` inside collection processing:

```
suspend fun getOffers(
    sellers: List<Seller>
): List<Offer> = coroutineScope {
    sellers
        .map { seller ->
            async { api.requestOffers(seller.id) }
        }
        .flatMap { it.await() }
}
```

The above approach is correct in many cases, but it has one downside:

if the list of sellers is big, sending so many requests at once would not be good neither for us nor for the server we are requesting from. Sure, this can be limited in the repository with a rate limiter, but we also might want to control it on the use side, for which we might use Flow. In this case, to limit the number of concurrent calls to 20, we can use flatMapMerge (one of the flow processing functions we will explain in the *Flow processing* chapter) with concurrency modifier set to 20.

```
suspend fun getOffers(
    sellers: List<Seller>
): List<Offer> = sellers
    .asFlow()
    .flatMapMerge(concurrency = 20) { seller ->
        suspend { api.requestOffers(seller.id) }.asFlow()
    }
    .toList()
```

Operating on Flow instead of on a collection gives us much more control over concurrency behavior, contexts, exceptions, and much more. We will discover these functionalities in the next chapters. This is where (in my experience) Flow is most useful. I hope you will see this clearly once we have covered all its different functionalities.

Finally, because they prefer a reactive style of programming, some teams like to use flow instead of suspending functions. Such a style became popular on Android, where RxJava was popular, but now Flow is often treated as a better alternative. In such teams, Flow is often used when only a single value is returned from functions. I prefer just suspending functions in such cases, but both approaches are valid.

As you can see, there are quite a few use cases for flows. In some projects, they will be used commonly, while in others they will be used only from time to time, but I hope you can see that they are useful and worth learning about.

Summary

In this chapter, we've introduced the concept of Flow. It represents a stream of asynchronously computed values that supports coroutines (unlike sequences). There are quite a few use cases where Flow is useful. We will explore them in the next chapters as we learn more about Flow capabilities.

Understanding `Flow`

Kotlin Coroutines Flow is a much simpler concept than most developers think. It is just a definition of which operations to execute. It's similar to a suspending lambda expression, but with some extra elements. In this chapter, I will show you how to implement the `Flow` interface and `flow` builder by transforming a lambda expression step by step. This should give you a deep understanding of how Flow works. This chapter is for curious minds who like to truly understand the tools they use. If this isn't you, feel free to skip this chapter. If you decide to continue reading it, I hope you enjoy it.

Understanding `Flow`

We'll start our story with a simple lambda expression. Each lambda expression can be defined once and then called multiple times.

```
fun main() {
    val f: () -> Unit = {
        print("A")
        print("B")
        print("C")
    }
    f() // ABC
    f() // ABC
}
```

To make it a bit spicier, let's make our lambda expression `suspend` and add some delay inside it. Notice that each call of such a lambda expression is sequential, so you shouldn't make another call until the previous one is finished.

```
suspend fun main() {
    val f: suspend () -> Unit = {
        print("A")
        delay(1000)
        print("B")
        delay(1000)
        print("C")
    }
    f()
    f()
}
// A
// (1 sec)
// B
// (1 sec)
// C
// A
// (1 sec)
// B
// (1 sec)
// C
```

A lambda expression might have a parameter that can represent a function. We will call this parameter emit. So, when you call the lambda expression f, you need to specify another lambda expression that will be used as emit.

```
suspend fun main() {
    val f: suspend ((String) -> Unit) -> Unit = { emit ->
        emit("A")
        emit("B")
        emit("C")
    }
    f { print(it) } // ABC
    f { print(it) } // ABC
}
```

The fact is that emit should also be a suspending function. Our function type is already getting quite complex, so we'll simplify it by defining a `FlowCollector` function interface with an abstract method named `emit`. We will use this interface instead of the function type. The trick is that functional interfaces can be defined with lambda expressions, therefore we don't need to change the `f` call.

```kotlin
import kotlin.*

fun interface FlowCollector {
    suspend fun emit(value: String)
}

suspend fun main() {
    val f: suspend (FlowCollector) -> Unit = {
        it.emit("A")
        it.emit("B")
        it.emit("C")
    }
    f { print(it) } // ABC
    f { print(it) } // ABC
}
```

Calling `emit` on `it` is not convenient; instead, we'll make `FlowCollector` a receiver. Thanks to that, inside our lambda expression there is a receiver (`this` keyword) of type `FlowCollector`. This means we can call `this.emit` or just `emit`. The `f` invocation still stays the same.

```kotlin
fun interface FlowCollector {
    suspend fun emit(value: String)
}

suspend fun main() {
    val f: suspend FlowCollector.() -> Unit = {
        emit("A")
        emit("B")
        emit("C")
    }
    f { print(it) } // ABC
    f { print(it) } // ABC
}
```

Instead of passing around lambda expressions, we prefer to have an object implementing an interface. We will call this interface Flow and wrap our definition with an object expression.

```kotlin
import kotlin.*

fun interface FlowCollector {
    suspend fun emit(value: String)
}

interface Flow {
    suspend fun collect(collector: FlowCollector)
}

suspend fun main() {
    val builder: suspend FlowCollector.() -> Unit = {
        emit("A")
        emit("B")
        emit("C")
    }
    val flow: Flow = object : Flow {
        override suspend fun collect(
            collector: FlowCollector
        ) {
            collector.builder()
        }
    }
    flow.collect { print(it) } // ABC
    flow.collect { print(it) } // ABC
}
```

Finally, let's define the flow builder function to simplify our flow creation.

```kotlin
import kotlin.*

fun interface FlowCollector {
    suspend fun emit(value: String)
}

interface Flow {
    suspend fun collect(collector: FlowCollector)
}

fun flow(
    builder: suspend FlowCollector.() -> Unit
) = object : Flow {
    override suspend fun collect(collector: FlowCollector) {
        collector.builder()
    }
}

suspend fun main() {
    val f: Flow = flow {
        emit("A")
        emit("B")
        emit("C")
    }
    f.collect { print(it) } // ABC
    f.collect { print(it) } // ABC
}
```

The last change we need is to replace String with a generic type parameter in order to allow emitting and collecting any type of value.

```
import kotlin.*

fun interface FlowCollector<T> {
    suspend fun emit(value: T)
}

interface Flow<T> {
    suspend fun collect(collector: FlowCollector<T>)
}

fun <T> flow(
    builder: suspend FlowCollector<T>.() -> Unit
) = object : Flow<T> {
    override suspend fun collect(
        collector: FlowCollector<T>
    ) {
        collector.builder()
    }
}

suspend fun main() {
    val f: Flow<String> = flow {
        emit("A")
        emit("B")
        emit("C")
    }
    f.collect { print(it) } // ABC
    f.collect { print(it) } // ABC
}
```

That's it! This is nearly exactly how Flow, FlowCollector, and flow are implemented. When you call collect, you invoke the lambda expression from the flow builder call. When this expression calls emit, it calls the lambda expression specified when collect was called. This is how it works.

The presented builder is the most basic way to create a flow. Later, we'll learn about other builders, but they generally just use flow under the hood.

```
public fun <T> Iterator<T>.asFlow(): Flow<T> = flow {
    forEach { value ->
        emit(value)
    }
}

public fun <T> Sequence<T>.asFlow(): Flow<T> = flow {
    forEach { value ->
        emit(value)
    }
}

public fun <T> flowOf(vararg elements: T): Flow<T> = flow {
    for (element in elements) {
        emit(element)
    }
}
```

How `Flow` processing works

`Flow` can be considered a bit more complicated than suspending lambda expressions with a receiver. However, its power lies in all the functions defined for its creation, processing, and observation. Most of them are actually very simple under the hood. We will learn about them in the next chapters, but I want you to have the intuition that most of them are very simple and can be easily constructed using `flow`, `collect`, and `emit`.

Consider the `map` function that transforms each element of a flow. It creates a new flow, so it uses the `flow` builder. When its flow is started, it needs to start the flow it wraps; so, inside the builder, it calls the `collect` method. Whenever an element is received, `map` transforms this element and then emits it to the new flow.

```
fun <T, R> Flow<T>.map(
    transformation: suspend (T) -> R
): Flow<R> = flow {
    collect {
        emit(transformation(it))
    }
}

suspend fun main() {
    flowOf("A", "B", "C")
        .map {
            delay(1000)
            it.lowercase()
        }
        .collect { println(it) }
}
// (1 sec)
// a
// (1 sec)
// b
// (1 sec)
// c
```

The behavior of most of the methods that we'll learn about in the next chapters is just as simple. It is important to understand this because it not only helps us better understand how our code works but also teaches us how to write similar functions.

```
fun <T> Flow<T>.filter(
    predicate: suspend (T) -> Boolean
): Flow<T> = flow {
    collect {
        if (predicate(it)) {
            emit(it)
        }
    }
}

fun <T> Flow<T>.onEach(
```

```
    action: suspend (T) -> Unit
): Flow<T> = flow {
    collect {
        action(it)
        emit(it)
    }
}

// simplified implementation
fun <T> Flow<T>.onStart(
    action: suspend () -> Unit
): Flow<T> = flow {
    action()
    collect {
        emit(it)
    }
}
```

Flow is synchronous

Notice that Flow is synchronous by nature, just like suspending functions: the collect call is suspended until the flow is completed. This also means that a flow doesn't start any new coroutines. Its concrete steps can do it, just like suspending functions can start coroutines, but this is not the default behavior for suspending functions. Most flow processing steps are executed synchronously, which is why a delay inside onEach introduces a delay **between** each element, not before all elements, as you might expect.

```
suspend fun main() {
    flowOf("A", "B", "C")
        .onEach { delay(1000) }
        .collect { println(it) }
}
// (1 sec)
// A
// (1 sec)
// B
// (1 sec)
// C
```

Flow and shared states

When you implement more complex algorithms for flow processing, you should know when you need to synchronize access to variables. Let's analyze the most important use cases. When you implement some custom flow processing functions, you can define mutable states inside the flow without any mechanism for synchronization because a flow step is synchronous by nature.

```kotlin
fun <T, K> Flow<T>.distinctBy(
    keySelector: (T) -> K
) = flow {
    val sentKeys = mutableSetOf<K>()
    collect { value ->
        val key = keySelector(value)
        if (key !in sentKeys) {
            sentKeys.add(key)
            emit(value)
        }
    }
}
```

Here is an example that is used inside a flow step and produces consistent results; the counter variable is always incremented to 1000.

```kotlin
fun Flow<*>.counter() = flow<Int> {
    var counter = 0
    collect {
        counter++
        // to make it busy for a while
        List(100) { Random.nextLong() }.shuffled().sorted()
        emit(counter)
    }
}

suspend fun main(): Unit = coroutineScope {
    val f1 = List(1000) { "$it" }.asFlow()
    val f2 = List(1000) { "$it" }.asFlow()
```

```
    .counter()
```

```
    launch { println(f1.counter().last()) } // 1000
    launch { println(f1.counter().last()) } // 1000
    launch { println(f2.last()) } // 1000
    launch { println(f2.last()) } // 1000
}
```

It is a common mistake to extract a variable from outside a flow step into a function. Such a variable is shared between all the coroutines that are collecting from the same flow. **It requires synchronization and is flow-specific, not flow-collection-specific.** Therefore, f2.last() returns 2000, not 1000, because it is a result of counting elements from two flow executions in parallel.

```
fun Flow<*>.counter(): Flow<Int> {
    var counter = 0
    return this.map {
        counter++
        // to make it busy for a while
        List(100) { Random.nextLong() }.shuffled().sorted()
        counter
    }
}
```

```
suspend fun main(): Unit = coroutineScope {
    val f1 = List(1_000) { "$it" }.asFlow()
    val f2 = List(1_000) { "$it" }.asFlow()
        .counter()

    launch { println(f1.counter().last()) } // 1000
    launch { println(f1.counter().last()) } // 1000
    launch { println(f2.last()) } // less than 2000
    launch { println(f2.last()) } // less than 2000
}
```

Finally, just as suspending functions using the same variables need synchronization, a variable used in a flow needs synchronization if it's defined outside a function, on the scope of a class, or at the top-level.

```
var counter = 0

fun Flow<*>.counter(): Flow<Int> = this.map {
    counter++
    // to make it busy for a while
    List(100) { Random.nextLong() }.shuffled().sorted()
    counter
}

suspend fun main(): Unit = coroutineScope {
    val f1 = List(1_000) { "$it" }.asFlow()
    val f2 = List(1_000) { "$it" }.asFlow()
        .counter()

    launch { println(f1.counter().last()) } // less than 4000
    launch { println(f1.counter().last()) } // less than 4000
    launch { println(f2.last()) } // less than 4000
    launch { println(f2.last()) } // less than 4000
}
```

Conclusion

Flow can be considered a bit more complicated than a suspending lambda expression with a receiver, and its processing functions just decorate it with new operations. There is no magic here: how Flow and most of its methods are defined is simple and straightforward.

Flow building

Each flow needs to start somewhere. There are many ways to do this, depending on what we need. In this chapter, we will focus on the most important options.

Flow from raw values

The simplest way to create a flow is by using the `flowOf` function, where we just define what values this flow should have(similar to the `listOf` function for a list).

```
suspend fun main() {
    flowOf(1, 2, 3, 4, 5)
        .collect { print(it) } // 12345
}
```

At times, we might also need a flow with no values. For this, we have the `emptyFlow()` function (similar to the `emptyList` function for a list).

```
suspend fun main() {
    emptyFlow<Int>()
        .collect { print(it) } // (nothing)
}
```

Converters

We can also convert every `Iterable`, `Iterator` or `Sequence` into a `Flow` using the `asFlow` function.

```
suspend fun main() {
    listOf(1, 2, 3, 4, 5)
        // or setOf(1, 2, 3, 4, 5)
        // or sequenceOf(1, 2, 3, 4, 5)
        .asFlow()
        .collect { print(it) } // 12345
}
```

These functions produce a flow of elements that are available immediately. They are useful to start a flow of elements that we can then
process using the flow processing functions.

Converting a function to a flow

Flow is frequently used to represent a single value delayed in time
(like a `Single` in RxJava). So, it makes sense to convert a suspending
function into a flow. The result of this function will be the only value
in this flow. For that, there is the `asFlow` extension function, which
works on function types (both `suspend () -> T` and `() -> T`). Here
it is used to convert a suspending lambda expression into `Flow`.

```
suspend fun main() {
    val function = suspend {
        // this is suspending lambda expression
        delay(1000)
        "UserName"
    }

    function.asFlow()
        .collect { println(it) }
}
// (1 sec)
// UserName
```

To convert a regular function, we need to reference it first. We do this
using :: in Kotlin.

```
suspend fun getUserName(): String {
    delay(1000)
    return "UserName"
}

suspend fun main() {
    ::getUserName
        .asFlow()
        .collect { println(it) }
}
// (1 sec)
// UserName
```

Flow and Reactive Streams

If you use Reactive Streams in your application (like Reactor[64], Rx-Java 2.x.[65] or RxJava 3.x[66]), you don't need to make big changes in your code. All objects like Flux, Flowable or Observable implement the Publisher interface, which can be converted to Flow with the asFlow function from the kotlinx-coroutines-reactive library.

```
suspend fun main() = coroutineScope {
    Flux.range(1, 5).asFlow()
        .collect { print(it) } // 12345
    Flowable.range(1, 5).asFlow()
        .collect { print(it) } // 12345
    Observable.range(1, 5).asFlow()
        .collect { print(it) } // 12345
}
```

To convert the other way around, you need more specific libraries. With kotlinx-coroutines-reactor, you can convert Flow to Flux. With kotlinx-coroutines-rx3 (or kotlinx-coroutines-rx2), you can convert Flow to Flowable or Observable.

```
suspend fun main(): Unit = coroutineScope {
    val flow = flowOf(1, 2, 3, 4, 5)

    flow.asFlux()
        .doOnNext { print(it) } // 12345
        .subscribe()

    flow.asFlowable()
        .subscribe { print(it) } // 12345

    flow.asObservable()
        .subscribe { print(it) } // 12345
}
```

---

[64]https://projectreactor.io/
[65]https://github.com/ReactiveX/RxJava
[66]https://github.com/ReactiveX/RxJava

Flow builders

The most popular way to make a flow is using the flow builder, which we've already used in previous chapters. It behaves similarly to sequence builder for building a sequence, or produce builder for building a channel. We start the builder with the flow function call, and inside its lambda expression we emit the next values using the emit function. We can also use emitAll to emit all the values from Channel or Flow (emitAll(flow) is shorthand for flow.collect { emit(it) }).

```
fun makeFlow(): Flow<Int> = flow {
    repeat(3) { num ->
        delay(1000)
        emit(num)
    }
}

suspend fun main() {
    makeFlow()
        .collect { println(it) }
}
// (1 sec)
// 0
// (1 sec)
// 1
// (1 sec)
// 2
```

This builder has already been used in previous chapters, and it will be used many times in the upcoming ones, so we will see many use cases for it. For now, I will just revisit one from the *Sequence builder* chapter. Here, the flow builder is used to produce a stream of users that need to be requested page by page from our network API.

```
fun allUsersFlow(
    api: UserApi
): Flow<User> = flow {
    var page = 0
    do {
        val users = api.takePage(page++) // suspending
        emitAll(users)
    } while (!users.isNullOrEmpty())
}
```

Understanding flow builder

The flow builder is the most basic way to create a flow. All other options are based on it.

```
public fun <T> flowOf(vararg elements: T): Flow<T> = flow {
    for (element in elements) {
        emit(element)
    }
}
```

When we understand how this builder works, we will understand how flow works. flow builder is very simple under the hood: it just creates an object implementing the Flow interface, which just calls the block function inside the collect method[67].

```
fun <T> flow(
    block: suspend FlowCollector<T>.() -> Unit
): Flow<T> = object : Flow<T>() {
    override suspend fun collect(collector: FlowCollector<T>){
        collector.block()
    }
}

interface Flow<out T> {
    suspend fun collect(collector: FlowCollector<T>)
```

---

[67]The code below is simplified. In real code, there would be an additional mechanism for releasing a continuation interceptor.

```
}

fun interface FlowCollector<in T> {
    suspend fun emit(value: T)
}
```

Knowing this, let's analyze how the following code works:

```
fun main() = runBlocking {
    flow { // 1
        emit("A")
        emit("B")
        emit("C")
    }.collect { value -> // 2
        println(value)
    }
}
// A
// B
// C
```

When we call a `flow` builder, we just create an object. However, calling `collect` means calling the `block` function on the `collector` interface. The `block` function in this example is the lambda expression defined at 1. Its receiver is the `collector`, which is defined at 2 with a lambda expression. When we define a function interface (like `FlowCollector`) using a lambda expression, the body of this lambda expression will be used as the implementation of the only function expected by this interface, that is `emit` in this case. So, the body of the `emit` function is `println(value)`. Thus, when we call `collect`, we start executing the lambda expression defined at 1, and when it calls `emit`, it calls the lambda expression defined at 2. This is how flow works. Everything else is built on top of that.

channelFlow

`Flow` is a cold data stream, so it produces values on demand when they are needed. If you think of the `allUsersFlow` presented above, the next page of users will be requested when the receiver asks for it. This is desired in some situations. For example, imagine that we are looking for a specific user. If it is in the first page, we don't need to request any more pages. To see this in practice, in the example below we produce the next elements using the `flow` builder. Notice that the next page is requested lazily when it is needed.

```kotlin
data class User(val name: String)

interface UserApi {
    suspend fun takePage(pageNumber: Int): List<User>
}

class FakeUserApi : UserApi {
    private val users = List(20) { User("User$it") }
    private val pageSize: Int = 3

    override suspend fun takePage(
        pageNumber: Int
    ): List<User> {
        delay(1000) // suspending
        return users
            .drop(pageSize * pageNumber)
            .take(pageSize)
    }
}

fun allUsersFlow(api: UserApi): Flow<User> = flow {
    var page = 0
    do {
        println("Fetching page $page")
        val users = api.takePage(page++) // suspending
        emitAll(users.asFlow())
    } while (!users.isNullOrEmpty())
}

suspend fun main() {
    val api = FakeUserApi()
    val users = allUsersFlow(api)
    val user = users
        .first {
```

```
            println("Checking $it")
            delay(1000) // suspending
            it.name == "User3"
        }
    println(user)
}
// Fetching page 0
// (1 sec)
// Checking User(name=User0)
// (1 sec)
// Checking User(name=User1)
// (1 sec)
// Checking User(name=User2)
// (1 sec)
// Fetching page 1
// (1 sec)
// Checking User(name=User3)
// (1 sec)
// User(name=User3)
```

On the other hand, we might have cases in which we want to fetch pages in advance when we are still processing the elements. Doing this in the presented case could lead to more network calls, but it might also produce a faster result. To achieve this, we would need independent production and consumption. Such independence is typical of hot data streams, like channels. So, we need a hybrid of Channel and Flow. Yes, this is supported: we just need to use the channelFlow function, which is like Flow because it implements the Flow interface. This builder is a regular function, and it is started with a terminal operation (like collect). It is also like a Channel because once it is started, it produces the values in a separate coroutine without waiting for the receiver. Therefore, fetching the next pages and checking users happens concurrently.

```kotlin
fun allUsersFlow(api: UserApi): Flow<User> = channelFlow {
    var page = 0
    do {
        println("Fetching page $page")
        val users = api.takePage(page++) // suspending
        users?.forEach { send(it) }
    } while (!users.isNullOrEmpty())
}

suspend fun main() {
    val api = FakeUserApi()
    val users = allUsersFlow(api)
    val user = users
        .first {
            println("Checking $it")
            delay(1000)
            it.name == "User3"
        }
    println(user)
}
// Fetching page 0
// (1 sec)
// Checking User(name=User0)
// Fetching page 1
// (1 sec)
// Checking User(name=User1)
// Fetching page 2
// (1 sec)
// Checking User(name=User2)
// Fetching page 3
// (1 sec)
// Checking User(name=User3)
// Fetching page 4
// (1 sec)
// User(name=User3)
```

Inside `channelFlow` we operate on `ProducerScope<T>`. `ProducerScope` is the same type as used by the `produce` builder. It implements `CoroutineScope`, so we can use it to start new coroutines with builders. To produce elements, we use send instead of emit. We can also access the channel or control it directly with SendChannel functions.

```
interface ProducerScope<in E> :
    CoroutineScope, SendChannel<E> {

    val channel: SendChannel<E>
}
```

A typical use case for channelFlow is when we need to independently compute values. To support this, channelFlow creates a coroutine scope, so we can directly start coroutine builders like launch. The code below would not work for flow because it does not create the scope needed by coroutine builders.

```
fun <T> Flow<T>.merge(other: Flow<T>): Flow<T> =
    channelFlow {
        launch {
            collect { send(it) }
        }
        other.collect { send(it) }
    }

fun <T> contextualFlow(): Flow<T> = channelFlow {
    launch(Dispatchers.IO) {
        send(computeIoValue())
    }
    launch(Dispatchers.Default) {
        send(computeCpuValue())
    }
}
```

Just like all the other coroutines, channelFlow doesn't finish until all its children are in a terminal state.

callbackFlow

Let's say that you need a flow of events you listen for, like user clicks or other kinds of actions. The listening process should

be independent from the process of handling these events, so
channelFlow would be a good candidate. However, there is a better
one: callbackFlow.

For a very long time, there was no difference between channelFlow
and callbackFlow. In version 1.3.4, small changes were introduced
to make it less error-prone when using callbacks. However, the
biggest difference is in how people understand these functions:
callbackFlow is for wrapping callbacks.

Inside callbackFlow, we also operate on ProducerScope<T>. Here are
a few functions that might be useful for wrapping callbacks:

- awaitClose { ... } - a function that suspends until the
  channel is closed. Once it is closed, it invokes its argument.
  awaitClose is very important for callbackFlow. Take a look
  at the example below. Without awaitClose, the coroutine will
  end immediately after registering a callback. This is natural
  for a coroutine: its body has ended and it has no children to
  wait for, so it ends. We use awaitClose (even with an empty
  body) to prevent this, and we listen for elements until the
  channel is closed in some other way.
- trySendBlocking(value) - similar to send, but it is blocking
  instead of suspending, so it can be used on non-suspending
  functions.
- close() - ends this channel.
- cancel(throwable) - ends this channel and sends an exception
  to the flow.

Here is a typical example of how callbackFlow is used:

```
fun flowFrom(api: CallbackBasedApi): Flow<T> = callbackFlow {
    val callback = object : Callback {
        override fun onNextValue(value: T) {
            trySendBlocking(value)
        }
        override fun onApiError(cause: Throwable) {
            cancel(CancellationException("API Error", cause))
        }
        override fun onCompleted() = channel.close()
    }
    api.register(callback)
    awaitClose { api.unregister(callback) }
}
```

Summary

In this chapter, we've reviewed different ways in which flows can be created. There are many functions for starting a flow, from simple ones like `flowOf` or `emptyFlow`, conversion `asFlow`, up to flow builders. The simplest flow builder is just a `flow` function, where you can use the `emit` function to produce the next values. There are also the `channelFlow` and `callbackFlow` builders, which create a flow that has some of the characteristics of Channel. Each of these functions has its own use cases, and it's useful to know them in order to leverage the full potential of Flow.

Flow lifecycle functions

Flow can be imagined as a pipe in which requests for next values flow
in one direction, and the corresponding produced values flow in the
other direction. When flow is completed or an exception occurs, this
information is also propagated and it closes the intermediate steps
on the way. So, as they all flow, we can listen for values, exceptions, or
other characteristic events (like starting or completing). To do this,
we use methods such as onEach, onStart, onCompletion, onEmpty and
catch. Let's explain these one by one.

onEach

To react to each flowing value, we use the onEach function.

```
suspend fun main() {
    flowOf(1, 2, 3, 4)
        .onEach { print(it) }
        .collect() // 1234
}
```

The onEach lambda expression is suspending, and elements are processed one after another in order (sequentially). So, if we add delay
in onEach, we will delay each value as it flows.

```
suspend fun main() {
    flowOf(1, 2)
        .onEach { delay(1000) }
        .collect { println(it) }
}
// (1 sec)
// 1
// (1 sec)
// 2
```

onStart

The onStart function sets a listener that should be called immediately once the flow is started, i.e., once the terminal operation is
called. It is important to note that onStart does not wait for the first
element: it is called when we request the first element.

```
suspend fun main() {
    flowOf(1, 2)
        .onEach { delay(1000) }
        .onStart { println("Before") }
        .collect { println(it) }
}
// Before
// (1 sec)
// 1
// (1 sec)
// 2
```

It is good to know that in onStart (as well as in onCompletion, onEmpty and catch) we can emit elements. Such elements will flow downstream from this place.

```
suspend fun main() {
    flowOf(1, 2)
        .onEach { delay(1000) }
        .onStart { emit(0) }
        .collect { println(it) }
}
// 0
// (1 sec)
// 1
// (1 sec)
// 2
```

onCompletion

There are a few ways in which a flow can be completed. The most common one is when the flow builder is done (i.e., the last element has been sent), although this also happens in the case of an uncaught exception or a coroutine cancellation. In all these cases, we can add a listener for flow completion by using the onCompletion method.

```kotlin
suspend fun main() = coroutineScope {
    flowOf(1, 2)
        .onEach { delay(1000) }
        .onCompletion { println("Completed") }
        .collect { println(it) }
}
// (1 sec)
// 1
// (1 sec)
// 2
// Completed
```

```kotlin
suspend fun main() = coroutineScope {
    val job = launch {
        flowOf(1, 2)
            .onEach { delay(1000) }
            .onCompletion { println("Completed") }
            .collect { println(it) }
    }
    delay(1100)
    job.cancel()
}
// (1 sec)
// 1
// (0.1 sec)
// Completed
```

In Android, we often use onStart to show a progress bar (the in-dicator that we are waiting for a network response), and we use onCompletion to hide it.

```
fun updateNews() {
    scope.launch {
        newsFlow()
            .onStart { showProgressBar() }
            .onCompletion { hideProgressBar() }
            .collect { view.showNews(it) }
    }
}
```

onEmpty

A flow might complete without emitting any value, which might be an indication of an unexpected event. For such cases, there is the onEmpty function, which invokes the given action when this flow completes without emitting any elements. onEmpty might then be used to emit some default value.

```
suspend fun main() = coroutineScope {
    flow<List<Int>> { delay(1000) }
        .onEmpty { emit(emptyList()) }
        .collect { println(it) }
}
// (1 sec)
// []
```

catch

At any point of flow building or processing, an exception might occur. Such an exception will flow down, closing each processing step on the way; however, it can be caught and managed. To do so, we can use the catch method. This listener receives the exception as an argument and allows you to perform recovering operations.

```
class MyError : Throwable("My error")

val flow = flow {
    emit(1)
    emit(2)
    throw MyError()
}

suspend fun main(): Unit {
    flow.onEach { println("Got $it") }
        .catch { println("Caught $it") }
        .collect { println("Collected $it") }
}
// Got 1
// Collected 1
// Got 2
// Collected 2
// Caught MyError: My error
```

In the example above, notice that onEach does not react to an exception. The same happens with other functions like map, filter etc. Only the onCompletion handler will be called.

The catch method stops an exception by catching it. The previous steps have already been completed, but catch can still emit new values and keep the rest of the flow alive.

```
val flow = flow {
    emit("Message1")
    throw MyError()
}

suspend fun main(): Unit {
    flow.catch { emit("Error") }
        .collect { println("Collected $it") }
}
// Collected Message1
// Collected Error
```

The catch will only react to the exceptions thrown in the function defined upstream (you can imagine that the exception needs to be caught as it flows down).

```kotlin
import kotlinx.coroutines.flow.*

suspend fun main(): Unit {
    flowOf( value: "Message1")
        .catch { emit( value: "Error") }
        .onEach { throw Error(it) }
        .collect { println("Collected $it") }
}
// Exception in thread "main" java.lang.Error: Message1
```

In Android, we often use catch to show exceptions that happened in a flow.

```kotlin
fun updateNews() {
    scope.launch {
        newsFlow()
            .catch { view.handleError(it) }
            .onStart { showProgressBar() }
            .onCompletion { hideProgressBar() }
            .collect { view.showNews(it) }
    }
}
```

We could also use catch to emit default data to display on the screen, such as an empty list.

```kotlin
fun updateNews() {
    scope.launch {
        newsFlow()
            .catch {
                view.handleError(it)
                emit(emptyList())
            }
            .onStart { showProgressBar() }
```

```
        .onCompletion { hideProgressBar() }
        .collect { view.showNews(it) }
    }
}
```

Uncaught exceptions

Uncaught exceptions in a flow immediately cancel this flow, and
collect rethrows this exception. This behavior is typical of suspending functions, and coroutineScope behaves the same way. Exceptions can be caught outside flow using the classic try-catch block.

```
val flow = flow {
    emit("Message1")
    throw MyError()
}

suspend fun main(): Unit {
    try {
        flow.collect { println("Collected $it") }
    } catch (e: MyError) {
        println("Caught")
    }
}
// Collected Message1
// Caught
```

Notice that using catch does not protect us from an exception in the
terminal operation (because catch cannot be placed after the last
operation). So, if there is an exception in the collect, it won't be
caught, and an error will be thrown.

```
val flow = flow {
    emit("Message1")
    emit("Message2")
}

suspend fun main(): Unit {
    flow.onStart { println("Before") }
        .catch { println("Caught $it") }
        .collect { throw MyError() }
}
// Before
// Exception in thread "..." MyError: My error
```

Therefore, it is common practice to move the operation from collect to onEach and place it before the catch. This is specifically useful if we suspect that collect might raise an exception. If we move the operation from collect, we can be sure that catch will catch all exceptions.

```
val flow = flow {
    emit("Message1")
    emit("Message2")
}

suspend fun main(): Unit {
    flow.onStart { println("Before") }
        .onEach { throw MyError() }
        .catch { println("Caught $it") }
        .collect()
}
// Before
// Caught MyError: My error
```

flowOn

Lambda expressions used as arguments for flow operations (like onEach, onStart, onCompletion, etc.) and its builders (like flow or channelFlow) are all suspending in nature. Suspending functions need to have a context and should be in relation to their parent (for

structured concurrency). So, you might be wondering where these
functions take their context from. The answer is: from the context
where `collect` is called.

```
fun usersFlow(): Flow<String> = flow {
    repeat(2) {
        val ctx = currentCoroutineContext()
        val name = ctx[CoroutineName]?.name
        emit("User$it in $name")
    }
}

suspend fun main() {
    val users = usersFlow()
    withContext(CoroutineName("Name1")) {
        users.collect { println(it) }
    }
    withContext(CoroutineName("Name2")) {
        users.collect { println(it) }
    }
}
// User0 in Name1
// User1 in Name1
// User0 in Name2
// User1 in Name2
```

How does this code work? The terminal operation call requests elements from upstream, thereby propagating the coroutine context.
However, it can also be modified by the `flowOn` function.

```
suspend fun present(place: String, message: String) {
    val ctx = coroutineContext
    val name = ctx[CoroutineName]?.name
    println("[$name] $message on $place")
}

fun messagesFlow(): Flow<String> = flow {
    present("flow builder", "Message")
    emit("Message")
```

```
}

suspend fun main() {
    val users = messagesFlow()
    withContext(CoroutineName("Name1")) {
        users
            .flowOn(CoroutineName("Name3"))
            .onEach { present("onEach", it) }
            .flowOn(CoroutineName("Name2"))
            .collect { present("collect", it) }
    }
}
// [Name3] Message on flow builder
// [Name2] Message on onEach
// [Name1] Message on collect
```

Remember that `flowOn` works only for functions that are upstream in the flow.

launchIn

`collect` is a suspending operation that suspends a coroutine until the flow is completed. It is common to wrap it with a `launch` builder so that flow processing can start on another coroutine. To help with such cases, there is the `launchIn` function, which launches `collect` in a new coroutine on the scope object passed as the only argument.

```
fun <T> Flow<T>.launchIn(scope: CoroutineScope): Job =
    scope.launch { collect() }
```

`launchIn` is often used to start flow processing in a separate coroutine.

```
suspend fun main(): Unit = coroutineScope {
    flowOf("User1", "User2")
        .onStart { println("Users:") }
        .onEach { println(it) }
        .launchIn(this)
}
// Users:
// User1
// User2
```

Summary

In this chapter, we've learned about different Flow functionalities. Now we know how to do something when our flow starts, when it is closing, or on each element; we also know how to catch exceptions and how to launch a flow in a new coroutine. These are typical tools that are widely used, especially in Android development. For instance, here is how a flow might be used on Android:

```
fun updateNews() {
    newsFlow()
        .onStart { showProgressBar() }
        .onCompletion { hideProgressBar() }
        .onEach { view.showNews(it) }
        .catch { view.handleError(it) }
        .launchIn(viewModelScope)
}
```

Flow processing

We've presented Flow as a pipe through which values flow. As they do so, they can be changed in different ways: dropped, multiplied, transformed, or combined. These operations between flow creation and the terminal operation are called Flow processing. In this chapter, we will learn about the functions we use for this.

> The functions presented here might remind you of the functions we use for Collection processing. This is no coincidence as they represent the same concepts, with the difference that flow elements can be spread in time.

map

The first important function we need to learn about is map, which transforms each flowing element according to its transformation function. So, if you have a flow of numbers and your operation is calculating the squares of these numbers, then the resulting flow will have the squares of these numbers.

```
suspend fun main() {
    flowOf(1, 2, 3) // [1, 2, 3]
        .map { it * it } // [1, 4, 9]
        .collect { print(it) } // 149
}
```

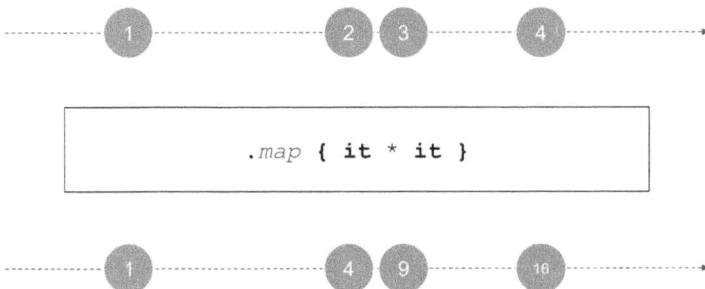

I will use the diagrams shown above to visualize how flow processing functions change elements over time. The horizontal line represents time, and the elements on this line are elements that are emitted in the flow at this point in time. The line above represents a flow before the presented operation, and the line below represents a flow after the operation. This diagram can also be used to represent multiple operations used one after another, like map and filter in the diagram below.

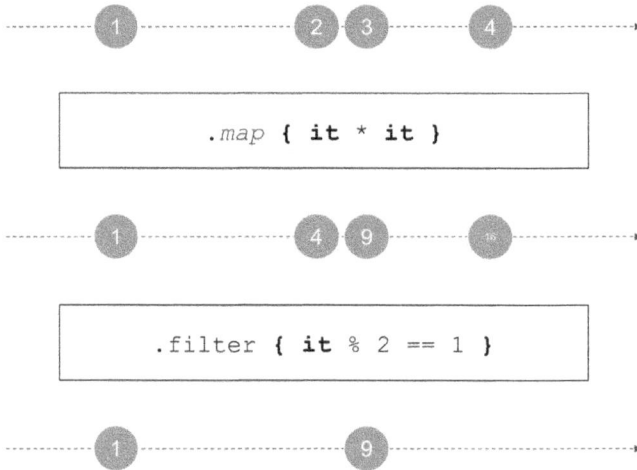

Most of the Flow processing functions are quite simple to implement with tools we already know from previous chapters. To implement map, we might use the flow builder to create a new flow. Then, we might collect elements from the previous flow and emit each collected element transformed. The implementation below is just a slightly simplified version of the actual one from the kotlinx.coroutines library.

```
fun <T, R> Flow<T>.map(
    transform: suspend (value: T) -> R
): Flow<R> = flow { // here we create a new flow
    collect { value -> // here we collect from receiver
        emit(transform(value))
    }
}
```

map is a very popular function. Its use cases include unpacking or converting values into a different type.

```
// Here we use map to have user actions from input events
fun actionsFlow(): Flow<UserAction> =
    observeInputEvents()
        .map { toAction(it.code) }

// Here we use map to convert from User to UserJson
fun getAllUser(): Flow<UserJson> =
    userRepository.getAllUsers()
        .map { it.toUserJson() }
```

filter

The next important function is filter, which returns a flow containing only values from the original flow that match the given predicate.

```
suspend fun main() {
    (1..10).asFlow() // [1, 2, 3, 4, 5, 6, 7, 8, 9, 10]
        .filter { it <= 5 } // [1, 2, 3, 4, 5]
        .filter { isEven(it) } // [2, 4]
        .collect { print(it) } // 24
}

fun isEven(num: Int): Boolean = num % 2 == 0
```

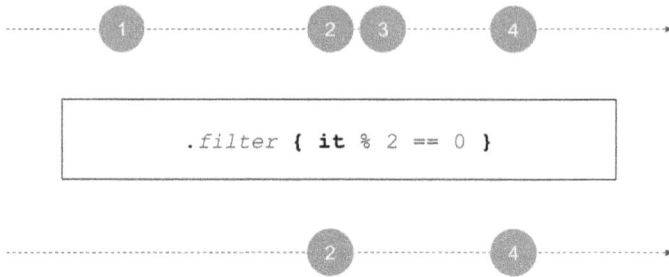

This function can also be implemented quite easily using the flow builder. We would just need to introduce an if statement with the predicate (instead of transformation).

```
fun <T> Flow<T>.filter(
    predicate: suspend (T) -> Boolean
): Flow<T> = flow { // here we create a new flow
    collect { value -> // here we collect from receiver
        if (predicate(value)) {
            emit(value)
        }
    }
}
```

filter is typically used to eliminate elements we are not interested in.

```
// Here we use filter to drop invalid actions
fun actionsFlow(): Flow<UserAction> =
    observeInputEvents()
        .filter { isValidAction(it.code) }
        .map { toAction(it.code) }
```

take and drop

We use take to pass only a certain number of elements.

```
suspend fun main() {
    ('A'..'Z').asFlow()
        .take(5) // [A, B, C, D, E]
        .collect { print(it) } // ABCDE
}
```

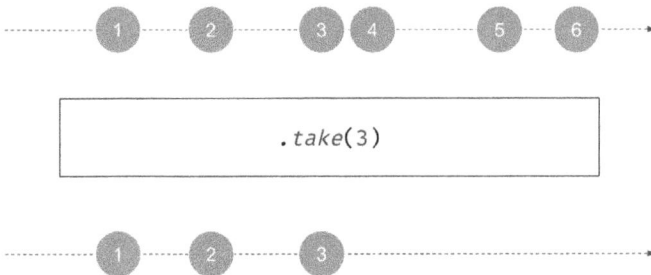

We use drop to ignore a certain number of elements.

```
suspend fun main() {
    ('A'..'Z').asFlow()
        .drop(20) // [U, V, W, X, Y, Z]
        .collect { print(it) } // UVWXYZ
}
```

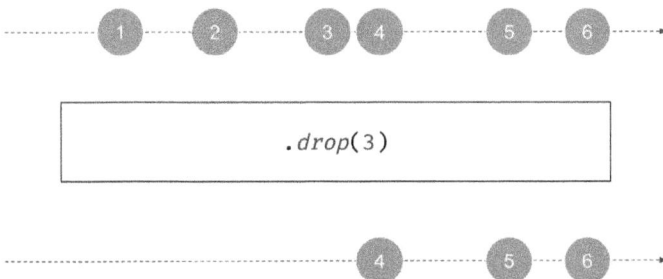

How does collection processing work?

We've seen quite a few flow processing and lifecycle functions. Their implementation is quite simple, so you can guess that there is no magic going on there. Most such functions can be implemented with `flow` builder and `collect` with a lambda. Here is a simple example of flow processing and some simplified `map` and `flowOf` implementations:

```kotlin
suspend fun main() {
    flowOf('a', 'b')
        .map { it.uppercase() }
        .collect { print(it) } // AB
}

fun <T, R> Flow<T>.map(
    transform: suspend (value: T) -> R
): Flow<R> = flow {
    collect { value ->
        emit(transform(value))
    }
}

fun <T> flowOf(vararg elements: T): Flow<T> = flow {
    for (element in elements) {
        emit(element)
    }
}
```

If you inline `filter` and `map` functions, you will end up with the following code (I added labels to the lambdas and comments with numbers).

```
suspend fun main() {
    flow map@{ // 1
        flow flowOf@{ // 2
            for (element in arrayOf('a', 'b')) { // 3
                this@flowOf.emit(element) // 4
            }
        }.collect { value -> // 5
            this@map.emit(value.uppercase()) // 6
        }
    }.collect { // 7
        print(it) // 8
    }
}
```

Let's analyze this step by step. We start a flow at 1 and collect it at 7. When we start collecting, we invoke the lambda @map (which starts at 1), which calls another builder at 2 and collects it at 5. When we collect, we start lambda @flowOn (which starts at 2). This lambda (at 2) iterates over an array with 'a' and 'b'. The first value 'a' is emitted at 4, which calls the lambda at 5. This lambda (at 5) transforms the value to 'A' and emits it to the flow @map, thus calling the lambda at 7. The value is printed; we then finish the lambda at 7 and resume the lambda at 6. It finishes, so we resume @flowOf at 4. We continue the iteration and emit 'b' at 4. So, we call the lambda at 5, transform the value to 'B', and emit it at 6 to the flow @map. The value is collected at 7 and printed at 8. The lambda at 7 is finished, so we resume the lambda at 6. This is finished, so we resume the lambda @flowOf at 4. This is also finished, so we resume the @map on collect at 5. Since there is nothing more, we reach the end of @map. With that, we resume the collect at 7, and we reach the end of the main function.

The same happens in most flow processing and lifecycle functions, so understanding this gives us quite a good understanding of how Flow works.

merge, zip and combine

Let's talk about combining two flows into one. There are a few ways to do this. The simplest involves merging the elements from two flows into one. No modifications are made, no matter from which flow elements originate. To do this, we use the top-level merge function.

```kotlin
suspend fun main() {
    val ints: Flow<Int> = flowOf(1, 2, 3)
    val doubles: Flow<Double> = flowOf(0.1, 0.2, 0.3)

    val together: Flow<Number> = merge(ints, doubles)
    print(together.toList())
    // [1, 0.1, 0.2, 0.3, 2, 3]
    // or [1, 0.1, 0.2, 0.3, 2, 3]
    // or [0.1, 1, 2, 3, 0.2, 0.3]
    // or any other combination
}
```

It is important to know that when we use `merge` the elements from one flow do not wait for another flow. For instance, in the example below, elements from the first flow are delayed, but this does not stop the elements from the second flow.

```kotlin
suspend fun main() {
    val ints: Flow<Int> = flowOf(1, 2, 3)
        .onEach { delay(1000) }
    val doubles: Flow<Double> = flowOf(0.1, 0.2, 0.3)

    val together: Flow<Number> = merge(ints, doubles)
    together.collect { println(it) }
}
```

```
// 0.1
// 0.2
// 0.3
// (1 sec)
// 1
// (1 sec)
// 2
// (1 sec)
// 3
```

We use `merge` when we have multiple sources of events that should lead to the same actions.

```
fun listenForMessages() {
    merge(userSentMessages, messagesNotifications)
        .onEach { displayMessage(it) }
        .launchIn(scope)
}
```

The next function is `zip`, which makes pairs from both flows. We also need to specify a function that decides how elements are paired (transformed into one what will be emitted in the new flow). Each element can only be part of one pair, so it needs to wait for its pair. Elements left without a pair are lost, so when the zipping of a flow is complete, the resulting flow is also complete (as is the other flow).

```
suspend fun main() {
    val flow1 = flowOf("A", "B", "C")
        .onEach { delay(400) }
    val flow2 = flowOf(1, 2, 3, 4)
        .onEach { delay(1000) }
    flow1.zip(flow2) { f1, f2 -> "${f1}_${f2}" }
        .collect { println(it) }
}
// (1 sec)
// A_1
// (1 sec)
// B_2
// (1 sec)
// C_3
```

```
flow1.zip(flow2) { f1, f2 -> "${f1}_${f2}" }
```

The zip function reminds me of the polonaise - a traditional Polish dance. One feature of this dance is that a line of pairs is separated down the middle, then these pairs reform when they meet again.

A still from the movie Pan Tadeusz, directed by Andrzej Wajda, presenting the polonaise dance.

The last important function when combining two flows is combine. Just like zip, it also forms pairs from elements, which have to wait for the slower flow to produce the first pair. However, the similarities to the polonaise dance end here. When we use combine, every new element replaces its predecessor. If the first pair has been formed already, it will produce a new pair together with the previous element from the other flow.

Notice that `zip` needs pairs, so it closes when the first flow closes. `combine` does not have such a limitation, so it will emit until both flows are closed.

```kotlin
suspend fun main() {
    val flow1 = flowOf("A", "B", "C")
        .onEach { delay(400) }
    val flow2 = flowOf(1, 2, 3, 4)
        .onEach { delay(1000) }
    flow1.combine(flow2) { f1, f2 -> "${f1}_${f2}" }
        .collect { println(it) }
}
// (1 sec)
// B_1
// (0.2 sec)
// C_1
// (0.8 sec)
// C_2
// (1 sec)
// C_3
// (1 sec)
// C_4
```

combine is typically used when we need to actively observe two sources of changes. If you want to have elements emitted whenever a change occurs, you can add initial values to each combined flow (to have the initial pair).

```
userUpdateFlow.onStart { emit(currentUser) }
```

A typical use case might be when a view needs to be either of two observable element changes. For example, when a notification badge depends on both the current state of a user and some notifications, we might observe them both and combine their changes to update a view.

```
userStateFlow
    .combine(notificationsFlow) { userState, notifications ->
        updateNotificationBadge(userState, notifications)
    }
    .collect()
```

fold and scan

If you use collection processing functions, you might recognize fold. It is used to combine all the values in this collection into one by applying an operation that combines two values into one for each element (starting from the initial value).

For example, if the initial value is 0 and the operation is addition, then the result is the sum of all the numbers: we first take the initial value 0; then, we add the first element 1 to it; to the result 1, we add the second number 2; to the result 3, we add the third number 3; to the result 6, we add the last number 4. The result of this operation, 10, is what will be returned from fold.

```
fun main() {
    val list = listOf(1, 2, 3, 4)
    val res = list.fold(0) { acc, i -> acc + i }
    println(res) // 10
    val res2 = list.fold(1) { acc, i -> acc * i }
    println(res2) // 24
}
```

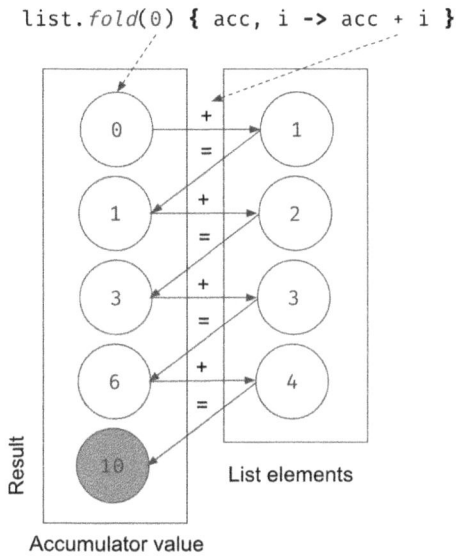

list.*fold*(0) { acc, i -> acc + i }

Result

Accumulator value

List elements

`fold` is a terminal operation. It can also be used for Flow, but it will suspend until this flow is completed (just like `collect`).

```
suspend fun main() {
    val list = flowOf(1, 2, 3, 4)
        .onEach { delay(1000) }
    val res = list.fold(0) { acc, i -> acc + i }
    println(res)
}
// (4 sec)
// 10
```

There is an alternative to `fold` called `scan`. It is an intermediate operation that produces all intermediate accumulator values.

```kotlin
fun main() {
    val list = listOf(1, 2, 3, 4)
    val res = list.scan(0) { acc, i -> acc + i }
    println(res) // [0, 1, 3, 6, 10]
}
```

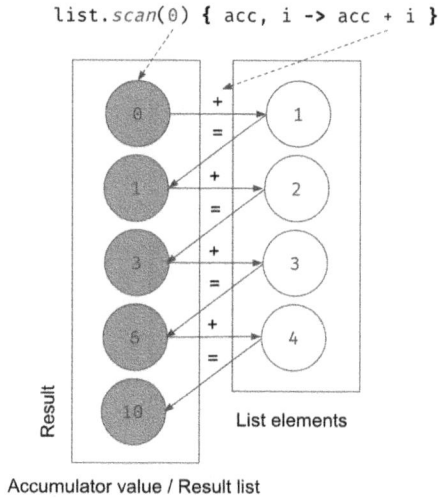

list.*scan*(0) **{** acc, i -> acc + i **}**

Accumulator value / Result list

scan is useful with Flow because it produces a new value immediately after receiving one from the previous step.

```kotlin
suspend fun main() {
    flowOf(1, 2, 3, 4)
        .onEach { delay(1000) }
        .scan(0) { acc, v -> acc + v }
        .collect { println(it) }
}
// 0
// (1 sec)
// 1
// (1 sec)
// 3
// (1 sec)
// 6
```

```
// (1 sec)
// 10
```

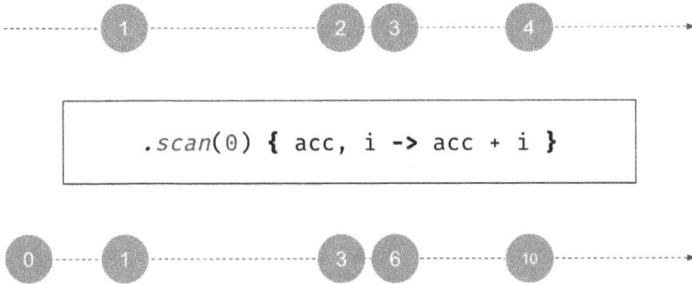

.scan(0) { acc, i -> acc + i }

We can implement scan easily using the flow builder and collect. We first emit the initial value, then with each new element we emit the result of the next value accumulation.

```
fun <T, R> Flow<T>.scan(
    initial: R,
    operation: suspend (accumulator: R, value: T) -> R
): Flow<R> = flow {
    var accumulator: R = initial
    emit(accumulator)
    collect { value ->
        accumulator = operation(accumulator, value)
        emit(accumulator)
    }
}
```

The typical use case for scan is when we have a flow of updates or changes, and we need an object that is the result of these changes.

```
val userStateFlow: Flow<User> = userChangesFlow
    .scan(user) { user, change -> user.withChange(change) }

val messagesListFlow: Flow<List<Message>> = messagesFlow
    .scan(messages) { acc, message -> acc + message }
```

flatMapConcat, flatMapMerge and flatMapLatest

Another well-known function for collections is flatMap. In the case
of collections, it is similar to a map, but the transformation function
needs to return a collection that is then flattened. For example, if you
have a list of departments, each of which has a list of employees, you
can use flatMap to make a list of all employees in all departments.

```
val allEmployees: List<Employee> = departments
    .flatMap { department -> department.employees }

// If we had used map, we would have a list of lists instead
val listOfListsOfEmployee: List<List<Employee>> = departments
    .map { department -> department.employees }
```

How should flatMap look on a flow? It seems intuitive that we might
expect its transformation function to return a flow that should then
be flattened. The problem is that flow elements can be spread in
time. So, should the flow produced from the second element wait
for the one produced from the first one, or should it process them
concurrently? Since there is no clear answer, there is no flatMap
function for Flow, but instead there are flatMapConcat, flatMapMerge
and flatMapLatest.

The flatMapConcat function processes the produced flows one after
another. So, the second flow can start when the first one is done.
In the following example, we make a flow from the characters "A",
"B", and "C". The flow produced by each of them includes these
characters and the numbers 1, 2, and 3, with a 1-second delay in
between.

```
fun flowFrom(elem: String) = flowOf(1, 2, 3)
    .onEach { delay(1000) }
    .map { "${it}_${elem} " }

suspend fun main() {
    flowOf("A", "B", "C")
        .flatMapConcat { flowFrom(it) }
        .collect { println(it) }
}
// (1 sec)
// 1_A
// (1 sec)
// 2_A
// (1 sec)
// 3_A
// (1 sec)
// 1_B
// (1 sec)
// 2_B
// (1 sec)
// 3_B
// (1 sec)
// 1_C
// (1 sec)
// 2_C
// (1 sec)
// 3_C
```

The second mentioned function, flatMapMerge, is the most intuitive to me. It processes produced flows concurrently.

```kotlin
fun flowFrom(elem: String) = flowOf(1, 2, 3)
    .onEach { delay(1000) }
    .map { "${it}_${elem} " }

suspend fun main() {
    flowOf("A", "B", "C")
        .flatMapMerge { flowFrom(it) }
        .collect { println(it) }
}
// (1 sec)
// 1_A
// 1_B
// 1_C
// (1 sec)
// 2_A
// 2_B
// 2_C
// (1 sec)
// 3_A
// 3_B
// 3_C
```

```
flowOf("A", "B", "C")
    .flatMapMerge { flowFrom(it) }
```

The number of flows that can be concurrently processed can be set using the concurrency parameter. The default value of this parameter is 16, but it can be changed in the JVM using the DEFAULT_-CONCURRENCY_PROPERTY_NAME property. Beware of this default limitation because if you use flatMapMerge on a flow with many elements, only 16 will be processed at the same time.

```
suspend fun main() {
    flowOf("A", "B", "C")
        .flatMapMerge(concurrency = 2) { flowFrom(it) }
        .collect { println(it) }
}
// (1 sec)
// 1_A
// 1_B
// (1 sec)
// 2_A
// 2_B
// (1 sec)
// 3_A
// 3_B
// (1 sec)
// 1_C
// (1 sec)
// 2_C
```

```
// (1 sec)
// 3_C
```

The typical use of flatMapMerge is when we need to request data for each element in a flow. For instance, we have a list of categories, and you need to request offers for each of them. You already know that you can do this with the async function. There are two advantages of using a flow with flatMapMerge instead:

- we can control the concurrency parameter and decide how many categories we want to fetch at the same time (to avoid sending hundreds of requests at the same time);
- we can return Flow and send the next elements as they arrive (so, on the function-use side, they can be handled immediately).

```
suspend fun getOffers(
    categories: List<Category>
): List<Offer> = coroutineScope {
    categories
        .map { async { api.requestOffers(it) } }
        .flatMap { it.await() }
}

// A better solution
suspend fun getOffers(
    categories: List<Category>
): Flow<Offer> = categories
    .asFlow()
    .flatMapMerge(concurrency = 20) {
        suspend { api.requestOffers(it) }.asFlow()
        // or flow { emit(api.requestOffers(it)) }
    }
```

The last function is flatMapLatest. It forgets about the previous flow once a new one appears. With every new value, the previous flow processing is forgotten. So, if there is no delay between "A", "B" and "C", then you will only see "1_C", "2_C", and "3_C".

```
fun flowFrom(elem: String) = flowOf(1, 2, 3)
    .onEach { delay(1000) }
    .map { "${it}_${elem} " }

suspend fun main() {
    flowOf("A", "B", "C")
        .flatMapLatest { flowFrom(it) }
        .collect { println(it) }
}
// (1 sec)
// 1_C
// (1 sec)
// 2_C
// (1 sec)
// 3_C
```

It gets more interesting when the elements from the initial flow are delayed. What happens in the example below is that (after 1.2 sec) "A" starts its flow, which was created using flowFrom. This flow produces an element "1_A" in 1 second, but 200 ms later "B" appears and this previous flow is closed and forgotten. "B" flow managed to produce "1_B" when "C" appeared and started producing its flow. This one will finally produce elements "1_C", "2_C", and "3_C", with a 1-second delay in between.

```kotlin
suspend fun main() {
    flowOf("A", "B", "C")
        .onEach { delay(1200) }
        .flatMapLatest { flowFrom(it) }
        .collect { println(it) }
}
// (2.2 sec)
// 1_A
// (1.2 sec)
// 1_B
// (1.2 sec)
// 1_C
// (1 sec)
// 2_C
// (1 sec)
// 3_C
```

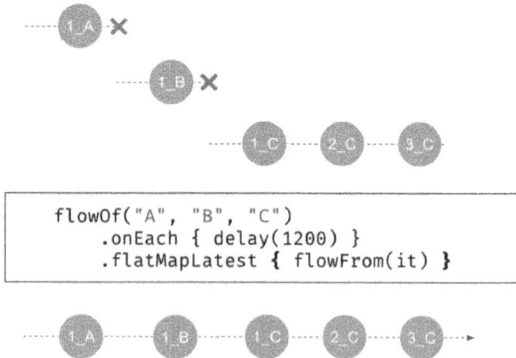

```kotlin
flowOf("A", "B", "C")
    .onEach { delay(1200) }
    .flatMapLatest { flowFrom(it) }
```

retry

An exception flows through a flow, closing each step one by one. These steps become inactive, so it is not possible to send messages after an exception, but each step gives you a reference to the previous ones, and this reference can be used to start this flow again. Based on this idea, Kotlin offers the retry and retryWhen functions. Here is a simplified implementation of retryWhen:

```kotlin
// Simplified implementation of retryWhen
fun <T> Flow<T>.retryWhen(
    predicate: suspend FlowCollector<T>.(
        cause: Throwable,
        attempt: Long,
    ) -> Boolean,
): Flow<T> = flow {
    var attempt = 0L
    do {
        val shallRetry = try {
            collect { emit(it) }
            false
        } catch (e: Throwable) {
            predicate(e, attempt++)
                .also { if (!it) throw e }
        }
    } while (shallRetry)
}
```

As you can see, retryWhen has a predicate which is checked whenever an exception occurs from the previous steps of the flow. This predicate decides if an exception should be ignored and previous steps started again, or if it should continue closing this flow. This is a universal retry function. In most cases, we want to specify that we want to retry a specific number of times and/or only when a certain class of exceptions occurs (like a network connection exception). For that, there is another function called retry, which uses retryWhen under the hood.

```kotlin
// Actual implementation of retry
fun <T> Flow<T>.retry(
    retries: Long = Long.MAX_VALUE,
    predicate: suspend (cause: Throwable) -> Boolean = {true}
): Flow<T> {
    require(retries > 0) {
        "Expected positive amount of retries, but had $retries"
    }
    return retryWhen { cause, attempt ->
        attempt < retries && predicate(cause)
```

```
    }
}
```

This is how `retry` works:

```
suspend fun main() {
    flow {
        emit(1)
        emit(2)
        error("E")
        emit(3)
    }.retry(3) {
        print(it.message)
        true
    }.collect { print(it) } // 12E12E12E12(exception thrown)
}
```

Let's see a few popular usages of these functions. I often see retries that always retry. For them, a popular reason to define a predicate is to specify some logging and introduce some delay between new connection attempts.

```
fun makeConnection(config: ConnectionConfig) = api
    .startConnection(config)
    .retry { e ->
        delay(1000)
        log.error(e) { "Error for $config" }
        true
    }
```

There is another popular practice which involves gradually increasing the delay between subsequent connection attempts. We can also implement a predicate that retries if an exception is or isn't of a certain type.

```
fun makeConnection(config: ConnectionConfig) = api
    .startConnection(config)
    .retryWhen { e, attempt ->
        delay(100 * attempt)
        log.error(e) { "Error for $config" }
        e is ApiException && e.code !in 400..499
    }
```

Distinct functions

```
// Simplified distinctUntilChanged implementation
fun <T> Flow<T>.distinctUntilChanged(): Flow<T> = flow {
    var previous: Any? = NOT_SET
    collect {
        if (previous == NOT_SET || previous != it) {
            emit(it)
            previous = it
        }
    }
}


private val NOT_SET = Any()
```

Another function I find very useful is distinctUntilChanged, which helps us eliminate repeating elements that are considered identical. Note that this function only eliminates elements that are identical to the corresponding **previous element.**

```
suspend fun main() {
    flowOf(1, 2, 2, 3, 2, 1, 1, 3)
        .distinctUntilChanged()
        .collect { print(it) } // 123213
}
```

There are also variants of this function. The first one, distinctUntilChangedBy, specifies a key selector to be compared in order to check if two elements are equal. The second one, distinctUntilChanged with a lambda expression, specifies how two elements should be compared (instead of equals, which is used by default).

```kotlin
data class User(val id: Int, val name: String) {
    override fun toString(): String = "[$id] $name"
}

suspend fun main() {
    val users = flowOf(
        User(1, "Alex"),
        User(1, "Bob"),
        User(2, "Bob"),
        User(2, "Celine")
    )

    println(users.distinctUntilChangedBy { it.id }.toList())
    // [[1] Alex, [2] Bob]
    println(users.distinctUntilChangedBy{ it.name }.toList())
    // [[1] Alex, [1] Bob, [2] Celine]
    println(users.distinctUntilChanged { prev, next ->
        prev.id == next.id || prev.name == next.name
    }.toList()) // [[1] Alex, [2] Bob]
    // [2] Bob was emitted,
    // because we compare to the previous emitted
}
```

Terminal operations

Finally, we have operations that end flow processing. These are
called terminal operations. Until now, we have only used collect,
but there are also others that are similar to those offered by collections and Sequence: count (counts the number of elements in the
flow), first and firstOrNull (to get the first element emitted by
the flow), fold and reduce (to accumulate elements into an object).
Terminal operations are suspended and they return the value once
the flow is complete (or they complete the flow themselves).

```
suspend fun main() {
    val flow = flowOf(1, 2, 3, 4) // [1, 2, 3, 4]
        .map { it * it } // [1, 4, 9, 16]

    println(flow.first()) // 1
    println(flow.count()) // 4

    println(flow.reduce { acc, value -> acc * value }) // 576
    println(flow.fold(0) { acc, value -> acc + value }) // 30
}
```

There are currently not many more terminal operations for flow, but if you need something different you can always implement it yourself. This is, for instance, how you can implement sum for a flow of Int:

```
suspend fun Flow<Int>.sum(): Int {
    var sum = 0
    collect { value ->
        sum += value
    }
    return sum
}
```

Similarly, you can implement nearly any terminal operation with just the collect method.

Summary

There are many tools that support Flow processing. It is good to have some idea about them because they are useful in both backend and Android development. Also, if you need some different functions, they can be implemented quite easily thanks to the collect method and the flow builder.

SharedFlow and StateFlow

Flow is typically cold, so its values are calculated on demand. However, there are cases in which we want multiple receivers to be subscribed to one source of changes. This is where we use Shared-Flow, which is conceptually similar to a mailing list. We also have StateFlow, which is similar to an observable value. Let's explain them both step by step.

SharedFlow

Let's start with `MutableSharedFlow`, which is like a broadcast channel: everyone can send (emit) messages which will be received by every coroutine that is listening (collecting).

```
suspend fun main(): Unit = coroutineScope {
    val mutableSharedFlow =
        MutableSharedFlow<String>(replay = 0)
    // or MutableSharedFlow<String>()

    launch {
        mutableSharedFlow.collect {
            println("#1 received $it")
        }
    }
    launch {
        mutableSharedFlow.collect {
            println("#2 received $it")
        }
    }

    delay(1000)
    mutableSharedFlow.emit("Message1")
    mutableSharedFlow.emit("Message2")
}
// (1 sec)
// #1 received Message1
// #2 received Message1
// #1 received Message2
```

```
// #2 received Message2
// (program never ends)
```

The above program never ends because the
coroutineScope is waiting for the coroutines that
were started with launch and which keep listening on
MutableSharedFlow. Apparently, MutableSharedFlow is
not closable, so the only way to fix this problem is to
cancel the whole scope.

MutableSharedFlow can also keep sending messages. If we set the
replay parameter (it defaults to 0), the defined number of last values
will be kept. If a coroutine now starts observing, it will receive these
values first. This cache can also be reset with resetReplayCache.

```
suspend fun main(): Unit = coroutineScope {
    val mutableSharedFlow = MutableSharedFlow<String>(
        replay = 2,
    )
    mutableSharedFlow.emit("Message1")
    mutableSharedFlow.emit("Message2")
    mutableSharedFlow.emit("Message3")

    println(mutableSharedFlow.replayCache)
    // [Message2, Message3]

    launch {
        mutableSharedFlow.collect {
            println("#1 received $it")
        }
        // #1 received Message2
        // #1 received Message3
    }

    delay(100)
    mutableSharedFlow.resetReplayCache()
    println(mutableSharedFlow.replayCache) // []
}
```

MutableSharedFlow is conceptually similar to RxJava
Subjects. When the replay parameter is set to 0, it

is similar to a PublishSubject. When replay is 1,
it is similar to a BehaviorSubject. When replay is
Int.MAX_VALUE, it is similar to ReplaySubject.

In Kotlin, we like to have a distinction between interfaces
that are used to only listen and those that are used to modify.
For instance, we've already seen the distinction between
SendChannel, ReceiveChannel and just Channel. The same rule
applies here. MutableSharedFlow inherits from both SharedFlow
and FlowCollector. The former inherits from Flow and is used to
observe, while FlowCollector is used to emit values.

```kotlin
interface MutableSharedFlow<T> :
    SharedFlow<T>, FlowCollector<T> {

    fun tryEmit(value: T): Boolean
    val subscriptionCount: StateFlow<Int>
    fun resetReplayCache()
}

interface SharedFlow<out T> : Flow<T> {
    val replayCache: List<T>
}

interface FlowCollector<in T> {
    suspend fun emit(value: T)
}
```

These interfaces are often used to expose only functions, to emit, or
only to collect.

```kotlin
suspend fun main(): Unit = coroutineScope {
    val mutableSharedFlow = MutableSharedFlow<String>()
    val sharedFlow: SharedFlow<String> = mutableSharedFlow
    val collector: FlowCollector<String> = mutableSharedFlow

    launch {
        mutableSharedFlow.collect {
            println("#1 received $it")
```

```
        }
    }
    launch {
        sharedFlow.collect {
            println("#2 received $it")
        }
    }

    delay(1000)
    mutableSharedFlow.emit("Message1")
    collector.emit("Message2")
}
// (1 sec)
// #1 received Message1
// #2 received Message1
// #1 received Message2
// #2 received Message2
```

Here is an example of typical usage on Android:

```
class UserProfileViewModel {
    private val _userChanges =
        MutableSharedFlow<UserChange>()
    val userChanges: SharedFlow<UserChange> = _userChanges

    fun onCreate() {
        viewModelScope.launch {
            userChanges.collect(::applyUserChange)
        }
    }

    fun onNameChanged(newName: String) {
        // ...
        _userChanges.emit(NameChange(newName))
    }

    fun onPublicKeyChanged(newPublicKey: String) {
        // ...
        _userChanges.emit(PublicKeyChange(newPublicKey))
```

```
        }
}
```

shareIn

Flow is often used to observe changes, like user actions, database
modifications, or new messages. We already know the different ways
in which these events can be processed and handled. We've learned
how to merge multiple flows into one. But what if multiple classes
are interested in these changes and we would like to turn one flow
into multiple flows? The solution is SharedFlow, and the easiest way
to turn a Flow into a SharedFlow is by using the shareIn function.

```kotlin
suspend fun main(): Unit = coroutineScope {
    val flow = flowOf("A", "B", "C")
        .onEach { delay(1000) }

    val sharedFlow: SharedFlow<String> = flow.shareIn(
        scope = this,
        started = SharingStarted.Eagerly,
        // replay = 0 (default)
    )

    delay(500)

    launch {
        sharedFlow.collect { println("#1 $it") }
    }

    delay(1000)

    launch {
        sharedFlow.collect { println("#2 $it") }
    }

    delay(1000)

    launch {
        sharedFlow.collect { println("#3 $it") }
```

```
    }
}
// (1 sec)
// #1 A
// (1 sec)
// #1 B
// #2 B
// (1 sec)
// #1 C
// #2 C
// #3 C
```

The shareIn function creates a SharedFlow and sends elements from its Flow. Since we need to start a coroutine to collect elements on flow, shareIn expects a coroutine scope as the first argument. The third argument is replay, which is 0 by default. The second argument is interesting: started determines when listening for values should start, depending on the number of listeners. The following options are supported:

- SharingStarted.Eagerly - immediately starts listening for values and sending them to a flow. Notice that if you have a limited replay value and your values appear before you start subscribing, you might lose some values (if your replay is 0, you will lose all such values).

```
suspend fun main(): Unit = coroutineScope {
    val flow = flowOf("A", "B", "C")

    val sharedFlow: SharedFlow<String> = flow.shareIn(
        scope = this,
        started = SharingStarted.Eagerly,
    )

    delay(100)
    launch {
        sharedFlow.collect { println("#1 $it") }
    }
    print("Done")
```

```
}
// (0.1 sec)
// Done
```

- `SharingStarted.Lazily` - starts listening when the first sub-scriber appears. This guarantees that this first subscriber gets all the emitted values, while subsequent subscribers are only guaranteed to get the most recent replay values. The upstream flow continues to be active even when all subscribers disappear, but only the most recent replay values are cached without subscribers.

```
suspend fun main(): Unit = coroutineScope {
    val flow1 = flowOf("A", "B", "C")
    val flow2 = flowOf("D")
        .onEach { delay(1000) }

    val sharedFlow = merge(flow1, flow2).shareIn(
        scope = this,
        started = SharingStarted.Lazily,
    )

    delay(100)
    launch {
        sharedFlow.collect { println("#1 $it") }
    }
    delay(1000)
    launch {
        sharedFlow.collect { println("#2 $it") }
    }
}
// (0.1 sec)
// #1 A
// #1 B
// #1 C
// (1 sec)
// #2 D
// #1 D
```

- WhileSubscribed() - starts listening on the flow when the first subscriber appears; it stops when the last subscriber disappears. If a new subscriber appears when our SharedFlow is stopped, it will start again. WhileSubscribed has additional optional configuration parameters: stopTimeoutMillis (how long to listen after the last subscriber disappears, 0 by default) and replayExpirationMillis (how long to keep replay after stopping, Long.MAX_VALUE by default).

```
suspend fun main(): Unit = coroutineScope {
    val flow = flowOf("A", "B", "C", "D")
        .onStart { println("Started") }
        .onCompletion { println("Finished") }
        .onEach { delay(1000) }

    val sharedFlow = flow.shareIn(
        scope = this,
        started = SharingStarted.WhileSubscribed(),
    )

    delay(3000)
    launch {
        println("#1 ${sharedFlow.first()}")
    }
    launch {
        println("#2 ${sharedFlow.take(2).toList()}")
    }
    delay(3000)
    launch {
        println("#3 ${sharedFlow.first()}")
    }
}
// (3 sec)
// Started
// (1 sec)
// #1 A
// (1 sec)
// #2 [A, B]
// Finished
```

```
// (1 sec)
// Started
// (1 sec)
// #3 A
// Finished
```

- It is also possible to define a custom strategy by implementing the SharingStarted interface.

Using shareIn is very convenient when multiple services are interested in the same changes. Let's say that you need to observe how stored locations change over time. This is how a DTO (Data Transfer Object) could be implemented on Android using the Room library:

```
@Dao
interface LocationDao {
    @Insert(onConflict = OnConflictStrategy.IGNORE)
    suspend fun insertLocation(location: Location)

    @Query("DELETE FROM location_table")
    suspend fun deleteLocations()

    @Query("SELECT * FROM location_table ORDER BY time")
    fun observeLocations(): Flow<List<Location>>
}
```

The problem is that if multiple services need to depend on these locations, then it would not be optimal for each of them to observe the database separately. Instead, we could make a service that listens to these changes and shares them into SharedFlow. This is where we will use shareIn. But how should we configure it? You need to decide for yourself. Do you want your subscribers to immediately receive the last list of locations? If so, set replay to 1. If you only want to react to change, set it to 0. How about started? WhileSubscribed() sounds best for this use case.

```
class LocationService(
    locationDao: LocationDao,
    scope: CoroutineScope
) {
    private val locations = locationDao.observeLocations()
        .shareIn(
            scope = scope,
            started = SharingStarted.WhileSubscribed(),
        )

    fun observeLocations(): Flow<List<Location>> = locations
}
```

> Beware! Do not create a new SharedFlow for each call.
> Create one, and store it in a property.

StateFlow

StateFlow is an extension of the SharedFlow concept. It works similarly to SharedFlow when the `replay` parameter is set to 1. It always stores one value, which can be accessed using the `value` property.

```
interface StateFlow<out T> : SharedFlow<T> {
    val value: T
}

interface MutableStateFlow<T> :
    StateFlow<T>, MutableSharedFlow<T> {

    override var value: T

    fun compareAndSet(expect: T, update: T): Boolean
}
```

> Please note how the `value` property is overridden inside
> `MutableStateFlow`. In Kotlin, an `open` `val` property can
> be overridden with a `var` property. `val` only allows get-
> ting a value (getter), while `var` also supports setting a new
> value (setter).

The initial value needs to be passed to the constructor. We both access and set the value using the `value` property. As you can see, `MutableStateFlow` is like an observable holder for a value.

```
suspend fun main() = coroutineScope {
    val state = MutableStateFlow("A")
    println(state.value) // A
    launch {
        state.collect { println("Value changed to $it") }
        // Value changed to A
    }

    delay(1000)
    state.value = "B" // Value changed to B

    delay(1000)
    launch {
        state.collect { println("and now it is $it") }
        // and now it is B
    }

    delay(1000)
    state.value = "C" // Value changed to C and now it is C
}
```

On Android, StateFlow is used as a modern alternative to LiveData. First, it has full support for coroutines. Second, it has an initial value, so it does not need to be nullable. So, StateFlow is often used on ViewModels to represent its state. This state is observed, and a view is displayed and updated on this basis.

```
class LatestNewsViewModel(
    private val newsRepository: NewsRepository
) : ViewModel() {
    private val _uiState =
        MutableStateFlow<NewsState>(LoadingNews)
    val uiState: StateFlow<NewsState> = _uiState

    fun onCreate() {
```

```
    scope.launch {
        _uiState.value =
            NewsLoaded(newsRepository.getNews())
    }
  }
}
```

Beware that StateFlow is conflated, so slower observers might not receive some intermediate state changes. To receive all events, use SharedFlow.

```
suspend fun main(): Unit = coroutineScope {
    val state = MutableStateFlow('X')

    launch {
        for (c in 'A'..'E') {
            delay(300)
            state.value = c
            // or state.emit(c)
        }
    }

    state.collect {
        delay(1000)
        println(it)
    }
}
// X
// C
// E
```

This behavior is by design. StateFlow represents the current state, and we might assume that nobody is interested in an outdated state.

stateIn

stateIn is a function that transforms Flow<T> into StateFlow<T>. It can only be called with a scope, but it is a suspending function. Remember that StateFlow needs to always have a value; so, if you don't specify it, then you need to wait until the first value is calculated.

```
suspend fun main() = coroutineScope {
    val flow = flowOf("A", "B", "C")
        .onEach { delay(1000) }
        .onEach { println("Produced $it") }
    val stateFlow: StateFlow<String> = flow.stateIn(this)

    println("Listening")
    println(stateFlow.value)
    stateFlow.collect { println("Received $it") }
}
// (1 sec)
// Produced A
// Listening
// A
// Received A
// (1 sec)
// Produced B
// Received B
// (1 sec)
// Produced C
// Received C
```

The second variant of stateIn is not suspending but it requires an initial value and a started mode. This mode has the same options as shareIn (as previously explained).

```
suspend fun main() = coroutineScope {
    val flow = flowOf("A", "B")
        .onEach { delay(1000) }
        .onEach { println("Produced $it") }

    val stateFlow: StateFlow<String> = flow.stateIn(
        scope = this,
        started = SharingStarted.Lazily,
        initialValue = "Empty"
    )

    println(stateFlow.value)
```

```
    delay(2000)
    stateFlow.collect { println("Received $it") }
}
// Empty
// (2 sec)
// Received Empty
// (1 sec)
// Produced A
// Received A
// (1 sec)
// Produced B
// Received B
```

We typically use stateIn when we want to observe a value from one source of changes. On the way, these changes can be processed, and in the end they can be observed by our views.

```
class LocationsViewModel(
    locationService: LocationService
) : ViewModel() {

    private val location = locationService.observeLocations()
        .map { it.toLocationsDisplay() }
        .stateIn(
            scope = viewModelScope,
            started = SharingStarted.Lazily,
            initialValue = LocationsDisplay.Loading,
        )

    // ...
}
```

Summary

In this chapter, we've learned about SharedFlow and StateFlow, both of which are especially important for Android developers as they are commonly used as a part of the MVVM pattern. Remember them and consider using them, especially if you use view models in Android development.

Testing flow

You should already have all the knowledge you need to properly test functions that return a flow. The rules for testing suspending functions are quite simple, but to ignite your imagination let's see a couple of examples of the most typical use cases, and the most important problems we need to deal with when testing flows.

Transformation functions

Most of the functions that return Flow call other functions that return Flow. This is the most common and simplest case, so we'll start from learning how to test such functions. Consider the following class:

```
class ObserveAppointmentsService(
    private val appointmentRepository: AppointmentRepository
) {
    fun observeAppointments(): Flow<List<Appointment>> =
        appointmentRepository
            .observeAppointments()
            .filterIsInstance<AppointmentsUpdate>()
            .map { it.appointments }
            .distinctUntilChanged()
            .retry {
                it is ApiException && it.code in 500..599
            }
}
```

The observeAppointments method decorates observeAppointments from AppointmentRepository with a couple of operations, including element filtering, mapping, elimination of repeating elements, and retrying in the case of certain kinds of exceptions. If you asked me to explain what this function does but with a separate sentence for each functionality, you would have a list of the unit tests this function should have:

- should keep only appointments from updates,
- should eliminate elements that are identical to the previous element,

- should retry if there is an API exception with the code 5XX.

To implement these tests, we need to fake or mock AppointmentRepository. For these tests, we could make a fake object whose observeAppointments function returns a constant Flow that will be used as a source. The simplest way to test a function like observeAppointments is by defining its source flow using flowOf, which creates a finite Flow in which time does not play a role. If time does not play a role in the function being tested, we can just transform its result into a list using the toList function, then compare it with the expected result in the assertions.

```kotlin
class FakeAppointmentRepository(
    private val flow: Flow<AppointmentsEvent>
) : AppointmentRepository {
    override fun observeAppointments() = flow
}


class ObserveAppointmentsServiceTest {
    val aDate1 = Instant.parse("2020-08-30T18:43:00Z")
    val anAppointment1 = Appointment("APP1", aDate1)
    val aDate2 = Instant.parse("2020-08-31T18:43:00Z")
    val anAppointment2 = Appointment("APP2", aDate2)

    @Test
    fun `should keep only appointments from...`() = runTest {
        // given
        val repo = FakeAppointmentRepository(
            flowOf(
                AppointmentsConfirmed,
                AppointmentsUpdate(listOf(anAppointment1)),
                AppointmentsUpdate(listOf(anAppointment2)),
                AppointmentsConfirmed,
            )
        )
        val service = ObserveAppointmentsService(repo)

        // when
        val result = service.observeAppointments().toList()
```

```
        // then
        assertEquals(
            listOf(
                listOf(anAppointment1),
                listOf(anAppointment2),
            ),
            result
        )
    }

    // ...
}
```

The second test could be implemented the same way, but I would like to introduce one more element that will make our test a bit more complicated and help us test what we haven't yet tested. The problem with tests like the one above is that they treat a flow just like a list; such an approach simplifies these tests, but they don't verify if elements are actually immediately transferred without any delays. Imagine that a developer added a delay to your flow transformation, as in the following code snippet. Such a change would not be detected by the above test.

```
class ObserveAppointmentsService(
    private val appointmentRepository: AppointmentRepository
) {
    fun observeAppointments(): Flow<List<Appointment>> =
        appointmentRepository
            .observeAppointments()
            .onEach { delay(1000) } // Will not influence
            // the above test
            .filterIsInstance<AppointmentsUpdate>()
            .map { it.appointments }
            .distinctUntilChanged()
            .retry {
                it is ApiException && it.code in 500..599
            }
}
```

Let's consider an even more extreme example where someone uses a list transformation instead of a flow transformation. This would be absolute nonsense, yet tests like the previous one would still pass.

```kotlin
class ObserveAppointmentsService(
    private val appointmentRepository: AppointmentRepository,
) {
    // Don't do that!
    fun observeAppointments(): Flow<List<Appointment>> =
        flow {
            val list = appointmentRepository
                .observeAppointments()
                .filterIsInstance<AppointmentsUpdate>()
                .map { it.appointments }
                .distinctUntilChanged()
                .retry {
                    it is ApiException && it.code in 500..599
                }
                .toList()
            emitAll(list)
        }
}
```

I like to have a test that verifies time dependencies, and for that, we need to use `runTest` and some `delay` in our source flow. The result flow needs to store information about when its elements were emitted, and we can verify the result in an assertion.

```kotlin
class ObserveAppointmentsServiceTest {
    // ...

    @Test
    fun `should eliminate elements that are...`() = runTest {
        // given
        val repo = FakeAppointmentRepository(flow {
            delay(1000)
            emit(AppointmentsUpdate(listOf(anAppointment1)))
            emit(AppointmentsUpdate(listOf(anAppointment1)))
            delay(1000)
            emit(AppointmentsUpdate(listOf(anAppointment2)))
```

```
            delay(1000)
            emit(AppointmentsUpdate(listOf(anAppointment2)))
            emit(AppointmentsUpdate(listOf(anAppointment1)))
        })
        val service = ObserveAppointmentsService(repo)

        // when
        val result = service.observeAppointments()
            .map { currentTime to it }
            .toList()

        // then
        assertEquals(
            listOf(
                1000L to listOf(anAppointment1),
                2000L to listOf(anAppointment2),
                3000L to listOf(anAppointment1),
            ), result
        )
    }


    // ...
}
```

Test name shortened due to limited page size - would not
be shortened in a real project.

Finally, consider the third functionality: "should retry when there
is an API exception with the code 5XX". If we returned a flow that
should not retry, we wouldn't test the retry behavior. If we returned
a flow that should retry, the function being tested would retry in-
finitely and would produce an infinite flow. The easiest way to test
an infinite flow is by limiting the number of its elements using take.

```
class ObserveAppointmentsServiceTest {
    // ...

    @Test
    fun `should retry when API exception...`() = runTest {
        // given
        val repo = FakeAppointmentRepository(flow {
            emit(AppointmentsUpdate(listOf(anAppointment1)))
            throw ApiException(502, "Some message")
        })
        val service = ObserveAppointmentsService(repo)

        // when
        val result = service.observeAppointments()
            .take(3)
            .toList()

        // then
        assertEquals(
            listOf(
                listOf(anAppointment1),
                listOf(anAppointment1),
                listOf(anAppointment1),
            ), result
        )
    }
}
```

We should also test "should not retry upon a non-API
exception" and "should not retry upon an API exception
with a non-5XX code", but I will skip these test cases in
this book.

Another option is to make a flow that first throws an exception that
should cause a retry, and then it throws one that should not. This
way, we can test not only a sample exception that should cause a
retry, but also one that should not.

```kotlin
class ObserveAppointmentsServiceTest {
    // ...

    @Test
    fun `should retry when API exception...`() = runTest {
        // given
        var retried = false
        val someException = object : Exception() {}
        val repo = FakeAppointmentRepository(flow {
            emit(AppointmentsUpdate(listOf(anAppointment1)))
            if (!retried) {
                retried = true
                throw ApiException(502, "Some message")
            } else {
                throw someException
            }
        })
        val service = ObserveAppointmentsService(repo)

        // when
        val result = service.observeAppointments()
            .catch<Any> { emit(it) }
            .toList()

        // then
        assertTrue(retried)
        assertEquals(
            listOf(
                listOf(anAppointment1),
                listOf(anAppointment1),
                someException,
            ), result
        )
    }
}
```

Testing infinite flows

Testing classes that use StateFlow or SharedFlow is a bit more complicated. First, they need a scope; if we define our test using runTest, this scope should be backgroundScope, not this, so our test does not await this scope's completion. Second, these flows are infinite, so they don't complete unless their scope is cancelled. There are a couple of ways to test infinite flows, which I will present by means of an example.

Consider the following service that can be used to observe messages from a specific user. This class also uses SharedFlow so no more than one connection to the source of messages is made, even if there are multiple observers. This means that observeMessages returns a flow that will never complete unless scope is cancelled.

```
class MessagesService(
    messagesSource: Flow<Message>,
    scope: CoroutineScope
) {
    private val source = messagesSource
        .shareIn(
            scope = scope,
            started = SharingStarted.WhileSubscribed()
        )

    fun observeMessages(fromUserId: String) = source
        .filter { it.fromUserId == fromUserId }
}
```

To better understand the problem, consider the following **failing** test:

```kotlin
class MessagesServiceTest {
    // Failing test!
    @Test
    fun `should emit messages from user`() = runTest {
        // given
        val source = flowOf(
            Message(fromUserId = "0", text = "A"),
            Message(fromUserId = "1", text = "B"),
            Message(fromUserId = "0", text = "C"),
        )
        val service = MessagesService(
            messagesSource = source,
            scope = backgroundScope,
        )

        // when
        val result = service.observeMessages("0")
            .toList() // Here we'll wait forever!

        // then
        assertEquals(
            listOf(
                Message(fromUserId = "0", text = "A"),
                Message(fromUserId = "0", text = "C"),
            ), result
        )
    }
}
```

The test above is suspended forever by `toList`. The simplest (and, sadly, most popular) solution to this problem uses `take` with a specific number of expected elements. The test below passes, but it loses a lot of information. Consider a message that should not have been emitted by `observeMessages` yet was, albeit in the next position. This situation would not be recognized by a unit test. A bigger problem is when someone makes a change in the code that makes it run forever. Finding the reason behind this is much harder than it would be if our test were implemented as in the following examples.

```kotlin
class MessagesServiceTest {
    @Test
    fun `should emit messages from user`() = runTest {
        // given
        val source = flowOf(
            Message(fromUserId = "0", text = "A"),
            Message(fromUserId = "1", text = "B"),
            Message(fromUserId = "0", text = "C"),
        )
        val service = MessagesService(
            messagesSource = source,
            scope = backgroundScope,
        )

        // when
        val result = service.observeMessages("0")
            .take(2)
            .toList()

        // then
        assertEquals(
            listOf(
                Message(fromUserId = "0", text = "A"),
                Message(fromUserId = "0", text = "C"),
            ), result
        )
    }
}
```

The next approach is to start our flow in `backgroundScope` and store all the elements it emits in a collection. This approach not only better shows us "what is" and "what should be" in failing cases; it also offers us much more flexibility with testing time. In the example below, I've added some delays to verify when messages are sent.

```kotlin
class MessagesServiceTest {
    @Test
    fun `should emit messages from user`() = runTest {
        // given
        val source = flow {
            emit(Message(fromUserId = "0", text = "A"))
            delay(1000)
            emit(Message(fromUserId = "1", text = "B"))
            emit(Message(fromUserId = "0", text = "C"))
        }
        val service = MessagesService(
            messagesSource = source,
            scope = backgroundScope,
        )

        // when
        val emittedMessages = mutableListOf<Message>()
        service.observeMessages("0")
            .onEach { emittedMessages.add(it) }
            .launchIn(backgroundScope)
        delay(1)

        // then
        assertEquals(
            listOf(
                Message(fromUserId = "0", text = "A"),
            ), emittedMessages
        )

        // when
        delay(1000)

        // then
        assertEquals(
            listOf(
                Message(fromUserId = "0", text = "A"),
                Message(fromUserId = "0", text = "C"),
            ), emittedMessages
        )
```

```
    }
}
```

A good alternative is the `toList` function, which is only observed for some duration. It offers less flexibility, but I like using it as it is simple and readable. This is how I implement and use such a function:

```kotlin
suspend fun <T> Flow<T>.toListDuring(
    duration: Duration
): List<T> = coroutineScope {
    val result = mutableListOf<T>()
    val job = launch {
        this@toListDuring.collect(result::add)
    }
    delay(duration)
    job.cancel()
    return@coroutineScope result
}

class MessagesServiceTest {
    @Test
    fun `should emit messages from user`() = runTest {
        // given
        val source = flow {
            emit(Message(fromUserId = "0", text = "A"))
            emit(Message(fromUserId = "1", text = "B"))
            emit(Message(fromUserId = "0", text = "C"))
        }
        val service = MessagesService(
            messagesSource = source,
            scope = backgroundScope,
        )

        // when
        val emittedMessages = service.observeMessages("0")
            .toListDuring(1.milliseconds)

        // then
        assertEquals(
```

```
        listOf(
            Message(fromUserId = "0", text = "A"),
            Message(fromUserId = "0", text = "C"),
        ), emittedMessages
    )
  }
}
```

It is also worth mentioning that there are libraries, like Turbine, that offer tools to simplify testing flows, that allow collecting by an object, and that can be used to wait for elements.

```
class MessagesServiceTest {
    @Test
    fun `should emit messages from user`() = runTest {
        // given
        val source = flow {
            emit(Message(fromUserId = "0", text = "A"))
            emit(Message(fromUserId = "1", text = "B"))
            emit(Message(fromUserId = "0", text = "C"))
        }
        val service = MessagesService(
            messagesSource = source,
            scope = backgroundScope,
        )

        // when
        val messagesTurbine = service.observeMessages("0")
            .testIn(backgroundScope)

        // then
        assertEquals(
            Message(fromUserId = "0", text = "A"),
            messagesTurbine.awaitItem()
        )
        assertEquals(
            Message(fromUserId = "0", text = "C"),
            messagesTurbine.awaitItem()
        )
```

```
        messagesTurbine.expectNoEvents()
    }
}
```

Turbine seems quite popular for testing flows, but I'm not a big fan of using third-party libraries when they're not really needed.

Determining how many connections were opened

One of the most important functionalities of `MessagesService` is that it should start only one connection to the source, no matter how many active observers we have.

```
// Starts at most one connection to the source
class MessagesService(
    messagesSource: Flow<Message>,
    scope: CoroutineScope
) {
    private val source = messagesSource
        .shareIn(
            scope = scope,
            started = SharingStarted.WhileSubscribed()
        )

    fun observeMessages(fromUserId: String) = source
        .filter { it.fromUserId == fromUserId }
}

// Can start multiple connections to the source
class MessagesService(
    messagesSource: Flow<Message>,
) {
    fun observeMessages(fromUserId: String) = messagesSource
        .filter { it.fromUserId == fromUserId }
}
```

The simplest way to test this behavior is by making a flow that counts how many subscribers it has. This can be done by incrementing a counter in `onStart` and decrementing it in `onCompletion`.

```kotlin
private val infiniteFlow =
    flow<Nothing> {
        while (true) {
            delay(100)
        }
    }

class MessagesServiceTest {
    // ...

    @Test
    fun `should start at most one connection`() = runTest {
        // given
        var connectionsCounter = 0
        val source = infiniteFlow
            .onStart { connectionsCounter++ }
            .onCompletion { connectionsCounter-- }
        val service = MessagesService(
            messagesSource = source,
            scope = backgroundScope,
        )

        // when
        service.observeMessages("0")
            .launchIn(backgroundScope)
        service.observeMessages("1")
            .launchIn(backgroundScope)
        service.observeMessages("0")
            .launchIn(backgroundScope)
        service.observeMessages("2")
            .launchIn(backgroundScope)
        delay(1000)

        // then
        assertEquals(1, connectionsCounter)
    }
}
```

Testing view models

Flow builder lets us describe how elements should be emitted from
the source, which is a simple and powerful method. However, there
is also another option: using SharedFlow as a source and emitting
elements in the test. I find this option especially useful for testing
view models.

```kotlin
class ChatViewModel(
    private val messagesService: MessagesService,
) : ViewModel() {
    private val _lastMessage =
        MutableStateFlow<String?>(null)
    val lastMessage: StateFlow<String?> = _lastMessage

    private val _messages =
        MutableStateFlow(emptyList<String>())
    val messages: StateFlow<List<String>> = _messages

    fun start(fromUserId: String) {
        messagesService.observeMessages(fromUserId)
            .onEach {
                val text = it.text
                _lastMessage.value = text
                _messages.value = _messages.value + text
            }
            .launchIn(viewModelScope)
    }
}

class ChatViewModelTest {
    @Test
    fun `should expose messages from user`() = runTest {
        // given
        val source = MutableSharedFlow<Message>()

        // when
        val viewModel = ChatViewModel(
            messagesService = FakeMessagesService(source)
```

```
    )
    viewModel.start("0")

    // then
    assertEquals(null, viewModel.lastMessage.value)
    assertEquals(emptyList(), viewModel.messages.value)

    // when
    source.emit(Message(fromUserId = "0", text = "ABC"))

    // then
    assertEquals("ABC", viewModel.lastMessage.value)
    assertEquals(listOf("ABC"), viewModel.messages.value)

    // when
    source.emit(Message(fromUserId = "0", text = "DEF"))
    source.emit(Message(fromUserId = "1", text = "GHI"))

    // then
    assertEquals("DEF", viewModel.lastMessage.value)
    assertEquals(
        listOf("ABC", "DEF"),
        viewModel.messages.value
    )
    }
}
```

This way, we can properly test our functions' behavior without depending on virtual time at all, and our unit test is simpler to read.

Summary

I hope this chapter has given you an overview of how we can test classes that use Flow. The logic, in general, is very similar to testing suspending functions, but Flow has its own specificities, and in this chapter,I'm I've shown different examples of how to deal with them.

Part 4: Kotlin Coroutines in practice

At this point, you have all the puzzles to use coroutines in real-life projects. The previous chapters cover all the elements, from using suspending functions to operating on flow. We've also seen some use cases and common mistakes. In this chapter, we will review them, and try to build a deeper understanding of how Kotlin Coroutines should be used in real-life projects, and how they should not be used. We will cover the most typical use cases and best practices. This chapter is built on top of the previous chapters, and it will often reference them. It should be your essential guideline and your summary.

Common use cases

Let's review the most common patterns that can be found in applications that are well implemented using Kotlin Coroutines. Most of these patterns are used on both the backend and Android.

Most modern applications can be divided into three layers:

- Data/Adapters Layer - The layer that is responsible for data storage or interaction with other systems. This layer mainly consists of repositories that can each contain one or more data sources. In this layer, our coroutines interact with other libraries, including some that might not support them.
- Domain Layer - The layer where our application business logic is implemented. It includes classes that encapsulate specific operations, like use cases, services, facades, etc. In this layer, coroutines are used to optimize our core processes.
- Presentation/API/UI layer - The layer that starts our application's processes. It might be considered an entry to our application. In this layer, we start coroutines and handle their execution results.

Each of those layers has different coroutine use cases. In the next sections of this chapter, I will describe the typical use cases for each of these layers.

Data/Adapters Layer

I will start by presenting typical Kotlin Coroutines use cases from the Data/Adapters Layer, which is where we implement repositories, providers, adapters, data sources, etc. This layer is relatively easy nowadays because many popular JVM libraries support Kotlin Coroutines either out of the box or with some additional dependencies.

As an example, we might use Retrofit, which is a popular library for network requests. It has out-of-the-box support for suspending functions. It is enough to add the `suspend` modifier to make its request definition functions suspending instead of blocking.

```
// Retrofit
class GithubApi {
    @GET("orgs/{organization}/repos?per_page=100")
    suspend fun getOrganizationRepos(
        @Path("organization") organization: String
    ): List<Repo>
}
```

Another good example is Room, which is a popular library for communication with SQLite databases on Android. It supports both the `suspend` modifier to make its functions suspending, as well as `Flow` for observing table states.

```
// Room
@Dao
interface LocationDao {
    @Insert
    suspend fun insertLocation(location: Location)

    @Query("DELETE FROM location_table")
    suspend fun deleteLocations()

    @Query("SELECT * FROM location_table ORDER BY time")
    fun observeLocations(): Flow<List<Location>>
}
```

Callback functions

If you need to use a library that does not support Kotlin Coroutines but instead forces you to use callback functions, turn them into suspending functions using the `suspendCancellableCoroutine`[68]. When a callback is called, the coroutine should be resumed using the `resume` method on `Continuation`. If this callback function is cancellable, it should be cancelled inside the `invokeOnCancellation` lambda expression[69].

---

[68]For details, see the *How does suspension work?* chapter, section *Resuming with a value.*

[69]For details, see the *Cancellation* chapter, section *invokeOnCompletion.*

```
suspend fun requestNews(): News {
    return suspendCancellableCoroutine<News> { cont ->
        val call = requestNewsApi { news ->
            cont.resume(news)
        }
        cont.invokeOnCancellation {
            call.cancel()
        }
    }
}
```

Callback functions that allow us to set separate functions for success
and failure can be implemented in a few different ways. We could
wrap over callback functions and return Result, and either resume
our coroutine with Result.success or with Result.failure.

```
suspend fun requestNews(): Result<News> {
    return suspendCancellableCoroutine<News> { cont ->
        val call = requestNewsApi(
            onSuccess = { news ->
                cont.resume(Result.success(news))
            },
            onError = { e ->
                cont.resume(Result.failure(e))
            }
        )
        cont.invokeOnCancellation {
            call.cancel()
        }
    }
}
```

Another option is to return a nullable value and either resume our
coroutine with the result data or with the null value.

```
suspend fun requestNews(): News? {
    return suspendCancellableCoroutine<News> { cont ->
        val call = requestNewsApi(
            onSuccess = { news -> cont.resume(news) },
            onError = { e -> cont.resume(null) }
        )
        cont.invokeOnCancellation {
            call.cancel()
        }
    }
}
```

The last popular option is to resume with a result in the case of callback function success or resume with an exception in case of failure. In the latter case, the exception is thrown from the suspension point[70].

```
suspend fun requestNews(): News {
    return suspendCancellableCoroutine<News> { cont ->
        val call = requestNewsApi(
            onSuccess = { news -> cont.resume(news) },
            onError = { e -> cont.resumeWithException(e) }
        )
        cont.invokeOnCancellation {
            call.cancel()
        }
    }
}
```

Blocking functions

Another common situation is when a library you use requires the use of blocking functions. You should never call blocking functions on regular suspending functions. In Kotlin Coroutines, we use threads with great precision, and blocking them is a big problem. If we block the thread from `Dispatchers.Main` on Android, our whole application freezes. If we block the thread from `Dispatchers.Default`, we

---

[70]For details, see the *How does suspension work?* chapter, section *Resume with an exception.*

can forget about efficient processor use. This is why we should never make a blocking call without first specifying the dispatcher[71].

When we need to make a blocking call, we should specify the dispatcher using `withContext`. In most cases, when we implement repositories in applications, it is enough to use `Dispatchers.IO`[72].

```kotlin
class DiscSaveRepository(
    private val discReader: DiscReader
) : SaveRepository {

    override suspend fun loadSave(name: String): SaveData =
        withContext(Dispatchers.IO) {
            discReader.read("save/$name")
        }
}
```

However, it's important to understand that `Dispatchers.IO` is limited to 64 threads, which might not be enough on the backend and Android. If every request needs to make a blocking call, and you have thousands of requests per second, the queue for these 64 threads might start growing quickly. In such a situation, you might consider using `limitedParallelism` on `Dispatchers.IO` to make a new dispatcher with an independent limit that is greater than 64 threads[73].

```kotlin
class LibraryGoogleAccountVerifier : GoogleAccountVerifier {
    private val dispatcher = Dispatchers.IO
        .limitedParallelism(100)

    private var verifier =
        GoogleIdTokenVerifier.Builder(..., ...)
    .setAudience(...)
    .build()

    override suspend fun getUserData(
```

---

[71]For details, see the *Dispatchers* chapter.

[72]For details, see the *Dispatchers* chapter, section *IO dispatcher*.

[73]For details, see the *Dispatchers* chapter, section *IO dispatcher with a custom pool of threads*.

```
        googleToken: String
    ): GoogleUserData? = withContext(dispatcher) {
        verifier.verify(googleToken)
            ?.payload
            ?.let {
                GoogleUserData(
                    email = it.email,
                    name = it.getString("given_name"),
                    surname = it.getString("family_name"),
                    imageUrl = it.getString("picture"),
                )
            }
    }
}
```

A dispatcher with a limit that is independent of `Dispatchers.IO` should be used whenever we suspect that our function might be called by so many coroutines that they might use a significant number of threads. In such cases, we do not want to block threads from `Dispatchers.IO` because we do not know which processes will wait until our process is finished.

When we implement a library, we often do not know how our functions will be used, and we should generally operate on dispatchers with independent pools of threads. What should be the limit of such dispatchers? You need to decide for yourself. If you make this a small number, coroutines might wait for one another. If you make it too big, you might use a lot of memory and CPU time on all these active threads.

```
class CertificateGenerator {
    private val dispatcher = Dispatchers.IO
        .limitedParallelism(5)

    suspend fun generate(data: CertificateData): UserData =
        withContext(dispatcher) {
            Runtime.getRuntime()
                .exec("generateCertificate " + data.toArgs())
        }
}
```

We should also ensure that all CPU-intensive processes run on
Dispatchers.Default, and all processes that modify the main view
run on Dispatchers.Main.immediate. For that, withContext might
also be useful.

```kotlin
suspend fun calculateModel() =
    withContext(Dispatchers.Default) {
        model.fit(
            dataset = newTrain,
            epochs = 10,
            batchSize = 100,
            verbose = false
        )
    }


suspend fun setUserName(name: String) =
    withContext(Dispatchers.Main.immediate) {
        userNameView.text = name
    }
```

Observing with Flow

Suspending functions are perfect for representing the process of
producing/fetching a single value; however, when we expect more
than one value, we should use Flow instead. We've seen one example
already: in the Room library, we use suspend functions to perform
a single database operation, and we use the Flow type to observe
changes in a table.

```kotlin
// Room
@Dao
interface LocationDao {
    @Insert(onConflict = OnConflictStrategy.IGNORE)
    suspend fun insertLocation(location: Location)

    @Query("DELETE FROM location_table")
    suspend fun deleteLocations()

    @Query("SELECT * FROM location_table ORDER BY time")
```

```
    fun observeLocations(): Flow<List<Location>>
}
```

We have a similar situation when we consider network calls. When we fetch a single value from an API, it is best to use a suspend function; however, when we set up a WebSocket and listen for messages, we should use `Flow` instead. To create such a flow (if the library we use does not support returning one), we should use `callbackFlow` (or `channelFlow`). Remember to end your builder with `awaitClose`[74].

```
fun listenMessages(): Flow<List<Message>> = callbackFlow {
    socket.on("NewMessage") { args ->
        trySendBlocking(args.toMessage())
    }
    awaitClose()
}
```

A popular use for `Flow` is observing UI events, like button clicks or text changes.

```
fun EditText.listenTextChange(): Flow<String> = callbackFlow {
    val watcher = doAfterTextChanged {
        trySendBlocking(it.toString())
    }
    awaitClose { removeTextChangedListener(watcher) }
}
```

Flow can also be used for other callback functions, and it should be used when these callbacks might produce multiple values.

---

[74]For details, see the *Flow building* chapter, section *callbackFlow*.

```kotlin
fun flowFrom(api: CallbackBasedApi): Flow<T> = callbackFlow {
    val callback = object : Callback {
        override fun onNextValue(value: T) {
            trySendBlocking(value)
        }
        override fun onApiError(cause: Throwable) {
            cancel(CancellationException("API Error", cause))
        }
        override fun onCompleted() = channel.close()
    }
    api.register(callback)
    awaitClose { api.unregister(callback) }
}
```

If you need to use a specific dispatcher in a flow builder, use `flowOn` on the produced flow[75].

```kotlin
fun fibonacciFlow(): Flow<BigDecimal> = flow {
    var a = BigDecimal.ZERO
    var b = BigDecimal.ONE
    emit(a)
    emit(b)
    while (true) {
        val temp = a
        a = b
        b += temp
        emit(b)
    }
}.flowOn(Dispatchers.Default)

fun filesContentFlow(path: String): Flow<String> =
    channelFlow {
        File(path).takeIf { it.exists() }
            ?.listFiles()
            ?.forEach {
                send(it.readText())
```

---

[75]For details, see the *Flow lifecycle functions* chapter, section *flowOn*.

```
        }
    }.flowOn(Dispatchers.IO)
```

Domain Layer

Now, let's discuss common Kotlin Coroutines use cases in the domain layer. This is where the business logic is implemented, therefore it's where we define use cases, services, facades, etc. **In this layer, we should avoid operating on coroutine scope objects and exposing suspending functions. The layer below this (the presentation layer) is responsible for starting coroutines on scope objects; in the domain layer, we should use coroutine scope functions to start coroutines.**

In practice, in the domain layer, we mainly have suspend functions that call other suspending functions.

```
class NetworkUserRepository(
    private val api: UserApi,
) : UserRepository {
    override suspend fun getUser(): User =
        api.getUser().toDomainUser()
}

class NetworkNewsService(
    private val newsRepo: NewsRepository,
    private val settings: SettingsRepository,
) {
    suspend fun getNews(): List<News> = newsRepo
        .getNews()
        .map { it.toDomainNews() }

    suspend fun getNewsSummary(): List<News> {
        val type = settings.getNewsSummaryType()
        return newsRepo.getNewsSummary(type)
    }
}
```

Concurrent calls

When we want two processes to happen in parallel, we should wrap our function body with `coroutineScope` and use `async` builder inside it to start each process that should run asynchronously.

```
suspend fun produceCurrentUser(): User = coroutineScope {
    val profile = async { repo.getProfile() }
    val friends = async { repo.getFriends() }
    User(profile.await(), friends.await())
}
```

It is essential to understand that this modification should only make these two processes run in parallel. All the other mechanisms, like cancellation, exception handling, or context passing, should stay the same. So, if you consider the produceCurrentUserSeq and produceCurrentUserPar functions below, the only important difference is that the first one is sequential, while the second one starts two parallel processes[76].

```
suspend fun produceCurrentUserSeq(): User {
    val profile = repo.getProfile()
    val friends = repo.getFriends()
    return User(profile, friends)
}
```

```
suspend fun produceCurrentUserPar(): User = coroutineScope {
    val profile = async { repo.getProfile() }
    val friends = async { repo.getFriends() }
    User(profile.await(), friends.await())
}
```

When we want to start two asynchronous processes and then await their completion, we can do that by creating a new coroutine for each of them using the async function; however, the same result can also be achieved if we start only one process using async and run the second one on the same coroutine. The following implementation of produceCurrentUserPar will have practically the same behavior as the previous one. Which option should be preferred? I think that most developers will prefer the first one, arguing that using async for each process we want to execute in parallel makes our code more readable. On the other hand, some developers will prefer the second option, arguing that it is more efficient because it uses fewer

---

[76]For details, see the *Coroutine Scope Functions* chapter.

coroutines and creates fewer objects. It is up to you to choose which option you prefer.

```
suspend fun produceCurrentUserPar(): User = coroutineScope {
    val profile = async { repo.getProfile() }
    val friends = repo.getFriends()
    User(profile.await(), friends)
}
```

```
suspend fun getArticlesForUser(
    userToken: String?,
): List<ArticleJson> = coroutineScope {
    val articles = async { articleRepository.getArticles() }
    val user = userService.getUser(userToken)
    articles.await()
        .filter { canSeeOnList(user, it) }
        .map { toArticleJson(it) }
}
```

We can use async together with collection processing functions to start an asynchronous process for each list element. In such cases, it is good practice to await results using the awaitAll function.

```
suspend fun getOffers(
    categories: List<Category>
): List<Offer> = coroutineScope {
    categories
        .map { async { api.requestOffers(it) } }
        .awaitAll()
        .flatten()
}
```

If you want to limit the number of concurrent calls, you can use a rate limiter. For example, the resilience4j library offers rate limiters for suspending functions. You can also transform your list into Flow and then use flatMapMerge with the concurrency parameter, which specifies how many concurrent calls you will send[77].

---

[77]For details, see the *Flow processing* chapter, section flatMapConcat, flatMapMerge, *and* flatMapLatest.

```
fun getOffers(
    categories: List<Category>
): Flow<List<Offer>> = categories
    .asFlow()
    .flatMapMerge(concurrency = 20) {
        suspend { api.requestOffers(it) }.asFlow()
        // or flow { emit(api.requestOffers(it)) }
    }
```

When you use coroutineScope, remember that an exception in any child coroutine will break the coroutine created by coroutineScope, cancel all its other children, and then throw an exception. This is the behavior we typically expect, but in some cases it doesn't suit us very well. When we want to start a number of concurrent processes that are considered independent, we should instead use supervisorScope, which ignores exceptions in its children[78].

```
suspend fun notifyAnalytics(actions: List<UserAction>) =
    supervisorScope {
        actions.forEach { action ->
            launch {
                notifyAnalytics(action)
            }
        }
    }
```

When we want to limit the execution time of a process, we can use withTimeout or withTimeoutOrNull, both of which cancel their process if it takes longer than the time specified by the argument[79].

```
suspend fun getUserOrNull(): User? =
    withTimeoutOrNull(5000) {
        fetchUser()
    }
```

---

[78]For details, see the *Coroutine Scope Functions* chapter, section *supervisorScope*.

[79]For details, see the *Coroutine Scope Functions* chapter, section *withTimeout*.

Flow transformations

Before we finish discussing this layer, we should also review the typical ways in which we process Flow. In most cases, we just use basic flow processing functions map, filter, or onEach, and occasionally less common functions like scan or flatMapMerge[80].

```kotlin
class UserStateProvider(
    private val userRepository: UserRepository
) {

    fun userStateFlow(): Flow<User> = userRepository
        .observeUserChanges()
        .filter { it.isSignificantChange }
        .scan(userRepository.currentUser()) { user, update ->
            user.with(update)
        }
        .map { it.toDomainUser() }
}
```

When you want to merge two flows together, you might use functions like merge, zip, or combine[81].

```kotlin
class ArticlesProvider(
    private val ktAcademy: KtAcademyRepository,
    private val kotlinBlog: KtAcademyRepository,
) {
    fun observeArticles(): Flow<Article> = merge(
        ktAcademy.observeArticles().map { it.toArticle() },
        kotlinBlog.observeArticles().map { it.toArticle() },
    )
}

class NotificationStatusProvider(
    private val userStateProvider: UserStateProvider,
    private val notificationsProvider: NotificationsProvider,
```

---

[80]For details, see the *Flow processing* chapter.
[81]For details, see the *Flow processing* chapter, section merge, zip, *and* combine.

```
    private val statusFactory: NotificationStatusFactory,
) {
    fun notificationStatusFlow(): NotificationStatus =
        notificationsProvider.observeNotifications()
            .filter { it.status == Notification.UNSEEN }
            .combine(userStateProvider.userStateFlow()) {
                    notifications, user ->
                statusFactory.produce(notifications, user)
            }
}
```

If you want a single flow to be observed by multiple coroutines, transform it to SharedFlow. A common way to do this is by using shareIn with a scope. To keep this flow active only when needed, use the WhileSubscribed option for the started parameter[82].

```
class LocationService(
    locationDao: LocationDao,
    scope: CoroutineScope
) {
    private val locations = locationDao.observeLocations()
        .shareIn(
            scope = scope,
            started = SharingStarted.WhileSubscribed(),
        )

    fun observeLocations(): Flow<List<Location>> = locations
}
```

Presentation/API/UI layer

The last layer we need to discuss is the Presentation layer, which is where coroutines are typically launched. In some types of applications, this layer is easiest because frameworks like Spring Boot or Ktor do the entire job for us. For example, in Spring Boot with Webflux, you can just add the suspend modifier in front of a controller function, and Spring will start this function in a coroutine.

---

[82]For details, see the *SharedFlow and StateFlow* chapter.

```
@Controller
class UserController(
    private val tokenService: TokenService,
    private val userService: UserService,
) {
    @GetMapping("/me")
    suspend fun findUser(
        @PathVariable userId: String,
        @RequestHeader("Authorization") authorization: String
    ): UserJson {
        val userId = tokenService.readUserId(authorization)
        val user = userService.findUserById(userId)
        return user.toJson()
    }
}
```

Similar support is provided by other libraries. On Android, we use Work Manager to schedule tasks. We can use the `CoroutineWorker` class and implement its `doWork` method to specify what should be done by a task. This method is a suspend function, so it will be started in a coroutine by the library, therefore we don't need to do this ourselves.

```
class CoroutineDownloadWorker(
    context: Context,
    params: WorkerParameters
) : CoroutineWorker(context, params) {

    override suspend fun doWork(): Result {
        val data = downloadSynchronously()
        saveData(data)
        return Result.success()
    }
}
```

However, in some other situations we need to start coroutines ourselves. For this we typically use `launch` on a scope object. On Android, thanks to `lifecycle-viewmodel-ktx`, we can use `viewModelScope` or `lifecycleScope` in most cases.

```kotlin
class UserProfileViewModel(
    private val loadProfileUseCase: LoadProfileUseCase,
    private val updateProfileUseCase: UpdateProfileUseCase,
) {
    private val userProfile =
        MutableSharedFlow<UserProfileData>()

    val userName: Flow<String> = userProfile
        .map { it.name }
    val userSurname: Flow<String> = userProfile
        .map { it.surname }
    // ...

    fun onCreate() {
        viewModelScope.launch {
            val userProfileData =
                loadProfileUseCase.execute()
            userProfile.value = userProfileData
            // ...
        }
    }

    fun onNameChanged(newName: String) {
        viewModelScope.launch {
            val newProfile = userProfile.copy(name = newName)
            userProfile.value = newProfile
            updateProfileUseCase.execute(newProfile)
        }
    }
}
```

Creating custom scope

When you do not have a library or class that can start a coroutine or create a scope, you might need to make a custom scope and use it to launch a coroutine.

```kotlin
class NotificationsSender(
    private val client: NotificationsClient,
    private val notificationScope: CoroutineScope,
) {
    fun sendNotifications(
        notifications: List<Notification>
    ) {
        for (n in notifications) {
            notificationScope.launch {
                client.send(n)
            }
        }
    }
}


class LatestNewsViewModel(
    private val newsRepository: NewsRepository
) : BaseViewModel() {
    private val _uiState =
        MutableStateFlow<NewsState>(LoadingNews)
    val uiState: StateFlow<NewsState> = _uiState

    fun onCreate() {
        scope.launch {
            _uiState.value =
                NewsLoaded(newsRepository.getNews())
        }
    }
}
```

We define a custom coroutine scope using the `CoroutineScope` function[83]. Inside it, it is practically standard practice to use `SupervisorJob`[84].

---

[83]For details, see the *Constructing a coroutine scope* chapter.

[84]To learn more about how `SupervisorJob` works, see the *Exception handling* chapter.

```
val analyticsScope = CoroutineScope(SupervisorJob())
```

Inside a scope definition, we might specify a dispatcher or an exception handler[85]. Scope objects can also be cancelled. Actually, on Android, most scopes are either cancelled or can cancel their children under some conditions, and the question "What scope should I use to run this process?" can often be simplified to "Under what conditions should this process be cancelled?". View models cancel their scopes when they are cleared. Work managers cancel scopes when the associated tasks are cancelled.

```
// Android example with cancellation and exception handler
abstract class BaseViewModel : ViewModel() {
    private val _failure: MutableLiveData<Throwable> =
        MutableLiveData()
    val failure: LiveData<Throwable> = _failure

    private val exceptionHandler =
        CoroutineExceptionHandler { _, throwable ->
            _failure.value = throwable
        }

    private val context =
        Dispatchers.Main + SupervisorJob() + exceptionHandler

    protected val scope = CoroutineScope(context)

    override fun onCleared() {
        context.cancelChildren()
    }
}
```

---

[85]For details, see the *Constructing a coroutine scope* chapter. Dispatchers and exception handlers are described in the *Dispatchers* and *Exception handling* chapters, respectively.

```
// Spring example with custom exception handler
@Configuration
class CoroutineScopeConfiguration {

    @Bean
    fun coroutineDispatcher(): CoroutineDispatcher =
        Dispatchers.Default

    @Bean
    fun exceptionHandler(): CoroutineExceptionHandler =
        CoroutineExceptionHandler { _, throwable ->
            FirebaseCrashlytics.getInstance()
                .recordException(throwable)
        }

    @Bean
    fun coroutineScope(
        coroutineDispatcher: CoroutineDispatcher,
        exceptionHandler: CoroutineExceptionHandler,
    ) = CoroutineScope(
        SupervisorJob() +
            coroutineDispatcher +
            exceptionHandler
    )
}
```

Using runBlocking

Instead of starting coroutines on a scope object, we can also use the
runBlocking function, which starts a coroutine and blocks the current thread until this coroutine is finished. Therefore, runBlocking
should only be used when we want to block a thread. The two most
common reasons why it is used are:

1. To wrap the main function. This is a correct use of runBlocking,
   because we need to block the thread until the coroutine started
   by runBlocking is finished.
2. To wrap test functions. In this case, we also need to block
   the test thread, so this test doesn't finish execution until the
   coroutine completes.

```kotlin
fun main() = runBlocking {
    // ...
}

class SomeTests {
    @Test
    fun someTest() = runBlocking {
        // ...
    }
}
```

Both these cases have more-modern alternatives. We can suspend the main function with `coroutineScope` or `runTest` in tests. This does not mean we should avoid using `runBlocking`, in some cases it might be enough for our needs.

```kotlin
suspend fun main() = coroutineScope {
    // ...
}

class SomeTests {
    @Test
    fun someTest() = runTest {
        // ...
    }
}
```

In other cases, we should avoid using `runBlocking`. Remember that `runBlocking` blocks the current thread, which should be avoided in Kotlin Coroutines. Use `runBlocking` only if you intentionally want to block the current thread.

```
class NotificationsSender(
    private val client: NotificationsClient,
    private val notificationScope: CoroutineScope,
) {
    @Measure
    fun sendNotifications(notifications: List<Notification>){
        val jobs = notifications.map { notification ->
            scope.launch {
                client.send(notification)
            }
        }
        // We block thread here until all notifications are
        // sent to make function execution measurement
        // give us correct execution time
        runBlocking { jobs.joinAll() }
    }
}
```

Working with Flow

When we observe flows, we often handle changes inside onEach, start our flow in another coroutine using launchIn, invoke some action when the flow is started using onStart, invoke some action when the flow is completed using onCompletion, and catch exceptions using catch. If we want to catch all the exceptions that might occur in a flow, specify catch on the last position[86].

```
fun updateNews() {
    newsFlow()
        .onStart { showProgressBar() }
        .onCompletion { hideProgressBar() }
        .onEach { view.showNews(it) }
        .catch { view.handleError(it) }
        .launchIn(viewModelScope)
}
```

On Android, it is popular to represent our application state inside properties of type MutableStateFlow inside view model classes[87].

---

[86]For details, see the *Flow lifecycle functions* chapter.
[87]For details, see the *SharedFlow and StateFlow* chapter.

These properties are observed by coroutines that update the view
based on their changes.

```kotlin
class NewsViewModel : BaseViewModel() {
    private val _loading = MutableStateFlow(false)
    val loading: StateFlow<Boolean> = _loading

    private val _news = MutableStateFlow(emptyList<News>())
    val news: StateFlow<List<News>> = _news

    fun onCreate() {
        newsFlow()
            .onStart { _loading.value = true }
            .onCompletion { _loading.value = false }
            .onEach { _news.value = it }
            .catch { _failure.value = it }
            .launchIn(viewModelScope)
    }
}

class LatestNewsActivity : AppCompatActivity() {
    @Inject
    val newsViewModel: NewsViewModel

    override fun onCreate(savedInstanceState: Bundle?) {
        // ...
        launchOnStarted {
            newsViewModel.loading.collect {
                progressBar.visbility =
                    if (it) View.VISIBLE else View.GONE
            }
        }
        launchOnStarted {
            newsViewModel.news.collect {
                newsList.adapter = NewsAdapter(it)
            }
        }
    }
}
```

When a property representing a state depends only on a single flow, we might use the `stateIn` method. Depending on the `started` parameter, this flow will be started eagerly (when this class is initialized), lazily (when the first coroutine starts collecting it), or while subscribed[88].

```kotlin
class NewsViewModel : BaseViewModel() {
    private val _loading = MutableStateFlow(false)
    val loading: StateFlow<Boolean> = _loading

    private val _news = MutableStateFlow(emptyList<News>())
    val newsState: StateFlow<List<News>> = newsFlow()
        .onStart { _loading.value = true }
        .onCompletion { _loading.value = false }
        .catch { _failure.value = it }
        .stateIn(
            scope = viewModelScope,
            started = SharingStarted.Lazily,
            initialValue = emptyList(),
        )
}


class LocationsViewModel(
    locationService: LocationService
) : ViewModel() {

    private val location = locationService.observeLocations()
        .map { it.toLocationsDisplay() }
        .stateIn(
            scope = viewModelScope,
            started = SharingStarted.Lazily,
            initialValue = LocationsDisplay.Loading,
        )

    // ...
}
```

[88]All these options are described in the *SharedFlow and StateFlow* chapter, subchapters *shareIn* and *stateIn*.

StateFlow should be used to represent a state. To have some events or updates observed by multiple coroutines, use SharedFlow.

```kotlin
class UserProfileViewModel {
    private val _userChanges =
        MutableSharedFlow<UserChange>()
    val userChanges: SharedFlow<UserChange> = _userChanges

    fun onCreate() {
        viewModelScope.launch {
            userChanges.collect(::applyUserChange)
        }
    }

    fun onNameChanged(newName: String) {
        // ...
        _userChanges.emit(NameChange(newName))
    }

    fun onPublicKeyChanged(newPublicKey: String) {
        // ...
        _userChanges.emit(PublicKeyChange(newPublicKey))
    }
}
```

Summary

I hope this chapter has given you some sense of how coroutines can be used, but these are not the only right approaches. Each project has its own unique style, and that's fine as long as the resulting behavior is correct. If a case that's used in this chapter seems strange to you, review the chapter where it was introduced. Feel free to invent your own use cases, but I hope you will also remember those presented here because they might help you in your applications.

Recipes

In this chapter, we will explore a collection of practical Kotlin Coroutine recipes that can help streamline your development process. These recipes have been tested and refined through use in multiple projects, so you can trust that they'll be a valuable addition to your toolkit.

These recipes, along with their accompanying unit tests, can be found in the following GitHub repository:

https://github.com/MarcinMoskala/kotlin-coroutines-recipes[89]

To make things even more convenient, the recipes have been published to Maven, allowing you to easily access them in your projects.

Recipe 1: Asynchronous map

An asynchronous map is something we have already discussed as a pattern, but I noticed it's so repetitive that it's worth extracting it into a function.

```
suspend fun <T, R> List<T>.mapAsync(
    transformation: suspend (T) -> R
): List<R> = coroutineScope {
    this@mapAsync.map { async { transformation(it) } }
        .awaitAll()
}


// Practical example use
suspend fun getBestStudent(
    semester: String,
    repo: StudentsRepository
): Student =
    repo.getStudentIds(semester)
        .mapAsync { repo.getStudent(it) }
        .maxBy { it.result }

// Practical example use
```

---

[89]https://github.com/MarcinMoskala/kotlin-coroutines-recipes

```kotlin
suspend fun getCourses(user: User): List<UserCourse> =
    courseRepository.getAllCourses()
        .mapAsync { composeUserCourse(user, it) }
        .filterNot { courseShouldBeHidden(user, it) }
        .sortedBy { it.state.ordinal }
```

Thanks to the `mapAsync` function, we're able to abstract away `map`, `awaitAll`, and `coroutineScope`. This makes implementing asynchronous mapping more straightforward and concise. To implement rate limiting and control the number of concurrent requests, we can utilize a semaphore.

```kotlin
suspend fun <T, R> List<T>.mapAsync(
    concurrencyLimit: Int = Int.MAX_VALUE,
    transformation: suspend (T) -> R
): List<R> = coroutineScope {
    val semaphore = Semaphore(concurrencyLimit)
    this@mapAsync.map {
        async {
            semaphore.withPermit {
                transformation(it)
            }
        }
    }.awaitAll()
}
```

By introducing an optional `concurrencyLimit` parameter to the `mapAsync` function, we can easily manage the number of concurrent requests, thus ensuring that our application remains responsive and efficient.

Recipe 2: Suspending Lazy Initialization

In Kotlin Coroutines, you may have noticed that sometimes suspending functions can be used in non-suspend lambda expressions, such as a `map`. This works because suspending functions can be called on non-suspend lambda expressions if these expressions are inlined, and `map` is an inline function. While this limitation is reasonable, it might restrict us from using certain functions we've grown accustomed to.

```
// Works because map is an inline function,
// so we can call suspend await in its lambda,
// even though this lambda itself is not suspending.
suspend fun getOffers(
    categories: List<Category>
): List<Offer> = coroutineScope {
    categories
        .map { async { api.requestOffers(it) } }
        .map { it.await() } // Prefer awaitAll
        .flatten()
}
```

For me, the most important example is the `lazy` delegate, which cannot be used with suspending functions.

```
suspend fun makeConnection(): Connection = TODO()

val connection by lazy { makeConnection() } // COMPILER ERROR
```

To make it possible, we need to implement our own `suspendLazy`. However, if a value calculation can be suspended, we would need a `suspend` getter, and for that we would need to have a `suspend` property. This is not supported in Kotlin, so instead we will make a function that generates a getter function.

```
fun <T> suspendLazy(
    initializer: suspend () -> T
): suspend () -> T {
    TODO()
}
```

First of all, we will use `Mutex` to prevent more than one coroutine from calculating the same value at the same time[90]. Note that `Mutex` cannot be substituted with a dispatcher that is limited to a single thread because we don't want more than one process calculating a value, even if the previous one is suspended. Next, we will set a variable for the calculated value. We will use `NOT_SET` as a flag that

---

[90]Details about `Mutex` can be found in the *The problem with shared states* chapter.

the value is not initialized yet. Now, our process which produces the value and secures it with a mutex should check whether the value has been calculated yet: if it hasn't, calculate it using the initializer function and then return the value.

```kotlin
private val NOT_SET = Any()

fun <T> suspendLazy(
    initializer: suspend () -> T
): suspend () -> T {
    val mutex = Mutex()
    var holder: Any? = NOT_SET

    return {
        if (holder !== NOT_SET) holder as T
        else mutex.withLock {
            if (holder === NOT_SET) holder = initializer()
            holder as T
        }
    }
}
```

Did you notice that this implementation has a memory leak? Once initializer has been used, we don't need to keep its reference, so we can free this lambda expression (and all the values it has captured) by setting initializer to null[91]. If we do this, we can change our condition and initialize the lazy value if the initializer is still not null. This is the implementation of suspending lazy I use:

```kotlin
fun <T> suspendLazy(
    initializer: suspend () -> T
): suspend () -> T {
    var initializer: (suspend () -> T)? = initializer
    val mutex = Mutex()
    var holder: Any? = Any()

    return {
```

---

[91]This problem is described in detail in *Effective Kotlin*, Item 50: *Eliminate obsolete object references*.

```kotlin
        if (initializer == null) holder as T
        else mutex.withLock {
            initializer?.let {
                holder = it()
                initializer = null
            }
            holder as T
        }
    }
}

// Example
suspend fun makeConnection(): String {
    println("Creating connection")
    delay(1000)
    return "Connection"
}

val getConnection = suspendLazy { makeConnection() }

suspend fun main() {
    println(getConnection())
    println(getConnection())
    println(getConnection())
}
// Creating connection
// (1 sec)
// (1 sec)
// Connection
// Connection
// Connection


// Practical example use
val userData: suspend () -> UserData = suspendLazy {
    service.fetchUserData()
}

suspend fun getUserData(): UserData = userData()
```

Recipe 3: Reusing connections

I showed you how SharedFlow can reuse a single flow so its values are emitted to multiple flows. This is a very important optimization, especially when this initial flow requires a persistent HTTP connection (like WebSocket or RSocket) or needs to observe a database. Let's focus for a moment on the persistent HTTP connection. Its maintenance is a serious cost, so we don't want to needlessly maintain two connections to receive the same data. This is why we will learn later in this book about transforming a flow into a shared flow in order to reuse a single connection.

```kotlin
class LocationService(
    locationDao: LocationDao,
    scope: CoroutineScope
) {
    private val locations = locationDao.observeLocations()
        .shareIn(
            scope = scope,
            started = SharingStarted.WhileSubscribed(),
        )

    fun observeLocations(): Flow<List<Location>> = locations
}
```

This pattern is useful for connections that are not parameterized, but what about those started with specific parameters? For instance, when you implement a messenger application and want to observe particular discussion threads. For such cases, I find the following ConnectionPool class very useful. When getConnection is called for the first time, it creates a state flow that makes a connection based on the flow specified in its builder. Notice that ConnectionPool uses state flows with WhileSubscribed, so they only keep connections active for as long as they are needed.

```kotlin
class ConnectionPool<K, V>(
    private val scope: CoroutineScope,
    private val builder: (K) -> Flow<V>,
) {
    private val connections = mutableMapOf<K, Flow<V>>()

    fun getConnection(key: K): Flow<V> = synchronized(this) {
        connections.getOrPut(key) {
            builder(key).shareIn(
                scope,
                started = SharingStarted.WhileSubscribed(),
            )
        }
    }
}

// Practical example use
private val scope = CoroutineScope(SupervisorJob())
private val messageConnections =
    ConnectionPool(scope) { threadId: String ->
        api.observeMessageThread(threadId)
    }

fun observeMessageThread(threadId: String) =
    messageConnections.getConnection(threadId)
```

Notice that the getConnection method uses a regular synchronization block. This is because it is a regular function, as all functions that return Flow should be. This synchronization secures access to the connections variable. The getConnection function should execute very quickly because it only defines a flow. A connection will be created when at least a single flow needs it. Notice that, thanks to the fact we're using WhileSubscribed, a connection will only be maintained when there is at least a single coroutine using it.

WhileSubscribed can be parameterized. These parameter values could be injected into ConnectionPool using a constructor, as in the example below.

```kotlin
class ConnectionPool<K, V>(
    private val scope: CoroutineScope,
    private val replay: Int = 0,
    private val stopTimeout: Duration,
    private val replayExpiration: Duration,
    private val builder: (K) -> Flow<V>,
) {
    private val connections = mutableMapOf<K, Flow<V>>()

    fun getConnection(key: K): Flow<V> = synchronized(this) {
        connections.getOrPut(key) {
            builder(key).shareIn(
                scope,
                started = SharingStarted.WhileSubscribed(
                    stopTimeoutMillis =
                    stopTimeout.inWholeMilliseconds,
                    replayExpirationMillis =
                    replayExpiration.inWholeMilliseconds,
                ),
                replay = replay,
            )
        }
    }
}
```

Recipe 4: Coroutine races

As I mentioned in the *Select* chapter, to start a couple of suspending
processes and await the result of the one that finishes first, we can
use the `raceOf` function from the Splitties library. However, I am
not a fan of depending on a library just to use a function that can be
implemented in a couple of lines. So, this is my implementation of
`raceOf`:

```kotlin
suspend fun <T> raceOf(
    racer: suspend CoroutineScope.() -> T,
    vararg racers: suspend CoroutineScope.() -> T
): T = coroutineScope {
    select {
        (listOf(racer) + racers).forEach { racer ->
            async { racer() }.onAwait {
                coroutineContext.job.cancelChildren()
                it
            }
        }
    }
}

// Example use
suspend fun a(): String {
    delay(1000)
    return "A"
}

suspend fun b(): String {
    delay(2000)
    return "B"
}

suspend fun c(): String {
    delay(3000)
    return "C"
}

suspend fun main(): Unit = coroutineScope {
    println(raceOf({ c() }))
    // (3 sec)
    // C
    println(raceOf({ b() }, { a() }))
    // (1 sec)
    // A
    println(raceOf({ b() }, { c() }))
    // (2 sec)
```

```
    // B
    println(raceOf({ b() }, { a() }, { c() }))
    // (1 sec)
    // A
}
```

```
// Practical example use
suspend fun fetchUserData(): UserData = raceOf(
    { service1.fetchUserData() },
    { service2.fetchUserData() }
)
```

Recipe 5: Retrying a suspending process

Since we live in the real world, we need to face the fact that unexpected errors might occur. When you request some data from a service, it might be temporarily unavailable, your network connection might be broken, or anything else might happen. One of the ways we handle such situations is by implementing an automatic reply to try again if a process fails.

We've already learned that we retry a flow using the `retry` or `retryWhen` methods.

```
fun makeConnection(config: ConnectionConfig) = api
    .startConnection(config)
    .retryWhen { e, attempt ->
        val times = 2.0.pow(attempt.toDouble()).toInt()
        delay(maxOf(10_000L, 100L * times))
        log.error(e) { "Error for $config" }
        e is ApiException && e.code !in 400..499
    }
```

There is no such function for retrying regular suspending processes, but the simplest solution could just be a loop that retries the process until it succeeds.

```kotlin
inline fun <T> retry(operation: () -> T): T {
    while (true) {
        try {
            return operation()
        } catch (e: Throwable) {
            // no-op
        }
    }
}

// Usage
suspend fun requestData(): String {
    if (Random.nextInt(0, 10) == 0) {
        return "ABC"
    } else {
        error("Error")
    }
}

suspend fun main(): Unit = coroutineScope {
    println(retry { requestData() })
}
// (1 sec)
// ABC


// Practical example use
suspend fun checkConnection(): Boolean = retryWhen(
    predicate = { _, retries -> retries < 3 },
    operation = { api.connected() }
)
```

The problem is that there is no such thing as a standard reply. When we implement such a mechanism, we often want to include:

- the conditions under which the process should be retried, often based on the number of retries and the exception type,
- increasing delay between retries,
- exception and information logging.

I know two good approaches to implementing `retry`. The first involves defining a universal function like `retryWhen` that can be easily parametrized on the use side. The following snippet presents my implementation of such a function and includes two important features:

- it never retries cancellation exceptions so as not to harm the cancellation mechanism,
- it adds previous exceptions as suppressed exceptions, so they are displayed when the final exception is thrown out of the function.

```
inline fun <T> retryWhen(
    predicate: (Throwable, retries: Int) -> Boolean,
    operation: () -> T
): T {
    var retries = 0
    var fromDownstream: Throwable? = null
    while (true) {
        try {
            return operation()
        } catch (e: Throwable) {
            if (fromDownstream != null) {
                e.addSuppressed(fromDownstream)
            }
            fromDownstream = e
            if (e is CancellationException ||
                !predicate(e, retries++)
            ) {
                throw e
            }
        }
    }
}

// Usage
suspend fun requestWithRetry() = retryWhen(
    predicate = { e, retries ->
        val times = 2.0.pow(attempt.toDouble()).toInt()
```

```
        delay(maxOf(10_000L, 100L * times))
        log.error(e) { "Retried" }
        retries < 10 && e is IllegalStateException
    }
) {
    requestData()
}
```

The second approach is to implement an application-specific `retry`
function that is predefined for how we want to retry in this application. Here is an example of how such a function might look:

```
inline suspend fun <T> retry(
    operation: () -> T
): T {
    var retries = 0
    while (true) {
        try {
            return operation()
        } catch (e: Exception) {
            val times = 2.0.pow(attempt.toDouble()).toInt()
            delay(maxOf(10_000L, 100L * times))
            if (e is CancellationException || retries >= 10){
                throw e
            }
            retries++
            log.error(e) { "Retrying" }
        }
    }
}

// Usage
suspend fun requestWithRetry() = retry {
    requestData()
}
```

There is a popular algorithm for retrying that is called the expo-
nential backoff[92], where after each failed retry, there is a growing

---

[92]https://en.wikipedia.org/wiki/Exponential_backoff

backoff delay. It is based on the idea that the longer we wait, the
less likely it is that the error will occur again. You can find its
implementation in my recipes' repository. Here is how it can be
used:

```kotlin
suspend fun fetchUser(): User = retryBackoff(
    minDelay = 1.seconds,
    maxDelay = 10.seconds, // optional
    maxAttempts = 10, // optional
    backoffFactor = 1.5, // optional
    jitterFactor = 0.5, // optional
    beforeRetry = { cause, _, -> // optional
        println("Retrying after $cause")
    },
    retriesExhausted = { cause -> // optional
        println("Retries exhausted after $cause")
    },
) {
    api.fetchUser()
}

fun observeUserUpdates(): Flow<User> = api
    .observeUserUpdates()
    .retryBackoff(
        minDelay = 1.seconds,
        maxDelay = 1.minutes, // optional
        maxAttempts = 30, // optional
        backoffFactor = 2.0, // optional
        jitterFactor = 0.1, // optional
        beforeRetry = { cause, _, _ -> // optional
            println("Retrying after $cause")
        },
        retriesExhausted = { cause -> // optional
            println("Retries exhausted after $cause")
        },
    )
```

Summary

In this section, I've presented a couple of recipes I use in my projects. I hope they will help you not only with the presented problems but also with implementing your own unique recipes.

Using coroutines from other languages

Different languages have different approaches to concurrency. In Java, it is common to start and block threads, but this practically never happens in JavaScript, where async processes are represented by promises and async functions. This means we need to learn how to define an API in Kotlin for developers from different platforms, but we also need to learn some of the limitations of certain platforms. In this chapter, we will learn which Kotlin features are platform-specific and how to adjust Kotlin coroutines for platform specificity if you want to expose an API to other popular languages.

Threads on different platforms

JavaScript operates on a single thread[93], so you can't force a thread to sleep. This is why there is no runBlocking function in Kotlin/JS. If you want to run your Kotlin code on the JS platform, you must forget about blocking threads. You can still use runTest for testing, which returns a promise in Kotlin/JS.

For the same reason, we cannot use Dispatchers.IO in Kotlin/JS because Dispatchers.IO is currently Kotlin/JVM-specific. However, I don't find this problematic: we should use Dispatchers.IO when we need to block threads, and that should only happen when we interoperate with JVM or native APIs.

Transforming suspending into non-suspending functions

We already know what to do when we need to transform blocking or callback functions into suspending functions. But what if we need to do the opposite and use our suspending functions from languages other than Kotlin? As we've seen in the *Coroutines under the hood* chapter, suspending functions need Continuation, which must be provided by Kotlin. We need to find a way to overcome this for other languages, and since Kotlin is a multiplatform language, these other languages might include all JVM languages (Java, Scala,

---

[93]This statement is not completely true because multiple threads can be used on npm, and there is the Web Workers API for browsers to start processes on different threads; however, JavaScript can generally be considered single-threaded.

Groovy, Clojure, ...), JavaScript languages (JavaScript, TypeScript), or native languages (Swift, C++, C, ...). Let's see the most important options that are available to us.

Let's say that you implement a multiplatform library using suspending functions, and as its API you expose the following façade[94]:

```kotlin
class AnkiConnector(
    // ...
) {
    suspend fun checkConnection(): Boolean = ...

    suspend fun getDeckNames(): List<String> = ...

    suspend fun pushDeck(
        deckName: String,
        markdown: String
    ): AnkiConnectorResult = ...

    suspend fun pullDeck(
        deckName: String,
        currentMarkdown: String
    ): AnkiConnectorResult = ...
}
```

We might assume that we cannot call suspending functions from languages other than Kotlin, so if you want your library to support other languages, you need to specify an alternative.

Transforming suspend functions into blocking functions

On Kotlin/JVM and Kolin/Native, the easiest option is to transform our suspending functions into blocking functions using `runBlocking`. This isn't the best solution, but it is the easiest.

When you define a library, you can provide a wrapper class defining blocking functions for the classes you want to expose in your API.

---

[94]This is a simplified facade from my AnkiMarkdown project.

```kotlin
class AnkiConnectorBlocking {
    private val connector = AnkiConnector(/*...*/)

    fun checkConnection(): Boolean = runBlocking {
        connector.checkConnection()
    }

    fun getDeckNames(): List<String> = runBlocking {
        connector.getDeckNames()
    }

    fun pushDeck(
        deckName: String,
        markdown: String
    ): AnkiConnectorResult = runBlocking {
        connector.pushDeck(deckName, markdown)
    }

    fun pullDeck(
        deckName: String,
        currentMarkdown: String
    ): AnkiConnectorResult = runBlocking {
        connector.pullDeck(deckName, currentMarkdown)
    }
}
```

If you want to write classes that might be used by Kotlin and other languages, you might define your blocking variants next to suspend variants.

```kotlin
class AnkiConnector(
    // ...
) {
    suspend fun checkConnection(): Boolean = ...

    fun checkConnectionBlocking(): Boolean = runBlocking {
        connector.checkConnection()
    }
```

```
    // ...
}
```

You can already find Kotlin plugins that generate such blocking variants implicitly for properly annotated functions. An example of such a plugin is kotlin-jvm-blocking-bridge.

```
class AnkiConnector(
    // ...
) {
    @JvmBlockingBridge
    suspend fun checkConnection(): Boolean = ...
}
```

```
// Java
class JavaTest {
    public static void main(String[] args) {
        AnkiConnector connector = new AnkiConnector();
        boolean connection = connector.checkConnection();
        // ...
    }
}
```

Transforming suspend functions into callback functions

Another popular option is to transform suspending functions into callback functions. For that, we need to define a scope and use it to start coroutines for each function. In the example below, I call my callbacks with Result, which represents a success when the wrapper function has finished, or it represents a failure in the case of an exception. I also made this callback function return Cancellable, which can be used to cancel the execution of a particular function.

```kotlin
class AnkiConnectorCallback {
    private val connector = AnkiConnector(/*...*/)
    private val scope = CoroutineScope(SupervisorJob())

    fun checkConnection(
        callback: (Result<Boolean>) -> Unit
    ): Cancellable = toCallback(callback) {
        connector.checkConnection()
    }

    fun getDeckNames(
        callback: (Result<List<String>>) -> Unit
    ): Cancellable = toCallback(callback) {
        connector.getDeckNames()
    }

    fun pushDeck(
        deckName: String,
        markdown: String,
        callback: (Result<AnkiConnectorResult>) -> Unit
    ): Cancellable = toCallback(callback) {
        connector.pushDeck(deckName, markdown)
    }

    fun pullDeck(
        deckName: String,
        currentMarkdown: String,
        callback: (Result<AnkiConnectorResult>) -> Unit
    ): Cancellable = toCallback(callback) {
        connector.pullDeck(deckName, currentMarkdown)
    }

    fun <T> toCallback(
        callback: (Result<T>) -> Unit,
        body: suspend () -> T
    ): Cancellable {
        val job = scope.launch {
            try {
                val result = body()
```

```
                    callback(Result.success(result))
            } catch (t: Throwable) {
                callback(Result.failure(t))
            }
        }
        return Cancellable(job)
    }

    class Cancellable(private val job: Job) {
        fun cancel() {
            job.cancel()
        }
    }
}
```

Platform-specific options

Many platforms have their own ways of representing references to asynchronous tasks. In JavaScript, for instance, this is a Promise. To start a suspending function and expose its return value as a Promise which can be used in JavaScript to await this task, we can use the promise coroutine builder. Of course, this only works in Kotlin/JS.

```
@JsExport
@JsName("AnkiConnector")
class AnkiConnectorJs {
    private val connector = AnkiConnector(/*...*/)
    private val scope = CoroutineScope(SupervisorJob())

    fun checkConnection(): Promise<Boolean> = scope.promise {
        connector.checkConnection()
    }

    fun getDeckNames(): Promise<Array<String>> =
        scope.promise {
            connector.getDeckNames().toTypedArray()
        }

    fun pushDeck(
```

```kotlin
        deckName: String,
        markdown: String
    ): Promise<AnkiConnectorResult> = scope.promise {
        connector.pushDeck(deckName, markdown)
    }

    fun pullDeck(
        deckName: String,
        currentMarkdown: String
    ): Promise<AnkiConnectorResult> = scope.promise {
        connector.pullDeck(deckName, currentMarkdown)
    }
}
```

In Kotlin/JVM, we might want to return a `CompletableFuture` from Java stdlib. For that, we should use the `future` coroutine builder.

```kotlin
class AnkiConnectorFuture {
    private val connector = AnkiConnector(/*...*/)
    private val scope = CoroutineScope(SupervisorJob())

    fun checkConnection(): CompletableFuture<Boolean> =
        scope.future {
            connector.checkConnection()
        }

    fun getDeckNames(): CompletableFuture<List<String>> =
        scope.future {
            connector.getDeckNames()
        }

    fun pushDeck(
        deckName: String,
        markdown: String
    ): CompletableFuture<AnkiConnectorResult> = scope.future {
        connector.pushDeck(deckName, markdown)
    }

    fun pullDeck(
```

```
        deckName: String,
        currentMarkdown: String
    ): CompletableFuture<AnkiConnectorResult> = scope.future {
        connector.pullDeck(deckName, currentMarkdown)
    }
}
```

We might also transform our functions into objects from external libraries, like RxJava, which is very popular on the JVM. To transform suspending functions into RxJava objects, like `Single` or `Observable`, Kotlin provides a set of dependencies. For instance, to transform a suspending function into a `Single` from RxJava 3.x, we can use the `kotlinx-coroutines-rx3` dependency and the `rxSingle` function.

```
class AnkiConnectorBlocking {
    private val connector = AnkiConnector(/*...*/)

    fun checkConnection(): Single<Boolean> = rxSingle {
        connector.checkConnection()
    }

    fun getDeckNames(): Single<List<String>> = rxSingle {
        connector.getDeckNames()
    }

    fun pushDeck(
        deckName: String,
        markdown: String
    ): Single<AnkiConnectorResult> = rxSingle {
        connector.pushDeck(deckName, markdown)
    }

    fun pullDeck(
        deckName: String,
        currentMarkdown: String
    ): Single<AnkiConnectorResult> = rxSingle {
        connector.pullDeck(deckName, currentMarkdown)
    }
}
```

Calling suspending functions from other languages

In some of the projects I've worked on, previous developers decided to write tests using the Spock framework and Groovy, but this became problematic when we started using Kotlin Coroutines in those projects. We could not avoid calling suspending functions in unit tests because those were often the functions we were testing. It was also too hard to migrate all those tests from Groovy to Kotlin.

The easiest solution to this problem is to use `runBlocking` to construct a continuation in the other language, such as Java. This can be done in the following way.

```java
// Java
public class MainJava {
    public static void main(String[] args) {
        AnkiConnector connector = new AnkiConnector();
        boolean connected;
        try {
            connected = BuildersKt.runBlocking(
                    EmptyCoroutineContext.INSTANCE,
                    (s, c) -> connector.checkConnection(c)
            );
        } catch (InterruptedException e) {
            throw new RuntimeException(e);
        }
        // ...
    }
}
```

Three things make this function inconvenient to use:

1. `BuildersKt` is maybe not the best name.
2. We need to specify some context, even though `EmptyCoroutineContext` suffices in our case.
3. We always need to deal with the `InterruptedException` that `runBlocking` throws if the blocked thread is interrupted.

To help us improve this code, we can implement a wrapper function.

```
// Java
class SuspendUtils {
    public static <T> T runBlocking(
        Function<Continuation<? super T>, T> func
    ) {
        try {
            return BuildersKt.runBlocking(
                EmptyCoroutineContext.INSTANCE,
                (s, c) -> func.apply(c)
            );
        } catch (InterruptedException e) {
            throw new RuntimeException(e);
        }
    }
}

public class MainJava {
    public static void main(String[] args) {
        AnkiConnector connector = new AnkiConnector();
        boolean connected = SuspendUtils.runBlocking((c) ->
            connector.checkConnection(c)
        );
        // ...
    }
}
```

Flow and Reactive Streams

We've already discussed this topic in the *Flow building* chapter, but you can use simple conversion functions if you need to transform between `Flow` and libraries representing reactive streams (like Reactor[95], RxJava 2.x.[96] or RxJava 3.x[97]).

All objects like `Flux`, `Flowable`, or `Observable` implement the `Publisher` interface from the Java standard library, which can be converted to `Flow` with the `asFlow` function from the `kotlinx-coroutines-reactive` library.

[95]https://projectreactor.io/
[96]https://github.com/ReactiveX/RxJava
[97]https://github.com/ReactiveX/RxJava

```kotlin
suspend fun main() = coroutineScope {
    Flux.range(1, 5).asFlow()
        .collect { print(it) } // 12345
    Flowable.range(1, 5).asFlow()
        .collect { print(it) } // 12345
    Observable.range(1, 5).asFlow()
        .collect { print(it) } // 12345
}
```

To convert the other way around, you need more specific libraries.
With `kotlinx-coroutines-reactor`, you can convert `Flow` to `Flux`.
With `kotlinx-coroutines-rx3` (or `kotlinx-coroutines-rx2`), you can
convert `Flow` to `Flowable` or `Observable`.

```kotlin
suspend fun main(): Unit = coroutineScope {
    val flow = flowOf(1, 2, 3, 4, 5)

    flow.asFlux()
        .doOnNext { print(it) } // 12345
        .subscribe()

    flow.asFlowable()
        .subscribe { print(it) } // 12345

    flow.asObservable()
        .subscribe { print(it) } // 12345
}
```

You can also define simple functions to observe a flow on the JVM or
to block the current thread until a flow is completed.

```kotlin
// Kotlin
object FlowUtils {
    private val scope = CoroutineScope(SupervisorJob())

    @JvmStatic
    @JvmOverloads
    fun <T> observe(
        flow: Flow<T>,
```

```
        onNext: OnNext<T>? = null,
        onError: OnError? = null,
        onCompletion: OnCompletion? = null,
    ) {
        scope.launch {
            flow.onCompletion { onCompletion?.handle() }
                .onEach { onNext?.handle(it) }
                .catch { onError?.handle(it) }
                .collect()
        }
    }

    @JvmStatic
    @JvmOverloads
    fun <T> observeBlocking(
        flow: Flow<T>,
        onNext: OnNext<T>? = null,
        onError: OnError? = null,
        onCompletion: OnCompletion? = null,
    ) = runBlocking {
        flow.onCompletion { onCompletion?.handle() }
            .onEach { onNext?.handle(it) }
            .catch { onError?.handle(it) }
            .collect()
    }

    fun interface OnNext<T> {
        fun handle(value: T)
    }

    fun interface OnError {
        fun handle(value: Throwable)
    }

    fun interface OnCompletion {
        fun handle()
    }
}
```

```
class FlowTest {
    fun test(): Flow<String> = flow {
        emit("A")
        delay(1000)
        emit("B")
    }
}
```

```
// Java
public class Main {
    public static void main(String[] args) {
        FlowTest obj = new FlowTest();
        FlowUtils.observeBlocking(
                obj.test(),
                System.out::println
        );
    }
}
// A
// (1 sec)
// B
```

I don't see much utility in converting `Flow` into `Promise` or `CompletableFuture`. `Flow` can represent many values, but `Promise` or `CompletableFuture` can represent only one.

Summary

In this section, we've learned about some limitations of coroutines on different platforms. We've also learned how to transform Kotlin Coroutine concepts so they can be used in other languages. The two most basic techniques are transforming suspending functions into either blocking or callback functions. A flow can be transformed into an object from a library like RxJava or Reactor, or it can be wrapped with a class that can be used in other languages. However, there are also many platform-specific options. I hope you will find this chapter useful when you need to use Kotlin Coroutines from other languages.

Launching coroutines vs. suspending functions

Let's consider a use case where you need to perform a number of concurrent actions. There are two kinds of functions that can be used for this:

- a regular function operating on a coroutine scope object,
- a suspending function.

```kotlin
class NotificationsSender(
    private val client: NotificationsClient,
    private val notificationScope: CoroutineScope,
) {
    fun sendNotifications(
        notifications: List<Notification>
    ) {
        for (n in notifications) {
            notificationScope.launch {
                client.send(n)
            }
        }
    }
}


class NotificationsSender(
    private val client: NotificationsClient,
) {
    suspend fun sendNotifications(
        notifications: List<Notification>
    ) = supervisorScope {
        for (n in notifications) {
            launch {
                client.send(n)
            }
        }
    }
}
```

These two options might look similar in some ways, but they represent essentially different use cases. To see some essential differences, you don't even need to read their bodies.

When we know that a regular function starts coroutines, we know it needs to use a scope object. Such functions typically only start coroutines and don't await their completion, so sendNotifications will most likely take milliseconds to execute. Starting coroutines on an external scope also means that exceptions in these coroutines will be handled by this scope (most often printed and ignored). These coroutines will inherit context from the scope object, so we need to cancel the scope to cancel them.

```
class NotificationsSender(
    private val client: NotificationsClient,
    private val notificationScope: CoroutineScope,
) {
    // Does not wait for started coroutines
    // Exceptions are handled by the scope
    // Takes context from the scope
    // and builds relationship to the scope
    fun sendNotifications(
        notifications: List<Notification>
    ) {
        // ...
    }
}
```

When we know that a suspending function starts coroutines, we can assume that this function will not finish until all the coroutines are finished. Such sendNotifications will suspend until the last notification is fully handled. This is an important synchronization mechanism. We also know that suspending functions don't cancel their parent. Instead, they might throw or silence exceptions, just like regular functions can throw or silence exceptions. The coroutines started by such a function should inherit context from and build relationships with the function that called them.

```
class NotificationsSender(
    private val client: NotificationsClient,
) {
    // Waits for its coroutines
    // Handles exceptions
    // Takes context and builds relationship to
    // the coroutine that started it
    suspend fun sendNotifications(
        notifications: List<Notification>
    ) {
        // ...
    }
}
```

Both these use cases are important in our applications. When we have a choice, we should prefer suspending functions as they are easier to control and synchronize. But coroutines need to start somewhere, and for that we use regular functions with a scope object.

In some applications, we might have a situation where we need to mix these two kinds of functions when we need suspending functions that also start external processes on an outer scope.

Consider a function that needs to execute some operations that are an essential part of its execution, but it also needs to start an independent process. In the example below, the process of sending an event is considered an external process, so it is started on an external scope. Thanks to this:

- updateUser will not wait until the sendEvent execution is completed.
- the sendEvent process will not be cancelled when the coroutine that started updateUser is cancelled. (This makes sense because user synchronization has completed anyway.)
- eventsScope decides what the context should be for sending events, and whether or not this event should happen. (If eventsScope is not active, no event will be sent.)

```kotlin
suspend fun updateUser() = coroutineScope {
    val apiUserAsync = async { api.fetchUser() }
    val dbUserAsync = async { db.getUser() }
    val apiUser = apiUserAsync.await()
    val dbUser = dbUserAsync.await()

    if (apiUser.lastUpdate > dbUser.lastUpdate) {
        db.updateUser(apiUser)
    } {
        api.updateUser(dbUser)
    }

    eventsScope.launch { sendEvent(UserSunchronized) }
}
```

In some situations, this hybrid behavior is what we want in our
applications, but it should be used wisely.

Best practices

I will finish this book with my humble set of best practices. They've all been discussed in the book already, so you might treat this as a brief summary, but I hope it will help you remember and apply them in your everyday practice.

Don't use async with an immediate await

It makes no sense to define an asynchronous task with `async` if we want to await its completion without doing any operations during that time.

```
// Don't
suspend fun getUser(): User = coroutineScope {
    val user = async { repo.getUser() }.await()
    user.toUser()
}

// Do
suspend fun getUser(): User {
    val user = repo.getUser()
    return user.toUser()
}
```

There are cases where this transformation is not so simple. If you need a scope, instead of `async { ... }.await()`, use `coroutineScope`. If you need to set a context, use `withContext`.

When you start a few async tasks, all of them except the last one need to use `async`. In this case, I suggest using `async` for all of them for readability.

```kotlin
fun showNews() {
    viewModelScope.launch {
        val config = async { getConfigFromApi() }
        val news = async { getNewsFromApi(config.await()) }
        val user = async { getUserFromApi() } // async not
        // necessary here, but useful for readability
        view.showNews(user.await(), news.await())
    }
}
```

Use `coroutineScope` instead of `withContext(EmptyCoroutineContext)`

The only difference between `withContext` and `coroutineScope` is that `withContext` can override context, so instead of `withContext(EmptyCoroutineContext)`, use `coroutineScope`.

Use awaitAll

The `awaitAll` function should be preferred over `map { it.await() }` because it stops waiting when the first async task throws an exception, while `map { it.await() }` awaits these coroutines one after another until this process reaches one that fails.

Suspending functions should be safe to call from any thread

When you call a suspending function, you shouldn't be worried that it might block the thread you're currently using. This is especially important on Android, where we often use `Dispatchers.Main`; however, it is also important on the backend, where you might be using a dispatcher limited to a single thread for synchronization.

Each suspending function that needs to make blocking calls should use `Dispatchers.IO` or a custom dispatcher that is designed to be blocked. Each dispatcher that might be CPU-intensive should use `Dispatchers.Default` or `Dispatchers.Default` with limited parallelism. These dispatchers should be set using `withContext` so that function calls don't need to set these dispatchers themselves.

```
class DiscSaveRepository(
    private val discReader: DiscReader
) : SaveRepository {

    override suspend fun loadSave(name: String): SaveData =
        withContext(Dispatchers.IO) {
            discReader.read("save/$name")
        }
}
```

Functions that return `Flow` should specify a dispatcher using `flowOn`, which changes the context for all the steps **above** it, so it is typically used as the last step in a function.

Whether or not `Dispatchers.Main.immediate` should be used explicitly in suspending functions that update Android views is a controversial topic. Your decision should depend on your project's policy. We don't need to use it in layers where `Dispatchers.Main` is considered the default dispatcher, like in the presentation layer in many Android projects.

If you want to unit test these classes, remember that you need to inject a dispatcher so it can be overridden for unit testing.

```
class DiscSaveRepository(
    private val discReader: DiscReader,
    private val dispatcher: CoroutineContext = Dispatchers.IO
) : SaveRepository {

    override suspend fun loadSave(name: String): SaveData =
        withContext(dispatcher) {
            discReader.read("save/$name")
        }
}
```

Use `Dispatchers.Main.immediate` instead of `Dispatchers.Main`

`Dispatchers.Main.immediate` is an optimized version of `Dispatchers.Main` that avoids coroutine redispatching if it isn't necessary. We generally prefer to use it.

```
suspend fun showUser(user: User) =
    withContext(Dispatchers.Main.immediate) {
        userNameElement.text = user.name
        // ...
    }
```

Remember to use `yield` in heavy functions

It is good practice to use `yield` in suspending functions between
blocks of non-suspended CPU-intensive or time-intensive
operations. This function suspends and immediately resumes
the coroutine, thus it supports cancellation. Calling `yield` also
allows redispatching, thanks to which one process will not starve
other processes.

```
suspend fun cpuIntensiveOperations() =
    withContext(Dispatchers.Default) {
        cpuIntensiveOperation1()
        yield()
        cpuIntensiveOperation2()
        yield()
        cpuIntensiveOperation3()
    }
```

Inside coroutine builders, you can also use `ensureActive`.

Understand that suspending functions await completion of their children

A parent coroutine cannot complete before its children, and coroutine scope functions, like `coroutineScope` or `withContext`, suspend
their parent until their coroutines are completed. As a result, they
await all the coroutines they've started.

```
suspend fun longTask() = coroutineScope {
    launch {
        delay(1000)
        println("Done 1")
    }
    launch {
        delay(2000)
        println("Done 2")
    }
}

suspend fun main() {
    println("Before")
    longTask()
    println("After")
}
// Before
// (1 sec)
// Done 1
// (1 sec)
// Done 2
// After
```

Notice that ending a coroutine scope function with launch makes no sense because nothing would change if we deleted it.

```
suspend fun updateUser() = coroutineScope {
    // ...

    // Don't
    launch { sendEvent(UserSunchronized) }
}
```

We expect suspending functions to await completion of coroutines they've started. They can overcome this expectation by using an external scope, but we should avoid doing this if there is no good reason.

```
suspend fun updateUser() = coroutineScope {
    // ...

    eventsScope.launch { sendEvent(UserSunchronized) }
}
```

Understand that Job is not inherited: it is used as a parent

One of the biggest misunderstandings which causes mistakes in projects using Kotlin Coroutines comes from the fact that the Job context is the only context that is not inherited. Instead, a Job from a parent or argument is used as the parent of a coroutine.

Let's take a look at some examples. Adding SupervisorJob as a coroutine builder argument is pointless as it changes nothing.

```
// Don't
fun main() = runBlocking(SupervisorJob()) {
    launch {
        delay(1000)
        throw Error()
    }
    launch {
        delay(2000)
        println("Done")
    }
    launch {
        delay(3000)
        println("Done")
    }
}
// (1 sec)
// Error...
```

Job is the only context that is not inherited. Each coroutine needs its own job, and passing a job to a coroutine makes the passed job the **parent** of this coroutine job. So, in the snippet above, SupervisorJob is the parent of runBlocking. When a child has an exception, this exception propagates to the runBlocking coroutine, breaks the Job coroutine, cancels its children, and throws an exception. The fact that SupervisorJob is a parent has no practical implication.

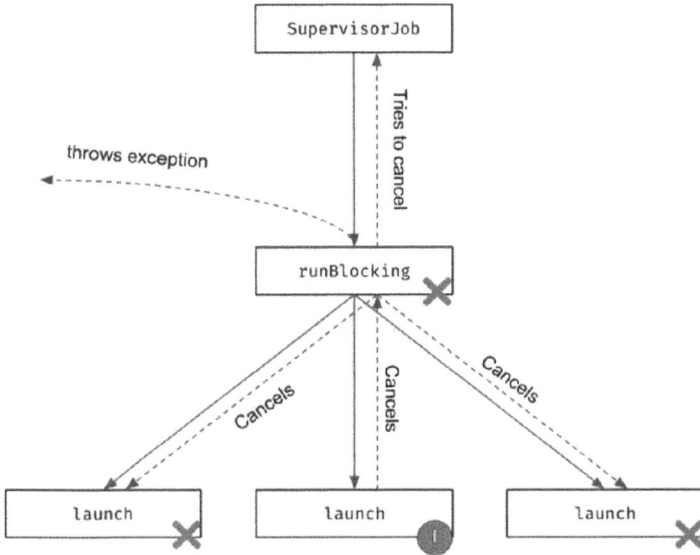

I see a similar mistake even more often when withContext is used together with SupervisorJob.

```
// Don't
suspend fun sendNotifications(
    notifications: List<Notification>
) = withContext(SupervisorJob()) {
    for (notification in notifications) {
        launch {
            client.send(notification)
        }
    }
}
```

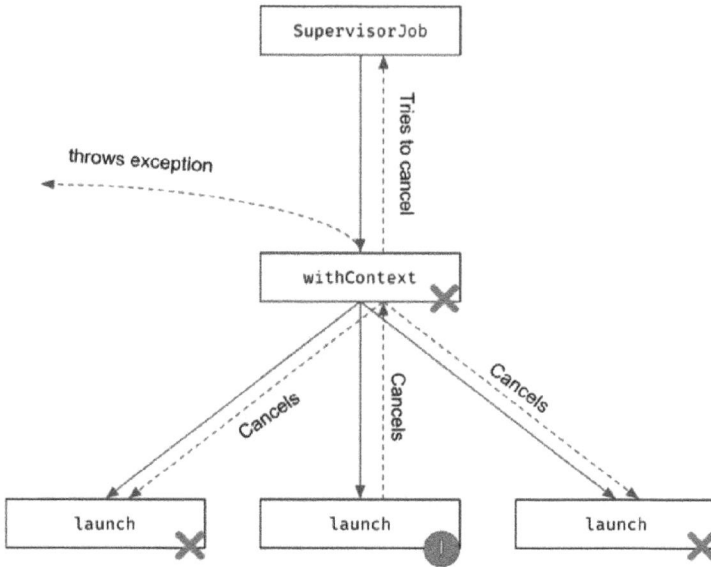

Using `SupervisorJob` this way is pointless. When I see this, I can generally guess that the intention is to silence exceptions in children. The proper way to do this is to use `supervisorScope`, which ignores exceptions in its direct children.

```kotlin
// Do
suspend fun sendNotifications(
    notifications: List<Notification>
) = supervisorScope {
    for (notification in notifications) {
        launch {
            client.send(notification)
        }
    }
}
```

Using `withContext(Job())` is pointless and should also be considered a mistake.

Don't break structured concurrency

The mistakes we presented above are not only pointless but also harmful. Whenever you set an explicit Job as a coroutine context, you break the relationship with this coroutine's parent. Take a look at the example below. The problem with using Job as an argument to the coroutine is that it is set as the parent of this coroutine. As a result, withContext is not a child of the coroutine that called this function. When this coroutine is cancelled, our coroutine will not be, therefore the processes inside it will continue and waste our resources. Using an external job or scope breaks structured concurrency, prevents proper cancellation, and leads to memory leaks as a result.

```
// Don't
suspend fun getPosts() = withContext(Job()) {
    val user = async { userService.currentUser() }
    val posts = async { postsService.getAll() }
    posts.await()
        .filterCanSee(user.await())
}
```

Use SupervisorJob when creating CoroutineScope

When we create a scope, we can freely assume that we don't want an exception in one coroutine that was started using this scope to cancel all the other coroutines. For that, we need to use SupervisorJob instead of Job, which is used by default.

```
// Don't
val scope = CoroutineScope(Job())

// Do
val scope = CoroutineScope(SupervisorJob())
```

Consider cancelling scope children

Once a scope has been cancelled, it cannot be used again. If you want to cancel all the tasks started on a scope but you might want to keep this scope active, cancel its children. Keeping a scope active costs nothing.

```kotlin
fun onCleared() {
    // Consider doing
    scope.coroutineContext.cancelChildren()

    // Instead of
    scope.cancel()
}
```

On Android, instead of defining and cancelling custom scopes, you should use the viewModelScope, lifecycleScope and lifecycle-aware coroutine scopes from the ktx libraries because these are cancelled automatically.

Before using a scope, consider under which conditions it is cancelled

One of my favorite heuristics for using Kotlin Coroutines on Android is "choosing what scope you should use is choosing when you want this coroutine cancelled". Each view model provides its own viewModelScope, which is cancelled when this view model is finalized. Each lifecycle owner has its own lifecycleScope, which is cancelled when this lifecycle is completed. We use these scopes instead of some shared global scope because we want our coroutines cancelled when they are not needed. Starting a coroutine on another scope means it will be cancelled under other conditions. Coroutines started on GlobalScope will never be cancelled.

```kotlin
class MainViewModel : ViewModel() {
    val scope = CoroutineScope(SupervisorJob())

    fun onCreate() {
        viewModelScope.launch {
            // Will be cancelled with MainViewModel
            launch { task1() }
            // Will never be cancelled
            GlobalScope.launch { task2() }
            // Will be cancelled when we cancel scope
            scope.launch { task2() }
        }
    }
}
```

Don't use GlobalScope

It is too easy to use GlobalScope, so it might be tempting, but I would avoid doing that and instead create at least a very simple scope with only SupervisorJob as its context.

```
val scope = CoroutineScope(SupervisorJob())

fun example() {
    // Don't
    GlobalScope.launch { task() }

    // Do
    scope.launch { task() }
}
```

GlobalScope means no relation, no cancellation, and is hard to override for testing. Even if GlobalScope is all you need now, defining a meaningful scope might be helpful in the future.

```
// GlobalScope definition
public object GlobalScope : CoroutineScope {
    override val coroutineContext: CoroutineContext
        get() = EmptyCoroutineContext
}
```

Avoid using Job builder, except for constructing a scope

When you create a job using the Job function, it is created in the active state regardless of the state of its children. Even if some children have completed, this doesn't mean their parents have also completed.

```
suspend fun main(): Unit = coroutineScope {
    val job = Job()
    launch(job) {
        delay(1000)
        println("Text 1")
    }
    launch(job) {
        delay(2000)
        println("Text 2")
    }
    job.join() // Here we will await forever
    println("Will not be printed")
}
// (1 sec)
// Text 1
```

It is possible for such a Job to complete, but only if its complete
method is first called and its state is then changed from "Active" to
"Completing", where it waits until its children are finished. However, you cannot start new coroutines on completing or completed
jobs. A more practical approach is to use a job reference to await its
children (job.children.forEach { it.join() }). In most cases, the
simplest solution is to await the job returned by a coroutine builder.
Most common cases include storing the active task job in a variable,
or collecting the jobs of all the started coroutines.

```
class SomeService {
    private var job: Job? = null
    private val scope = CoroutineScope(SupervisorJob())

    // Every time we start a new task,
    // we cancel the previous one.
    fun startTask() {
        cancelTask()
        job = scope.launch {
            // ...
        }
    }

    fun cancelTask() {
```

```
        job?.cancel()
    }
}


class SomeService {
    private var jobs: List<Job> = emptyList()
    private val scope = CoroutineScope(SupervisorJob())

    fun startTask() {
        jobs += scope.launch {
            // ...
        }
    }

    fun cancelTask() {
        jobs.forEach { it.cancel() }
    }
}
```

My general recommendation is to avoid using Job builder, except when constructing a scope.

Functions that return Flow should not be suspending

A flow represents a certain process that is started using the collect function. Functions that return Flow define such processes, and their execution is postponed until these processes are started. This is very different from suspending functions, which are supposed to execute processes themselves. Mixing these two concepts is counterintuitive and problematic.

As an example, consider that you need a function that fetches services to observe and then observes them. This is a problematic implementation:

```kotlin
// Don't use suspending functions returning Flow
suspend fun observeNewsServices(): Flow<News> {
    val newsServices = fetchNewsServices()
    return newsServices
        .asFlow()
        .flatMapMerge { it.observe() }
}

suspend fun main() {
    val flow = observeNewsServices() // Fetching services
    // ...
    flow.collect { println(it) } // Start observing
}
```

It is counterintuitive that part of the process is executed when observeNewsServices is called, and part is executed when we start collecting. Also, if we collect later, we will still use news items that were fetched in the past. This is problematic and counterintuitive. We expect that functions that return Flow pack the whole process into this flow.

To improve the function above, the most common intervention involves packing suspend calls into a flow.

```kotlin
fun observeNewsServices(): Flow<News> {
    return flow { emitAll(fetchNewsServices().asFlow()) }
        .flatMapMerge { it.observe() }
}

suspend fun main() {
    val flow = observeNewsServices()
    // ...
    flow.collect { println(it) }
    // Fetching services
    // Start observing
}
```

An alternative is, as always, to make a suspending function that awaits the completion of its process.

```
suspend fun fetchNewsFromServices(): List<News> {
    return fetchNewsServices()
        .mapAsync { it.observe() }
        .flatten()
}

suspend fun main() {
    val news = fetchNewsFromServices()
    // Fetching services
    // Start observing
    // ...
}
```

Prefer a suspending function instead of Flow when you expect only one value

I will finish this collection with the most controversial suggestion. Consider the function below. What values do you expect its flow to emit?

```
interface UserRepository {
    fun getUser(): Flow<User>
}
```

I would expect it to emit a user whenever it is changed, not only the current state. This is because the Flow type represents a source of values. To represent a single deferred value, we use suspending functions.

```
interface UserRepository {
    suspend fun getUser(): User
}
```

Contrary to this rule, many applications, especially Android applications, use Flow instead of suspending functions wherever possible. I understand the reasons behind this: some teams have used RxJava before and they don't want to change their habits. As my friend said, "I'm a RxJava senior, but a Kotlin Coroutines junior. I don't like being a junior, but Flow is like RxJava, so maybe I am a Flow mid".

On Android, developers have one more reason. It's become popular to represent mutable states using StateFlow, and Flow can be easily transformed into StateFlow using the `stateIn` function. So, operating on Flow is convenient.

```kotlin
class LocationsViewModel(
    locationService: LocationService
) : ViewModel() {

    private val location = locationService.observeLocations()
        .map { it.toLocationsDisplay() }
        .stateIn(
            scope = viewModelScope,
            started = SharingStarted.Lazily,
            initialValue = LocationsDisplay.Loading,
        )

    // ...
}
```

If you join a team that uses Flow everywhere, it's best to follow your team's conventions. Every team has its own style and practices. However, if you can choose - maybe because you're designing a greenfield project, or maybe because you've just introduced coroutines - I suggest you don't use flow where you expect only a single value. This will make your code simpler, easier to understand, and more efficient.

Before we close this chapter, I want you to remember this sentence: Best practices sometimes need to be violated; they are guidelines for standard situations, not rules for every situation.

The End

All good things must come to an end, and the same is sadly true of this book. Of course, there is still much more to say about Kotlin Coroutines, but I believe we've covered the essentials well. Now it is your turn to start using this knowledge in practice and deepen your understanding.

This and the following pages were intentionally left empty, feel free to use them for your notes and reflections.

Notes

The End

Notes

Notes

Notes

Notes

Notes

Notes

Notes

Notes

The End

Notes

Notes

Notes

Notes

460 The End

Notes

Notes

Notes

Notes

Notes